The Huston Smith Reader

The publisher gratefully acknowledges the generous support of the Humanities Endowment Fund of the University of California Press Foundation.

The Huston Smith Reader

Edited, with an Introduction, by

Jeffery Paine

UNIVERSITY OF CALIFORNIA PRESS

Berkeley   Los Angeles   London

University of California Press, one of the most distinguished
university presses in the United States, enriches lives around the
world by advancing scholarship in the humanities, social sciences,
and natural sciences. Its activities are supported by the UC Press
Foundation and by philanthropic contributions from individuals
and institutions. For more information, visit www.ucpress.edu.

University of California Press
Berkeley and Los Angeles, California

University of California Press, Ltd.
London, England

For acknowledgment of previous publication, please see credits, page 255.

Library of Congress Cataloging-in-Publication Data

Smith, Huston.
    The Huston Smith reader / edited with an introduction by Jeffery
Paine.
        p.   cm.
    Includes bibliographical references.
    ISBN 978-0-520-27022-0 (cloth : alk. paper)
    1. Religion.   2. Religions.   I. Paine, Jeffery, 1944–   II. Title.
    BL27.S39   2012
    200—dc23   2011030335

Manufactured in the United States of America

21   20   19   18   17   16   15   14   13   12
10   9   8   7   6   5   4   3   2   1

In keeping with a commitment to support environmentally responsible
and sustainable printing practices, UC Press has printed this book
on Rolland Enviro100, a 100% post-consumer fiber paper that is FSC
certified, deinked, processed chlorine-free, and manufactured with
renewable biogas energy. It is acid-free and EcoLogo certified.

CONTENTS

The contents of this volume are easy to describe: they are the best essays and excerpts from Huston Smith's many books, chosen for their relevance and resonance today. In his "Welcome" Huston observes how most Readers have a random, meandering character, but this one is, or hopes to be, more than the sum of its parts.

For here, as one selection succeeds another, something about the elusive nature of religion itself is revealed. An analogy to language may be useful. A second language allows you to begin to see—beyond the idiosyncrasies of your native English or Mandarin—what language itself is and does. Likewise when you encounter sympathetically a second religion: you begin to detect the larger unstated background, the sorrowing and the goodness, the meaninglessness and the ingenuity, the humanness in the universe, out of which all religions arise. This Reader attempts to give such a bird's-eye view of the whole shebang.

In its organization the book follows a schemata Huston used when he investigated "reality" or selfhood, ascending and descending level by level through the several worlds we live in simultaneously. The book begins personally, with Huston confiding his personal experience. From there it widens out into the immediate world, the various kinds of everyday circumstances, surrounding him (and us). The third section ventures further (or deeper), into the sphere of religions itself, which suffuses mundane existence with understanding and, possibly, tools for enhancing it. In the penultimate section, Huston situates even religious experiences in a larger framework—the Big Picture or unconditional worldview—where things finite yield a more infinite aspect. This Reader thus makes, in a sense, a little tour from Berkeley, California, to the ends of the cosmos. Yet it might be truer to say that it goes nowhere at all: each sphere of life, and each section in the Reader, contains a subtle reflection of the others: and so we end with Huston personally again, as he tells about being ninety and encountering God.

Bookkeeping. The one of Huston's books not excerpted here is the one for which he is most famous. *The World's Religions* reads best as a whole, and with three million copies in print, you can, if you have not already read it, easily acquire a copy. Some of the selections here have been lightly edited, to avoid repeating material already discussed in another essay or dated, now-obscure references. Only a few pieces are particularly challenging (notably "The Levels of Reality" and "The Levels of Selfhood"), but they seem worth it. Writing about religion can at times be complex and difficult, Huston observed and quoted C. S. Lewis, "as difficult as modern physics, and for the same reason." Huston is overall a pleasing and accessible stylist, though, and most chapters here provide that literary pleasure.

Once, while delivering a public lecture, Huston could find no chalk to make his point on the blackboard. "Never mind," he said, "I'll write it in air and you will see it vividly." This volume records what Huston said on those better occasions when he had, as it were, a blackboard and chalk in hand.

Who is Huston Smith? The answer seems straightforward. He is a retired college professor in Berkeley who taught at various universities, and he wrote books, one of which sold incredibly well. Oh yes, there's one thing more. Huston Smith did something that nobody, no one else in the history of the world, had done or even had thought to do before.

What has Huston done that no one else had done? Simply this: he was a practitioner of practically all the major world's religions, a unique feat in the annals of spirituality. There used to be on official forms a box where you had to write in your religion; Huston would have had a hard time squeezing into that small space Judeo-Christianity, Hinduism, Buddhism, and Islam.

In the beginning: Huston was born in 1919 to missionary parents in China. To that little boy Christianity was the only religion there was, identical with faith, synonymous with spirituality itself. Next: as a young man Huston met a Hindu swami in St. Louis—the only true saint he feels he ever met—and the scales, as it were, fell from his eyes. Before he had been like the bumpkin who thinks his language—English, Inuit, or whatever—is the only language there is. When Huston learned there were other languages, or rather other religions, other worlds opened for him, and for the next decade he practiced Hinduism. In middle age Huston discovered Hinduism's stepchild, Buddhism. He had not suspected there could be such a thing: a spiritual path rooted not in faith but in experience, and at the root of experience was not Original Sin to be overcome but an innate perfection to be realized. For ten years Huston sought out Buddhist teachers and gurus, stayed in a Zen monastery in Kyoto, and strove for *satori,* or enlightenment. Huston had by then acquired the knack of knocking on unfamiliar religious doors, and it felt natural to now enter into Islam. He studied the Koran, joined a *tariqa,* or secret Muslim fraternity, prayed facing Mecca five times a day, and enjoyed a devotee's personal relation to Allah. His experience of polymorphous spirituality led him to write *The World's Religions,* which has sold nearly three million copies, but Huston did not pursue the different religions in order to write a book about them. He had no checklist to go down, faith by faith. In moving from Christianity to Hinduism and from Hinduism to Buddhism and from there to Islam, he was also exploring unexamined parts of himself. He decided to show others, by writing and teaching, how to do similarly, how to have the greatest inward adventure of all.

The fact that he, that anyone, could cross all religious boundaries may have some implication for our troubled geopolitical planet. For centuries, before 1900, say, the major religions were largely either ignorant of or hostile to one another. By the time Huston began teaching in the 1940s, an interfaith dialogue was under way that paid respects to the validity of faiths other than one's own. After midcentury visionaries like Thomas Merton and Thich Nhat Hanh went even further and explored other spiritual traditions to enhance their religion of origin. But Huston went furthest of all: he approached Islam, Buddhism, Hinduism, and Judeo-Christianity as though each represented a different aspect of his inner self, each providing another piece in the jigsaw puzzle of being human. At the present time when religious-sponsored hatred is a planet-threatening disease, Huston's antidote of this further possiblity should hold some interest.

This may be the most ambitious book some readers will have held in their hands. *The World's Religions,* written a half century ago, helped establish comparative religion as a field of study, and the book exerted an appeal far beyond academia. *The World's Religions,* however, is only the upper tip of the iceberg. Huston's larger ambition—visible here, as one essay succeeds and complements another— is a planet-wide, centuries-long scavenger hunt: through all historical time and all human geography he rummaged for whatever might enrich the inward life of one living today. All eras—prehistorical, ancient, medieval, modern, postmodern, and post-postmodern—are his time frame; the round earth—the civilizations of Far East China and Japan, India and Tibet, the Judeo-Christian West, and Native America—are his playing field. He would peel "reality" back to see what's there in dimensions not visible to the naked eye; he would do the same for human selfhood, descending stratum by stratum, exploring personhood's remote nooks and crannies. Possibly no one will be so intellectually intrepid again. At least not if he or she wishes to remain academically respectable.

In fact, Huston's outsized vision was not easily accommodated in modern academia. At MIT, though his courses were the most popular in the philosophy department, his colleagues mistrusted someone who not only taught religion, but actually appeared to believe it. Students came to do graduate work under Huston, but MIT forbade him to teach graduate students. Near the end of his teaching career, at a religious studies association meeting, Huston made his eloquent Grand Summation. He had not only taught the world religions, he declared, but he had humbly tried—as a professor and as a human being—to live by their living wisdom. His mission had been to provide his students a better world, a resacramentalized understanding, wherein to dwell. When his speech ended, instead of applause there was cold, stony indifference. Such a declamation might have been normal in Socrates' Athens; at a contemporary religious studies meeting, in the university today, Huston's passion sounded questionable, if not exactly a reportable offense.

Huston did not think, however, that what was taught in a class should stay in the classroom; he wanted it replicated, not contradicted, in how one—particularly how he—lived outside of teaching hours. Almost as much as for *The World's Religion*, Huston is known for being a professionally lovely man. When the TV interviewer Bill Moyers met Huston, Moyers was so charmed that he created a five-part TV series on Huston for PBS. *The Wisdom of Huston Smith* showed the correlation between the man and the knowledge, between Huston's *worldview* (he prefers that word over *religion*) and how he embodied that worldview in day-to-day life. We might thus want to steal a glance through the window, to first gain a personal sense of the living thinker behind his written-down thoughts.

For a full portrait of Huston the place to look is his memoirs, *Tales of Wonder.* Given the limited space here, I propose doing something far more modest. If I recall my first encounters with Huston, it is because they are of small, manageable size and have the advantage that I know about them. They also have the advantage of being typical. Everyone, I gather, reports something similar when first meeting Huston.

Our first meeting happened almost by chance. My publisher sent Huston a manuscript of mine requesting a blurb, which he with characteristic generosity supplied; Huston also wrote me personally and ended his note with a polite, "If you are ever in the Bay Area, stop by."

I was going to the Bay Area, for one day before heading to Northern California, so—what the hell—I phoned him. Hardly surprising, he was unavailable that particular day: he was famous and on the go, especially for someone already past his eighty-fifth year. I let the prospect drop, but in his cracking voice he said, "No, wait. If you are going *to* Northern California, you have to come *back*. What day back?"

That day he would be there, but the problem was, though Huston began going deaf in his early fifties and can read lips perfectly, he cannot lip-read over the telephone. Unable to hear, he said, "I will now proceed down the hours of the day. Stop me at the right one. Eight. Nine. Ten. Eleven. Twelve. One. Two. Three—" "That one," I yelled.

At three P.M. on that day Huston was waiting at the Berkeley BART station. He was charming from the word go. "So you're not just a writer," he joked. "You're a human being, too." Huston started the car, saying, "On the drive home, we'll observe the Buddha's Noble Silence. That way, who knows, maybe we'll get there alive." Someone else might have whined, *Too damned old, can't talk and drive at the same time,* but Huston, with his allusion to the Buddha, converted it into something of a game. At his house, as he got out of the car osteoporosis had his body hunched over practically in the shape of a question mark. He saw me looking and said, "I know. But it's workable."

Once inside, conversation ranged. No subject was off-limits. Huston told of the tragedy much on his mind, of his beloved granddaughter's murder (described at length in *Tales of Wonder*). He described how a reporter had rudely asked him, "Is your faith in God shaken now?" Huston considered it the most foolish question ever put to him: Human tragedies do not invalidate the possibility of hallowed sacredness but, to the contrary, make it more necessary. Switching from his private life to his work, Huston reported just finishing *The Soul of Christianity*, and he had, he said, two more books in him to write. After that he would break his pencil, or rather turn off his computer, and read everything that he had never had time to. At present he was reading a wonderful book, *Don Quixote.* Before driving me back to the BART station, he asked, "Would you want the manuscript of *The Soul of Christianity*? Or too cumbersome for the plane?" It seemed more than mere hospitality to a passing guest. The question appeared quietly addressed as much to himself: What else can I do? How can I enhance this present moment, to nudge it toward indelibility? Every turn of the day presents either an obstacle or an opportunity, and Huston wants to maximize each, including this one, into an opportunity realized.

Obstacles metamorphose into opportunities? I recalled how over the phone Huston had arranged our appointment time: semi-deafness was not to be an obstacle. Nor was his inability to converse on the drive home; nor was his osteoporosis. Huston is a modern religious figure who shows that religion is more than theological truths and greater than moral precepts. Religion, for Huston, seems to be what allows you to take the difficult, the unacceptable, the unthinkable (such as his granddaughter's death), and, denying nothing, allows you to bear it, sorrow as the tragic other side of love. Such was my reflection as I got on the BART train.

Our next visit came about when I was to interview Huston for a magazine article about spirituality and aging. He was by then more housebound, no need to designate an hour, just say that on such-and-such a day I'd be coming. But such-

and-such a day followed, as sometimes happens, after such-and-such a night. That morning I awoke too debauched to interview a groundhog. But I roused myself and once at his house talked of this and that, and in a superficial way it could hardly have been more pleasant. At the end Huston exclaimed, "So enjoyable. This wasn't an interview. It was a social occasion. And what a wonderful one!"

How gracious was Huston's remark, especially considering—though it sounded like a compliment—I could detect his disappointment. Although eighty-eight he still wanted the intellectual give-and-take, wanted to be stimulated and challenged: his mind wanted a symposium. The visit (though embarrassing to me) showed the powerlessness of age to diminish the eagerness and engagement of his mind. As for the magazine article, Huston had given me, without my needing to ask a single question, a demonstration of the vigor of spirituality and aging.

The following year his publisher asked me if I would work with Huston on his memoirs. I would have done it for free. I wanted to take down the dictation of ninety years of a better way to live, to learn the secrets of remaking adversity into its opposite. *The World's Religions* (and the world religions) exist *out there:* this would like taking a front-row seat—as the reader here has such a seat—and seeing the mind behind them from *within.*

To return to the beginning. For the life arc Huston was to traverse there was no earlier precedent. From the vantage point of a century ago, his career would have been flatly inconceivable. He grew up a missionary's son in a Chinese village that had no electricity, no running water, no movies, no radio, and no newspaper. Saint Augustine or Plutarch would not have suffered future shock there. As a missionary's son, Huston was a devout Christian with an unshakable faith. Today, some ninety years later, he is a devout Christian with faith unshakable. The beginning and the ending, though they sound similar, are worlds apart. *Worldview* (from the German *Weltanschauung*) is a favorite word of Huston's, for good reason. To get from point A to point Z, from there to here, he had to discard one worldview after another, the way a gangly youth sheds clothes he's outgrown. Or to use a different metaphor: A historical building, because of zoning regulations, retains its old facade but is entirely renovated inside. Likewise, his serene childhood Christianity Huston has refurbished from within, with panelings and moldings hardly known to Christianity before.

At age sixteen Huston left China to attend college in America. His ship sailing across the Pacific crossed centuries, from a missionary backwater in Asia to high-tech America, with its wheels turning and churning, all science and rationality and material progress. At age sixteen Huston felt that this-worldly sleek modernity was heaven on earth, salvation in secular terms. He mastered this secularized salvation oddly from a theologian, the renowned Henry Wieman, his professor at the University of Chicago (and subsequently his father-in-law), who had advanced religion to the point where it could dispense with, well, religion. Unitarians—so runs an old joke—believe in one God *at most*. In Wieman's theology the Creator has been replaced by the creative process, which is extraordinary but not supernatural; Christ the Redeemer, replaced by a Jesus who catalyzes his disciples' creative ability to transcend societal limitations. In his twenties Huston believed in this heavenly city in the earthly here and now where everyone would be educated, equal, materially satisfied, and emotionally content. This is the modern Enlightenment (and for a while Huston's) vision: remove theological distraction, focus on what we can rationally control, and we may improve this present world until we need no other. All the founding fathers of the modern world, from Lenin and Sun Yat-sen to Atatürk and Nehru, had subscribed to some version of this beautiful secular dream.

Huston watched that semi-utopian dream—so new, so shining, so promising—shatter into pieces. All the world, Africa and Asia and the Middle East, was expected to xerox into secular middle-class replicas of Euro-America. The purveyors of this visionary modernism were caught off-guard and stunned when religious fundamentalists—instead of fading into inconsequence—began assuming control of politics and governments. Huston was early in perceiving the limitations in the Enlightenment vision. If Huston was prescient, though, it was because a worldview in which spirituality was marginalized had failed to satisfy him personally. Although he fought for racial and economic justice, from his childhood lingered more elusive longings and meanings that no civil polity, no matter how just, can fulfill. If the physical world is all, Huston thought, then we are like condemned prisoners on death row, trying to forget our situation by ordering up as tasty a last meal as possible.

All the "principal architects of the modern mind" (as he calls them in *Why Religion Matters*) had thought in a way Huston was ceasing to think. The intellectual headmasters of *l'école moderne* had all been, he now realized, rabidly antireligious. One had likened religion to a drug (Marx); another compared it to useless extra baggage (Darwin); a third, to a slave's mentality (Nietzsche); while the fourth dismissed it in one word, an illusion (Freud). Huston would hear similar disparagements about his chosen field his whole professional life. His colleagues would wonder, sometimes aloud, how anyone so likable and intelligent could believe such mumbo-jumbo and not only believe it but actually teach it in a classroom. At MIT a social scientist came up to Huston and with a witty double entendre asked, "Do you know the difference between you and me? I count and you don't."

His secular period now behind him, Huston was counting in a different way, or rather counting on something else. Indeed, he may well have become the first person of such prominence in contemporary academia to take religion seriously. The religion department, in the few universities that then had one, had a bias, strange to say, against the very thing they taught. For the modern study of religion took place within the modern view of reality, which denies to religion (unlike politics, say, or economics) a legitimacy of its own. What was taught as religion was in effect sociology or history or anthropology, using religion as its case study. When Huston read John Updike's *Roger's Version,* he found a passage he could have written himself. A Jesus freak confronts the professor of religion:

> What you call religion around here is what other people call sociology. That's how you teach it, right? Everything from the Gospels to *The Golden Bough,* Martin Luther to Martin Luther King, it all happened, it's historical fact, it's anthropology, it's ancient texts, it's humanly *interesting,* right? But that's so safe. How can you go wrong? Not even the worst atheist in the world denies that people have been religious. . . . [S]tudying all that stuff doesn't say *anything,* doesn't *commit* you to anything, except some perfectly harmless, humane cultural history. What I'm coming to talk to you about is God as a *fact,* a fact about to burst upon us, right up out of Nature.

The courses Huston offered in world religions did not play it safe. He tried to teach students about the vast unexplored human possibilities that he was in the process of learning himself through encountering the world's religions.

For instance? The most important thing Huston discovered was that there are radically different ways of being. Different people have contrary emotional responses to the same social stimulus; they give the same phenomenon opposite interpretations and then mistake that interpretation for the objective world. Venturing beyond Judeo-Christianity, Huston was amazed: all people believe alike even less than they all physically look alike. Dissimilar predispositions had proliferated into divers paths to salvation. In Hinduism, for instance, there are four basic human temperaments, hence there are four kinds of yogis. There are *karma* yogis (e.g., Gandhi) who attain liberation through action, and there are *bhakti* yogis (e.g., Saint Francis or Mother Teresa) who have great feeling and love their way to salvation. *Raja* yogis (e.g., the Buddha) meditate their way there, while *jnana* yogis reach the ultimate goal through intellect or vision. Thus Huston came to realize that the world is incorrigibly plural. And in a shock of recognition Huston identified himself as a *jnana* yogi, somebody who could use his intelligence, his teaching and writing, to help resacramentalize the world.

How can life be resacramentalized? Huston realized: Not easily, not merely by thinking it so. Lasting salvation rarely occurs in a book-lined study, and the words Huston wrote in such places reflected what he had experienced outside of them. He traveled to Japan and India; he sought out sages and swamis; he lived in ashrams and monasteries; he participated in retreats and *sesshins* and *kumbla melas*. He also spent time on Native American Indian reservations and befriended psychics and experimented with hallucinogenic drugs, for ways to enhance and ennoble the human pilgrimage.

Back in the 1960s when you said you'd returned from a trip, you might be asked, *Which kind?* Huston was interested in both kinds, voyages outward and voyages inward. Indeed, some cultural histories remember Huston less for what he wrote than for what he ingested. Although his use of mescaline was infrequent, Huston never denied the importance of his experience. In the blink of an eye, or rather in swallowing a pill, the curtains seemed to part, opening up another, the mystic's world(view).

The curtains part. On New Year's Eve, 1961, when Huston took two tabs of mescaline at Timothy Leary's house, it might have been odd if he hadn't. Far from bearing a stigma, hallucinogenic drugs then carried a positive connotation, a gateway to elusive wisdom. Huston recalled William James's experience after taking nitrous oxide (laughing gas):

> Our normal waking consciousness . . . is but one special type of consciousness, whilst all about it, parted from it by the filmiest of screens, there lie potential forms of consciousness entirely different . . . . [A]pply the requisite stimulus, and at a touch they are there in all there completeness . . . . No account of the universe in its totality can be final which leaves these other forms of consciousness quite disregarded.

Huston had read these sentences before; on the night of January 1, at Leary's house, he lived them. Mescaline allowed the mystical vision he knew from books to rise up through his senses. After taking the mescaline, his awareness crossed through the gateway of the three dimensions into normally hidden aspects of existence that evidently had been waiting there, as James had said, behind the thinnest of partitions. He laughed to think how the great religious visionaries of history, had they experiences like this—and they probably had—were just a bunch of hack reporters. In a suburban house in Newton, Massachusetts, Huston had become a visionary himself—"one who not merely believes in the existence of a more momentous world than this one but who has actually visited it." Certain hallucinogenic (or "entheogenic") drugs, he saw, could occasion genuine religious experiences, even if—unlike Judaism, say, or Native American spirituality—they do not solidify into an enduring religious life.

That Huston achieved his mystical experience through drugs, which were a "tool" of his particular time, does not discredit it or him. He wanted to be more than a professor; he would be the person who says, *I am here, I am not aloof, I and the world are not separate.* Thus after World War II, when America went from isolationism to becoming an international power, how fitting it was that Huston then reinterpreted religion using a global perspective. After the atom bomb dropped on Hiroshima he joined other concerned intellectuals to oppose nuclear proliferation. Later he invited Martin Luther King Jr. to help end segregation at Washington University, and later still he protested America's war in Vietnam. During the 1960s, in the years of student activism, Huston went from lecturing formally to a give-and-take interaction in his classes, modeled on Martin Buber's *I and Thou*. As feminist consciousness grew, he corrected his ingrained male-superiority bias and treated his female students with equal if not greater respect. Do such things have anything to do with religion? No, and yes. Unless you would be a holy hermit, Huston thought, you must quit the cloister of abstract theories and go out and engage the spirit of your times.

Which raises a question: Was there a unique "spiritual" character to Huston's era? And what was it like to be a religious person, a *jnana* yogi, during the twentieth century? Let's take a look.

Everything has a history—the rise and fall of nations, the novel, even the forms of intimate relationships—so it would be hardly surprising were there a subterranean history of spirituality, too. Huston was an attentive, attuned observer of the unexpected spiritual developments unfolding in his time. For example, he studied how the lamas fleeing the holocaust in Tibet reshaped their medieval religion into contemporary, verifiable experience. Even innovations in technology, which Huston's life span was agog with, can color the complexion of religious truth. To cite one example: people who died used to stay dead, but now medical technology can occasionally resuscitate the corpse. In these near-death experiences (NDEs) the resurrected, reporting their "other side" experience, seem for the first time to actually demonstrate death terminating people's life but not their consciousness. Huston's *modus operandus* was not merely to observe and record but also to participate in the changed and changing human inwardness of the twentieth century. He may have begun his life as a Christian and may be a Christian today, yet through such involvement—through his love-hate relationship with science, for instance, or in his exploration of other faiths—he has reinterpreted what Christianity can mean today.

In 1896 Andrew Dickson White published his influential *A History of the Warfare of Science with Theology in Christendom,* and that war was still waging when Huston was young. He recognized how in modernity science had replaced religion as the force that would redeem the world; it was science (and a social scientist) that told Huston that he did not count. Huston took up the challenge: in books and essays he argued that while science was valid and valuable, "scientism"—a materialist worldview extrapolated from science—was unproven, hence even unscientific. Yet even as he wrote, science was changing its tune.

Dark matter, observer-determined reality, particles interacting across millions of light-years, and so on, all were so fantastical as to make angels dancing on pinheads seem positively mundane. Huston was almost incredulous: science was on his side now? Folks who believe in more than what can be vouchsafed by the five senses used to be dismissed as poets or lunatics; now they were called physicists and cosmologists. "Science that saddled us with reductionistic materialism is going beyond that position," Huston exulted. "Materialism is now old hat." Science, formerly the rebuttal to a speculative or nonmaterialist worldview, had become its corroboration. The mountain had come to Muhammad.

It was a new era. Huston felt its newness in the changed way religions were relating to one another. Throughout history each faith had been largely sequestered in its own territory or ideology. Now they were suddenly in each other's face: far had become near, and a slight familiarity with one's religious neighbors was a good reason for hating them. Each religion, feeling hemmed in and threatened on an ever more claustrophobic globe, developed a militant fundamentalist strain that was preaching hate or, worse, lighting dynamite. Yet there was also, across at the other end of the spectrum, a "liberal" concern as religion became plural, *religions*. It was the right and progressive thing to say that all were valid, but did that not dilute the absolute truth value of any particular one? If all religions are true, the worry was, then in a sense none are. Huston's response to this quandary was neither fundamentalism nor the "spiritual supermarket": he showed a third possibility besides jihad or ecumenical conference. He had practiced Judeo-Christianity, Hinduism, Buddhism, and Islam and gotten some benefit from each and more from all of them together. Why straitjacket yourself? Everyone has different personae—a wife can also be a mother, a daughter, and an accountant simultaneously—and Huston likened the world's religions to humanity's various personae. Personally he had tried them all on for size, and they all fit. This may be Huston's chief lesson for the twenty-first century (in one sentence): empathizing with your enemy/neighbor is better than blowing him—and in the process, yourself—to smithereens.

Huston knew the dark, destructive side of religion, yet he chose to write about its positive aspects for the same reason that one listens to good, not bad, music. How else, he said, can you gain some personal benefit from it? Throughout his career Huston, by taking religion so seriously, was looked on by his colleagues as an atavism, a curiosity, out of step with his times. Now, in retrospect, it seems that it was he who had his finger on the pulse, after all. This Reader conveys the best of Huston Smith's endeavors to understand, finger on the pulse, spirituality in our time. More than understand: not academic monographs, his writings themselves came to play a part in the story of religion, as he attempted to make it meaningful, and helpful, for his contemporaries.

WELCOME TO THE READER

A Reader is obviously a book, but it is a distinctive kind of book. Most books, be they novels or works that convey information, flow smoothly from beginning to end. Not so with most Readers; they can seem disjointed in the sequence of their chapters. In this particular Reader, however, there is a sequence as one section leads into the next, and the whole of it, I hope, not only coheres, but becomes greater than the sum of its parts.

Readers have a rationale, a reason for being published, and the rationale for this book was straightforward. I wanted to bring together essays and selections from books that I wrote at different times and that were published in a variety of places.

I wanted to do this because the reading public has changed. The first generation of readers has passed on, but the "worldview" that the essays present should continue to be of interest to everyone who has a reflective bent. Some chapters are likely to jolt readers, springing on them things they have not thought of before. We might think of this volume as a data bank of reminders that bring to conscious awareness what for the most part is simply taken for granted.

In any case, here it is. If the reader enjoys and learns from it, I will be very pleased.

Huston Smith
March 2011
Berkeley, California

BOOK ONE

A Personal Starting Point

No Wasted Journey

A Theological Autobiography

Socrates told his tribunal that he didn't fear his sentence because if death was the end it would be like falling into untroubled sleep, while if his soul migrated to another realm he would meet the heroes of the past and a just tribunal, which would make it no wasted journey. When I found that passage from the *Apology* inscribed on a historical marker in Athens, the words *no wasted journey* jumped out at me, for I was on my first trip around the world, and they captured my mood perfectly. Not only was girdling the globe not a waste. Neither was life's journey, for I was learning so much!

I mention this because, though the prospect of writing my memoirs has never appealed to me (not even for grandchildren), I have toyed with the thought of what an appropriate title might be were I to do so, and in early manhood, "No Wasted Journey" was the obvious choice. In my forties, though, it gave way to "That Strong Mercy," for I underwent a midlife crisis which only mercy (it felt like) pulled me through. And in these later years, "Bubble Blown and Lived In" displaces both preceding candidates. For though I am not a constructionist, it does feel (now) as if I have spent my years sweeping out a horizon of beliefs, soap-bubble thin, that I could live in.

How that bubble took shape, together with the iridescent colors that swim on its surface, I have been invited to recount. Some things that I wrote in the introduction to the book I co-authored with David Griffin, *Primordial Truth and Postmodern Theology*, apply equally to the start of my story, so my first several paragraphs will follow that earlier statement closely.

SEARCH

I was born of missionary parents in China, and spent my formative years there. I don't suppose one ever gets over that. Because we were the only Americans in our small town, my parents were my only role models, so I grew up assuming that missionaries were what Western children grew up to be. As a consequence, I came to the United States for college, thinking that I would return to China as soon as I was theologically accredited, but I had not reckoned with the West's dynamism. Never mind that my landing pass was Central Methodist College, enrollment six hundred, located in Fayette, Missouri, population three thousand. Compared with Changshu (or even Shanghai of that day) it was the Big Apple. Within two weeks China had faded into a happy memory; I wasn't going to squander my life in its backwater. The vocational shift this entailed, however, was small. Instead of being a missionary I would be a minister.

My junior year in college brought a second surprise: ideas jumped to life and began to take over. To some extent they must have gained on me gradually, but there came a night when I watched them preempt my life with the force of conversion. Returning from a meeting of a small honor society that gathered monthly for dessert and discussion in the home of its faculty sponsor, several of us lingered in the corridor of our dormitory to continue the arguments the evening had provoked—as unlikely a knot of peripatetics as ever assembled. My excitement had been mounting all evening, and around midnight it exploded, shattering mental stockades. It was as if a fourth dimension of space had opened and my mind was catapulting into it. And I had my entire life to explore those endless, awesome, portentous corridors. I wonder if I slept at all that night.

In retrospect it seems predestined, but at the time I could only see it as providential that the faculty sponsor of our discussion group was a protégé of Henry Nelson Wieman, who had founded the school of naturalistic theism almost single-handedly. Wieman was at the University of Chicago, so it was inevitable that I proceed there for my graduate study. Having earlier shifted my vocational intent from missionary to minister, I now moved next door again by opting to teach rather than preach—although in moments of misgiving I suspect that I have friends who think I never accomplished that move. When Charles Kingsley asked Charles Lamb if he would like to hear him preach, Lamb replied, "I don't think I have ever heard you do anything else." That's too close to home for comfort.

Because those vocational adjustments were obvious and small, they occasioned no soul-searching; but as I think back, I am surprised that I didn't find the collapse of my youthful supernaturalism disturbing. I entered the Divinity School of the University of Chicago a committed Wiemanite. Despite World War II—I was headed for the chaplaincy, but the war ended before I made it—Chicago was an exciting time for me. Via naturalistic theism, my vocation was clear. It would be to align the two most powerful forces in history: science and religion. I was a very young man, and fresh to the world's confusions.

I can remember as if it were yesterday the night in which that entire prospect, including its underlying naturalistic worldview, collapsed like a house of cards. It was four years later, in Berkeley—but before I relate what happened, I need to explain how I got there. Chicago proceeded as planned, with one surprise. Although in my first year I would not have believed that such a thing was possible, in the second year I discovered something better than Wieman's theology, namely, his daughter. Two years later we were married. We celebrated our golden wedding anniversary last fall.

As I was now a member of Wieman's family, he couldn't direct my dissertation, but he did suggest its topic. Stephen Pepper at the University of California had written his *World Hypotheses,* one of which was pragmatism (or contextualism, as he called it), which was close to Wieman's metaphysics; so he sent me to Pepper to explore the fit. With a wife and an infant child, I spent 1944–1945 in Berkeley writing my doctoral dissertation, "The Metaphysical Foundations of Contextualistic Philosophy of Religion."

In the course of that year I chanced on a book, *Pain, Sex, and Time,* by Gerald Heard, who is credited for moving Aldous Huxley from his *Brave New World* cynicism to the mysticism of *The Perennial Philosophy,* and reading it brought the collapse of my naturalism that I mentioned above. The mystics hadn't figured much in my formal education, but when I encountered a sympathetic presentation of their position, I responded from the soles of my feet on upward, saying, Yes, yes! More than any other outlook I had encountered, it was their vision, I was convinced, that disclosed the way things are.

Mysticism pointed toward the "mystical East," so, Ph.D. in hand and teaching now, I cut back on philosophy to devote roughly half my time (as I have ever since) to immersing myself in the world's religions; *immersing* is the right word, for I have always been devotee as much as scholar. During my eleven years at Washington University (1947–1958) this involved weekly tutorials with a swami of the Ramakrishna Order who grounded me in the Vedanta and set me to meditating. When I responded to MIT's call to strengthen its humanities program by adding philosophy to it (my years there were 1958–1973), I shifted my focus to Buddhism and undertook Vipassana [a type of meditation] practice in Burma, Zen training in Kyoto, and fieldwork among the Tibetans in their refugee monasteries in North India. Angry at the hammerlock that analytic philosophers had on the field—in those days Harvard, Princeton, and Cornell constituted a "Bermuda Triangle" in which "planes" that entered from outlying territories disappeared professionally—I welcomed a bid from Syracuse University to move from philosophy to religious studies, and invested my last decade in full-time teaching (1973–1983), primarily in its graduate program. Asia-wise, that decade brought Islam into my lived world, through Sufi *sheikhs* [spiritual masters] that I encountered in pre-Khomeini Iran and North Africa—their five Arabic prayers continue to frame my day. On retiring from Syracuse we moved to Berkeley to be close to our children and their families. Until this year I continued to teach half-time: semesters here and there across the country, an occasional course at the Graduate Theological Union, and the last three years at the University of California. The new incursion on my religious front has been the primal religions. I helped edit a book with Reuben Snake (a leader of the Native American Church), *One Nation Under God: The Triumph of the Native American Church,* to help restore to that Church the rights the Supreme Court stripped it of in its 1990 *Smith* decision.

This all sounds flagrantly eclectic, and I can't argue that it wasn't, for the truth of the matter is that in culling from the world's religions what was of use to me, I was largely ignoring their differences. What they said about reality seemed sufficiently alike to carry me as I stepped from one to another like a hunter crossing ice floes, but I had no real idea what to do with their differences. I had been avoiding that question for some time when, in the course of a year-long around-the-world seminar that I co-directed in 1969–1970, I ran into Professor S. H. Nasr in Iran, who pointed me to a small group of thinkers who had the answer I was looking for. Referred to sometimes as Perennialists, sometimes as Traditionalists, their roots were in the *sophia perennis* and "Great Chain of Being." René Guénon and Frithjof Schuon have been their chief twentieth-century spokesmen, and I also recognized the names of Ananda Coomaraswamy, Titus Burckhart, Martin Lings, and Professor Nasr himself. Meeting those men changed everything. As their position has remained in place for me since I encountered it, autobiography will enter into the rest of what I have to say only to indicate why I found its key features plausible.

DISCOVERY

In the foreword to his collection of essays by Perennialist writers, titled *The Sword of Gnosis,* Jacob Needleman puts his finger on what struck me first about these thinkers.

> [They] were not interested in the hypothesizing and the marshaling of piece-meal evidence that characterizes the work of most academicians. On close reading, I felt an extraordinary intellectual force radiating through their intricate prose. These men were out for the kill. For them, the study of spiritual traditions was a sword with which to destroy the illusions of contemporary man.

I shall come back to those illusions, but let me begin with the contrast with academicians. None of the teachers I had actively sought out—Huxley and Heard, Swami Satprakashananda, Goto Roshi, the Dalai Lama, and Sheikh Isa—had been academicians. They had served me as spiritual directors as much as informants; I know the ashrams, *viharas,* and monasteries of Asia better than I know its universities. When I found Schuon writing that "knowledge only saves us on condition that it engages all that we are: only when it constitutes a way which works and transforms, and which wounds our nature as the plough wounds the soil," I recognized him as standing in the line of my preceding mentors. With two additional resources. Schuon worked all the major traditions. And he was a theoretician, actively concerned with the way those traditions fit together.

The kingpin in constellating them, he insisted, is an absolute. Only poorly can life manage without one, for spiritual wholeness derives from a sense of certainty, and certainty is incompatible with relativism. Every absolute brings wholeness to some extent, but the wholeness increases as the absolute in question approximates the Absolute from which everything else derives and to which everything is accountable. For (as the opening lines of my *Forgotten Truth* state the point) "people have a profound need to believe that the truth they perceive is rooted in the unchanging depths of the universe; for were it not, could the truth be really important?" If a human life could be completely geared to the Absolute, its power would course through it unrestrictedly, and it would actually be a *jivanmukta,* a soul that is completely enlightened while still in its body.

So much (momentarily) for the Absolute, the One. What of the Many? As the succeeding sentence in *Forgotten Truth* puts the question, "How *can* we [hold our truth to be the Truth] when others see truth so differently?" As I think back on the matter, this is one of the two issues on which the Perennialists have helped me most. The other is the character of the modern world, which I shall take up in my closing section.

THE RELATION BETWEEN RELIGIONS

Having found Hindu, Buddhist, and Muslim (as well as Christian) teachers I had grown to revere, there was no way I was going to privilege one religion over the others. The question was where (within them) was there an absolute I could live by. (It needed to be an ontological absolute, not just a moral absolute, like tolerance or the golden rule, for only ontological realities wield objective power.) I knew that such an Absolute couldn't be slapped together from pieces gleaned here and there, for it was obvious that the power of the historical revelations derived from their respective patterns, or gestalts. To think that I could match such power by splicing *chi* [spiritual energy], say, to *pratiyasammutpada* [literally, "dependent arising"] and the logos made about as much sense as hoping to create a great work of art by pasting together pieces from my favorite paintings. Or creating a living organism from a heap of organ transplants.

The alternative seemed to be to find a single thread that runs through the various religions. This, though, ran into the problem of essentialism. Who is to say what the common essence of the world's religions is, and how could any account of it escape the signature of its proponent's language and perspective?

Caught as I was in this impasse, the Perennialists called my attention to a third possibility that resolved it: Don't search for a single essence that pervades the world's religions. Recognize them as multiple expressions of the Absolute, which is indescribable. One reason it is ineffable is that its essence is single, and knowing requires a knower and a known, which means that we are already in duality. The more understandable reason, though, is that descriptions proceed through forms, and the Absolute is formless.

This solution to the problem of the One and the Many has satisfied me since it first came to view, but I have had to recognize that it is not widely available because most people hear formlessness as lack. To them, if formless things exist at all, they are vague and abstract. Others, though, see matters differently. To distinguish the two types of people, Perennialists call the first type esoterics and the second exoterics.

The lives of exoterics are completely contained in the formal world. For them the formless is (as was just noted) abstract at best. It is incomplete. Lacking in important respects, it is not fully real. Esoterics, on the other hand, find reality overflowing its formal containers into formlessness, though this puts the cart before the horse. Because the formless is more real than the formed, the accurate assertion is that the formal world derives from the formless. The logical argument for the esoterics' position is that forms are finite and the Absolute is infinite, but for genuine esoterics the formless is more than a logical inference. It is an experienced reality. Through a distinctive mode of knowing (variously called *gnosis, noesis, intellectus, jnana,* and *prajna*) esoterics sense the formless to be more concrete, more real, than the world of forms. This is incomprehensible to exoterics because they conclude that an absolute that lacks formal divisions must lack the qualities those divisions fan out. But for esoterics, not only are those qualities in the Absolute; they are there in superessential, archetypal intensity and degree. Opposite of abstract, the Absolute is superconcrete.

I said that the Absolute is indefinable, but we need indications of its character, and these are what the great revelations provide. In doing so, they resemble telescopes that "triangulate" the Absolute like a distant star. What in varying degrees of explicitness they all proclaim is that the Absolute is richer in every positive attribute we know—power, beauty, intelligence, whatever—than we can possibly imagine. This all the major religions assert, and we can understand the logic of their claim. For the only satisfying reason that can be given for the way things are is that it is best that they be that way, so the mind instinctively attributes to what is ultimate the best that it can conceive. The alternative is to accept meaninglessness to some degree.

The consequence of this approach for the relation between religions runs something like this. As the superconcrete Absolute includes all forms, it can deploy them at will. In anthropomorphic (which isn't to say inaccurate) idiom, it chooses to do so in the great formal constellations we call revelations, crowding as much of itself into each as is possible under the formal limitations that finitude exacts. Because the esoteric takes the Absolute to be the formless source of these revelations, he or she can endorse their plurality as alternative voices in which the Absolute speaks to be understood by different audiences.

While this format gave me exactly what I was looking for—(a) an Absolute (b) that didn't require that I rank order the religions I work with—it carries a stubborn consequence. There is no way to satisfy both parts of this two-fold *desideratum* on the formal, exoteric plane. To which hard truth Perennialists add: If it is necessary to choose, it is better to adhere to the Absolute as truly and sufficiently disclosed in one's own revelation than to displace it with the "civil liberties" principle of religious parity, which is no more than a personally arrived at guide for conduct. Somewhere within these last two sentences I sense myself as parting company with my liberal friends in "the wider ecumenism," for they seem willing to reshape the forms of the great, originating revelations to two ends: politically, to reduce conflict by rounding off their sharp corners and rough edges, and theologically, to improve on their truths by learning from others. For my part, believing as I do that each of the enduring revelations already contains "truth sufficient unto salvation," I am not enthusiastic about tampering with them. The project smacks of precisely the sort of human fiddling with the revelations that Perennialists find themselves charged with when their position is mistaken for (a) the cafeteria approach or (b) articulated essentialism.

Continuing with the last point, the chief objection to Perennialism that I hear is that its universalism rides roughshod over differences. I suspect that many such critics would shift their attack from Perennialism's (presumed) New Age all-is-oneism to its (actual) conservatism if they understood that everything that esoterics say about such things, universalism included, presupposes the formed/unformed distinction I have outlined. I was a universalist long before I encountered Perennialism. Where it changed my thinking was in persuading me to balance my universalism with an equal regard for the differences that distinguish revelations. Schuon's *Transcendent Unity of Religions* really is transcendent—radically so in being formless. In our "formal" life, forms are decisively important; so important that the forms of revelation should be respected. The cosmologies and social mores of their day (which they assume) are negotiable, but for spiritual insight we do better to plumb their pronouncements than tinker with them. For those forms are not incidental to the clarity of the message they convey, which clarity accounts for their historical power.

So much for religious pluralism. What of the modern world? Jacob Needleman warned us that for Perennialists "the study of spiritual traditions [is] a sword with which to destroy the illusions of contemporary man." What are those illusions?

CRITIQUE OF THE MODERN WORLD

As long as the issue was the relations between religions, Perennialists was the appropriate name for the thinkers I identify with. When we turn to their view of modernity, it is their other appellation—Traditionalists—that makes their point.

It does so because Traditionalists consider the ethos by which people lived before the rise of modern science to be on balance more accurate than the scientistic one that has replaced it. Not (to repeat the point just mentioned) its science, which has been superseded, or its social mores, but its ontological vision. I wrote *Forgotten Truth* to celebrate that vision; and I wrote its sequel, *Beyond the Post-Modern Mind*, to expose the Procrustean epistemology—again, scientistic—that has caused traditional truth to be largely forgotten. I say forgotten rather than refuted, for there has been no refutation, merely an exchange of traditional ontology for one that derives from an epistemology that (in the short run, at least) caters to our material wants and wish to control, "the Old Adam." There are, of course, oceans of historical and psychological reasons for the West's having made this exchange, but no logical reasons. We simply slid into assuming that the most reliable viewfinder available to our human lot is the scientistic one that edits out spiritual truths in the way X-ray films omit the beauty of faces.

I know that this assessment will be disputed; though actually it is a good day when one encounters dispute, for typically it is simply ignored. When rejoinders are heard, they point out that the preceding paragraph doesn't even mention science; only scientism, with which (by tacit association) science is sneakily tarred.

That reply is useful, for it forces me to drop innuendo, come into the open, and say right out loud that science is scientism. I didn't have the wit (or was it courage?) to arrive at that conclusion by myself; a scientist at the University of Minnesota who teaches science to nonscience majors pointed it out to me at the close of an all-day workshop that I had devoted to distinguishing science from scientism and exempting it from the latter's pernicious effects. "Everything you said about the dangers of scientism is true," he said; "but there's one thing, Huston, that you still don't see. Science is scientism."

His assertion startled me, but on the long walk it provoked I came to see his point. If we define science as the procedures that scientists follow and the demonstrable results that thereby accrue, and scientism as the assumption that the scientific method is the most reliable method for arriving at truth and that the things that science works with are the most real things, thus defined, the two are clearly different. But here's the point. Although in principle it is easy to distinguish them, in practice it is almost impossible to do so. So scientism gets overlooked in the way the power plays that are imbedded in institutions get overlooked until the extraordinary eye of a Michel Foucault spots them and points them out.

The cause of the blur is the one that Baruch Spinoza stated abstractly: things tend to enlarge their domains until checked by other things. This applies to institutions as much as to individuals. The vanguard of science's expansionism is scientism, and it advances automatically unless checked. Religiously, it is important that it be checked, for the two are incompatible. So where are the guardians to keep scientism from sweeping the field? The Traditionalists are the most vigilant and astute watchdogs I see. And scientism is one area where I claim expertise, for my longest tour of duty (as they say in the military; fifteen years) was at MIT.

The chief places I have tried to keep an eye on scientism are:

1. Higher education. Rooted as the universities are in the scientific method, as a recent president of the Johns Hopkins University pointed out, they are *killing the spirit.*

2. Mainline theology. Looking up to their more prestigious counterparts at the universities, seminary professors tend to accommodate to their styles of thought. As those styles do not allow for a robust, alternative, ontological reality, our understanding of God has slipped ontologically. (When was the last time I heard the word *supernatural* from a lectern or pulpit?) This slip is having disastrous effects on mainline churches whose members are moving to evangelical churches, Asian religions, or New Age cults and frivolity in search of the unconventional reality that *homo religiosus* requires.

3. The science/religion dialogue, with evolution as a major checkpoint. The only definition of Darwinism that has survived its multiple permutations is that it is the theory that claims that our arrival as human beings can be explained naturalistically. Scientism must make this claim, but the evidence for it is no stronger than that which supports its theistic alternative. Yawning lacunae in the naturalistic scenario are being papered over with stopgap "god of the gaps" stratagems—the god here is Darwin—that are as blatant as those that theology has ever resorted to.

4. Deconstruction and postmodernism. These thinkers see through scientism, but their constructive proposals make the wrong mistake (as Yogi Berra would say) for being brilliant answers to the wrong question. The question of our time is no longer how to take things apart, but how to work responsibly at reassembling them. For as the opening speaker at the 1992 U.C.B./Robert Bellah–sponsored Good Society Conference put the point: "We have no maps and we don't know how to make them."

If those four one-liners seem extreme and my obsession with scientism a complete tapestry woven from a few threads of fact, I suggest that a reading of Bryan

Appleyard's *Understanding the Present* would alter those judgments. In it he asks us to imagine a missionary to an isolated tribe. Conversion is slow work until a child contracts a deadly disease and is saved by some penicillin the missionary has brought along. With that single stroke, Appleyard argues, it's all over for the world the tribe had known, and by extension for the traditional world generally. For the miracle its medicine men and priests couldn't accomplish, science delivers. And "science has shown itself unable to coexist with anything."

Speaking for myself, if the chiefs of the tribe could reason as follows: This white man knows things about our bodies and how to maintain them that we don't know, and we certainly thank him for sharing that knowledge with us. But it appears that knowledge of that sort tells us nothing about how we and the world got here, who we are in the fullness of our being, what happens to us after death, and whether there are beings of other kinds—immaterial beings, some of whom may be more intelligent, powerful, and virtuous than we are, the Great Spirit, for example. Nor does it tell us how we should live with one another. There seems to be no reason, therefore, why we can't accept the white man's medicine with gratitude while continuing to take seriously the wonderful explanatory myths that our ancestors entrusted to us.

If, as I say, the chiefs could reason this way and hold true to that reasoning, science would not be a problem. But they can't. We moderns and postmoderns can't. And I can't—not wholeheartedly, so scientized is the culture that encases me. But trying to change it is happiness enough.

2

The Way Things Are

TIMOTHY BENEKE Tell us how you started your day.

HUSTON SMITH I began with the Islamic morning prayer to Allah. That was followed by India's hatha yoga, and after that a chapter from the Bible—this morning it was the Gospel of John—which I tried to read reflectively, opening myself to such insights that might enter. Then I was ready for coffee.

BENEKE What do those practices do for you?

SMITH Rabbis say that the first word you should think of when you wake up in the morning is the word *God*. Not even *thank-you* should precede it. I begin my day with the Islamic morning prayer as an extension of that point. I say it in Arabic. Not that I know Arabic, but I learned to pronounce the prayer phonetically because Islam is one of the three religions that require their canonical, prescribed prayers to be said in their original tongues; the other two are Hinduism and Judaism. And, of course, I know what the Arabic syllables of the prayer mean.

BENEKE What do they mean? What do they mean to you?

SMITH A great deal. That so much of what is important in life could be packed into just seven short phrases is almost proof in itself that Islam is a revealed religion.

The prayer opens with "Praise be to Allah, Creator of the worlds." Right off we are given to understand that life is no accident. It has derived from an Ultimate Source that is divine. But what is the character of divinity? The prayer addresses that immediately, in its second line, "the merciful, the compassionate." The Sufis from whom I learned the prayer give different nuances to those two words. Allah is merciful in having created us, and he is compassionate in that he will restore us to himself when our lives end, in keeping with the Koranic assertion "unto Him all things return." Some Sufis use that verse to argue that everyone reaches heaven eventually. Unlike other Muslims, they see hell as a place where sins are burned away; no souls stay there forever. But to continue with the prayer: the assurances of its second line are comforting, but they run the danger of inducing complacency. So the third line counters that danger immediately by adding "ruler of the day of judgment." Not everything goes. Actions have consequences, so we had better watch our step.

Then comes what (from the human standpoint) is the crucial fourth line: "Thee do we worship, and thee do we ask for aid." I was taught that when you come to that central line in the prayer, you should take stock of how your day is going. If it's going well, you should accent the first phrase, "Thee do we worship," and pour out your gratitude like Niagara Falls. If, on the other hand, it is one of those days when you wonder how you are going to get through it, you ask for help: "Thee do we ask for aid." Swallow your pride and admit that we all need help at times.

Truth to tell, by then the prayer has done it for me. Its remaining three assertions basically recapitulate what has gone before and round it off. "Guide us on the straight path, the path of those on whom thou hast poured forth thy grace; not the path of those who have incurred thy wrath and gone astray."

BENEKE How long have you been saying the Muslim prayers—the same prayer, five times a day?

SMITH About twenty-five years. Bodily movements accompany the words, but if circumstances don't permit them—say you are in a shopping line or on a freeway when the hour of prayer arrives—you may say the prayer silently to yourself. The prescribed times for prayer—on awakening, at noon, mid-afternoon, sunset, and on retiring—frame the day nicely. Five times a day, distractions are suspended, and one's attention is drawn to the infinite.

BENEKE After the prayer you turn to yoga.

SMITH Hatha yoga centers me; it gets me into my body somewhat. Ambu, my yoga teacher in South India, would occasionally hold a pose for two hours. I hold the poses for about twenty seconds, a fair measure of the distance between our attainments.

What does hatha yoga do for me? I don't want to claim too much. In the eight steps of Patanjali's "raja yoga"—the way to God through psychophysical exercises—hatha yoga, which works with body postures, is the third step in the program that integrates body, mind, spirit. If you undertake that program seriously, you don't do hatha yoga, the body movements, unless you are also working on the minimal moral precepts that the first two preceding steps prescribe. And the eighty-four postures of hatha yoga lead to the lotus position, where you sit, legs folded, with each foot upturned on its opposing thigh. In that position, you proceed to the remaining five steps, where you work with breathing and meditation. That's raja yoga in its full sweep. I've done it along the way, but it's not my primary path, and now I can't say that hatha yoga does more than counter somewhat the stiffness that comes with age.

BENEKE And why do you follow this by reading the Bible?

SMITH That's more complicated. For over fifty years I've read a passage from one of the world's sacred texts before breakfast. I'm not the first person in history to undertake the spiritual quest, and it's only sensible to draw on the experiences of those who have preceded me. The Bhagavad Gita, the Tao Te Ching, the Koran, the Bible, and the like are data banks of what they learned, so I apprentice myself to them. They are my guides on the path.

So much for the general practice. Now, to why I'm currently reading the Bible? To answer that I have to review my odyssey briefly. My parents were Methodist missionaries in China, so I had a Protestant upbringing, and I was fortunate: it proved to be positive. It "took," so to speak. I find that many of my students look to me like wounded Christians, or wounded Jews, in that what came through to them was dogmatism—we have the truth and everybody else is going to hell—and moralism—don't do this, that, and the other. What came through to me from my religious upbringing was quite different: we are in good hands, and in gratitude for that fact it would be good if we bore one another's burdens.

China was a part of my childhood and youth, and since then I have spent about a decade immersing myself sequentially in the thought and practice of Hinduism, Buddhism, Islam, and the Native American traditions. That pretty much covers the bases except for Judaism, which came to me through a daughter who married a Conservative Jew and converted to his faith. My ongoing involvement (with my wife) in their kosher family means a lot to me. We have a grandson named Isaiah.

During the middle decades of my life it would have been more accurate to consider me a Vedantist, a Zennist, or whatever I was then immersed in, than as a Christian, but I never severed my Christian connections. In the last year or two, though, I've developed an interest in reconnecting with my Christian roots; there's a saying, I believe, that "the child is father of the man." In any case it feels like coming full circle. I have been approaching Christianity this time as if it were a foreign religion like the others I encountered, which in many ways traditional Christianity is in our modern, secular age. This calls for bringing to it the same openness and empathy I tried to direct to the other religions I have studied. Approaching it this way strips away many stereotypes. I'm finding that in its depths, St. Augustine,

Dionysius, Meister Eckhart—not the third-grade Christianity one hears from most pulpits—this new (to me) Christianity is more interesting than that of my childhood.

It poses a problem, though. In its emphasis on loving Christ, Christianity is the most *bhaktic* of the world's religions—*bhakti* being (in Hinduism's four yogas) the way to God through love—whereas I am primarily the *jnanic* type that gets mileage primarily through knowing God. Interestingly, that makes Christianity the most challenging of all the religions I've tried to work my way into. *Jnanic* Christians do exist, it's just that you have to hunt for them. The Church fathers were heavily *jnanic*. They are not read much anymore, but it was they who gave Christianity the theological sinews that have powered it. Anyway, I like challenges. Perhaps working with Christianity will round out a flat side in my personality.

If it does, that will be all to the good, but having touched on the four yogas—the way to God through knowledge, love, work, and meditation—I want to put in a word for my own primary yoga, the first of the four. The knowledge it works with is not rational knowledge. It has nothing to do with quantity of information or logical dexterity—the kind universities tend to prize. It is, rather, an intuitive awareness of things, a discernment of *the way things are*. What could be more important or interesting than that? In any case, that is the direction of my religious search. Religion for me is the search for the Real, and the effort to approximate one's life to it. Such approximation should be easy because the Real is so real, but in fact it is difficult, because we are so unreal. "So phony" is the slang way to put it.

BENEKE Have you been much involved with religious institutions over the years?

SMITH No, I haven't. For one thing they take time—G. B. Shaw said the worst thing about socialism was that it takes too many evenings. And beyond that, institutions are ambiguous. They bring out the bad in people along with the good; I don't know any institution, religious or otherwise, that is pretty through and through. But it has occurred to me of late that in remaining aloof from the institutional side of religion I've been something like a parasite. I live by the truth of the enduring religions, but I've done precious little to help the institutions that have kept those truths alive. I am working now on changing that—trying to repay some of my debt to these religions—and Christianity (as the faith I was born into and am currently focusing on) is the natural place to pitch in.

So I am going to church again. To resurrect a phrase from the 1960s, it feels like I'm "walking the talk" more. As for which church, a friend who knows me well says, "Huston, you are the only Confucian Methodist I know. The only reason you stay with the Methodist Church is filial piety and ancestor worship. It keeps you connected with your parents." There is something to that. As I say, my friend knows me well. But while I hold no special brief for the Methodist denomination or even Christianity vis-à-vis the other world religions, it's the tradition I was born into. And Christianity does house profundities; that's beyond question. So I am exploring them. That is a long answer to why I read the Bible this morning.

BENEKE   One of the major themes of your work is the idea that behind the major religious traditions lies a deep truth that most educated secular people do not understand. It is a metaphysical truth about the universe and eternity, which involves seeing the eternal in the temporal, and seeing all the universe as a manifestation of eternity. This consciousness of the world puts one's own personality and all its accidental qualities, like gender and nationality, in a different perspective, and alters one's orientation to life. I sense that you want passionately to convey this to people.

SMITH   Fair statement. As I suggested earlier, what is more important than the way things are? Sometimes when I give a talk I discover from questions that the audience is only really interested in social issues. I agree that these are important, and though we should all do more, I pay my dues on that front, I think. My wife and I were charter members of the Committee on Racial Equality (CORE) in St. Louis in the 1950s. I do everything I can for the Tibetans, and my book *One Nation Under God: The Triumph of the Native American Church* is on the injustice of the Supreme Court's infamous decision that stripped that Church of its constitutional rights.

Still, isn't it also important to find out the way things are? Religion has many facets, but if you skip the question of what finally exists, it looks pretty much like wheel-spinning to me, and it's hard for me to think of its practitioners as really serious about life's quest. Even practical dealings call for knowing the lay of the land, so to speak. Orientation. Life requires it if it is to be lived well, and orientation derives from knowing the nature of the universe.

Beyond all that, if what exists is in the end incredibly wonderful, to know that fact infuses one's life with energy, call it psychic or spiritual energy, as you wish. Joseph Campbell made that point when he wrote, "It would not be too much to say that myth is the secret opening through which the inexhaustible energies of the cosmos pour into human cultural manifestation." I agree with that assertion, while adding that, at that level, myth and religion are indistinguishable. So beyond the minimal payoff of knowing *where* you are—the payoff of orientation—if where you are turns out to be breathtakingly beautiful, how much greater the reward that comes from knowing—*seeing*—that.

BENEKE   Okay, so where are we? What is the lay of our land?

SMITH   It sounds glib when I put it into words—as bland as $E = MC^2$—but the truth is that absolute perfection reigns. In addition to being glib, it sounds dogmatic when I say it that categorically, but please understand that I see myself as basically a transmitter, reporting what the intellectual and spiritual giants of the past pretty much attest to in unison. Arthur Lovejoy in *The Great Chain of Being*—one of the classics of intellectual history—says that up to the late eighteenth century, when the scientific worldview began to take over, virtually every great sage and prophet the world over saw reality as a vast hierarchy ranging from the barest entities at the bottom, which barely escape nonbeing, all the way up to the *ens perfectissimum,* perfect being, at the top. My studies confirm this report.

I admit that it sounds outlandish to say that absolute perfection reigns, but I have two arguments in its defense. First, Einstein said that if quantum mechanics is true, the world is crazy. Well, experiments since his day have confirmed quantum mechanics, so the world is crazy—crazy from the standpoint of what our senses tell us the world is like. We accept that verdict because we have to; it comes from science. But when the mystics make the same point about the world in its reach for values, we back off because they can't prove their claims.

Look at Bosnia, we say, or the Holocaust; how are you going to square them with absolute perfection? Well, in something of the way a physicist would try to explain to an eight-year-old that the ratio of solid matter to space in the chair he is sitting on is of the order of a baseball to a ballpark, which is to say, not easily. But truth is not easy or obvious in religion any more than in physics. In both we need to get beyond the third grade.

My second rejoinder to people who dismiss absolute perfection out of hand is to point out that if you do that it leads to life being incoherent and not making sense. Either we settle for its not making sense, or we press to the hilt the possibility that it is the way it should be.

BENEKE Even a tumor in your lungs?

SMITH Yes, if we can see that tumor in its total context. We are back to the point that religion takes up where our routine reactions to life leave off. At the center of the religious life is a peculiar kind of joy, the prospect of a happy ending that blossoms from necessarily painful ordeals, the promise of human difficulties embraced and overcome. We don't see the complete picture.

Eighteen months ago our oldest daughter died of sarcoma, one of cancer's most vicious forms, though what cancer isn't vicious? The anguish our family experienced was like nothing any of us had remotely known before.

BENEKE Did you have doubts about the perfection of the universe? Were you angry at the universe?

SMITH Not angry. But of course I couldn't *feel* perfection then. Or more precisely, in a way I *did* feel it, but paradoxically, through my tears. It was as if shards of perfection pierced my sobs through the heroic way our daughter and her immediate family rose to her death. These experiences gave me the conviction that her death was not the last word.

This is quite apart from my own experience. The point is that the only person who has a right to say that things are exactly as they should be is someone who at the time he or she is speaking is feeling the heel of the oppressor's boot smashing down on their face. If you can say it then, it is real. Otherwise, it is Pollyanna escapism.

BENEKE   The most famous example I know of is Aldous Huxley, dying of cancer, saying, "Yes this is painful, but look at the perfection of the universe." I can at times experience the universe as a manifestation of eternity, some great being behind the universe. I can to a degree transcend my own immediate pedestrian needs and involvement, but when this happens I experience extraordinary wonder and terror as well. Castaneda talks about balancing the wonder of being human with the terror of being human. Religion is about this sense of deep belonging in the universe, but I am not so sure that it is benign or friendly.

SMITH   I distinguish between my thoughts and my emotions here. The Hindus speak of the *jivanmukta,* a person who, perfectly enlightened, is uninterruptedly aware of the perfection of things while still in his or her body. They cite Ramana Maharshi [a Hindu spiritual leader] as an instance. For my part, much as I revere Ramana, I'm not sure that even his bliss was unvarying. For several decades now I don't recall that my head has doubted the perfection of things, but experiencing it is a different matter. I doubt that within these mortal coils it is possible to quiet the emotional waves of ups and downs that are our human lot. But my head sees farther than my emotions, and when I'm depressed I can hear it saying, "Poor Huston. He's got the spiritual flu, but he'll get over it."

There is more to be said about the tumor in the lungs, however. One of the reasons I did not doubt God or the eternal during the seven and a half months of our daughter's dying—I touched on this earlier, but want to spell out—was the way she and her immediate family rose to the showdown. Her life had had its normal joys and defeats, but the spiritual work that she accomplished in those thirty or so weeks of dying was more than enough for a lifetime. Her sarcoma cancer began in the abdomen and spread rapidly, exerting pressure on her vital organs. But even when her condition had her at the breaking point, her farewells to us, her parents, in our last two visits were "I have no complaints" and "I am at peace." Her last words to her husband and children (Kendra and I arrived minutes too late) were, "I see the sea. I smell the sea. It is because it is so near." She always loved the sea. I think it symbolized life for her.

BENEKE   A lot of us lapse readily into self-pity when we are sick or in anguish and think that the universe stinks.

SMITH   I have told you what I believe, but I don't think there is proof as to who is right. Life comes to each of us like a huge Rorschach blot, and people fall into four classes in the way they interpret it. First, there is the atheist who says there is no God. Next comes the polytheist who says there are many gods, gods here meaning disembodied spirits of whatever sorts. Then there is the monotheist who says there is one God. And finally, the mystic for whom there is *only* God. None, many, one, and only. Using God as the measuring rod, these are the basic ways we can interpret the universe. There is no way to prove which way is right.

BENEKE   I don't hear you using the word *faith.*

SMITH   That is because the word is so free-floating. Everyone who has not given up has faith in something. If not in God, then in science, life, himself, the future, something. My favorite definition of faith is "the choice of the most meaningful hypothesis."

BENEKE   That sounds a little like William James's pragmatism, which would have us believe things because of their positive effects on us.

SMITH   That was James the psychologist, carrying over into James the philosopher. I'm not a pragmatist; I do not believe in believing in things because of their beneficial effects on us. I reject the argument that says, "Here is this mysterious Rorschach blot, *life.* Let's interpret it optimistically because that energizes us and makes us feel good." To hell with that line of thought! The question isn't what revs us up and makes us feel good, but what is true.

BENEKE   And your intuitive discernment, your *jnanic* faculty as you call it, tells you that the universe is perfect.

SMITH   Yes, but I don't rely solely or even primarily on my own intuition here. The chief reason I accept it is that it conforms to "the winnowed wisdom of the human race," as I like to think of the enduring religions in their convergent metaphysical claims. The word *wisdom* needs to be qualified, though. Not everything in the "wisdom traditions" is wise. Modern science has retired their cosmologies; and their social formulas—master/slave, gender relations, and the like—must constantly be reviewed in the light of historical changes and our continuing search for justice. It is their convergent vision of ultimate reality, the Big Picture, that impresses me more than any of the alternatives that modernity has produced.

BENEKE   Could you tell us precisely what you experience when you "intuitively discern" the perfection of things?

SMITH   Something like Plato's experience when he said, "First a shudder runs through you, and then the old awe steals over you." I would not mind stopping with that, but other sensations can be added. Excitement. Exhilaration. Confidence. Selflessness and compassion. Peace.

BENEKE Underlying religion is the problem of death. Socrates defined philosophy as practice in the art of dying. You embody the traditional notion of the philosopher as a seeker of wisdom, someone who is concerned with the great questions of life. What do you think happens when we die?

SMITH I need to hesitate for a moment, for this is another place where it's easy to sound glib. The only honest answer is, *Who knows?* This is the ultimate mystery. Still, the mind keeps searching for answers, or at least for insights.

To pass into death is an adventure, for sure. Near the moment of his passing, Henry James said, "This is the distinguished moment." What the passage does is to raise again the question of final perfection. I believe in universal salvation, which is to say that everyone eventually comes to something like Dante's beatific vision, which phases out of time into the Eternal Now. That term isn't easy to understand. I have heard even theologians deride eternity as boring. That flagrantly misrepresents the concept. Boredom presupposes time that endures without changes, whereas eternity is outside of time.

BENEKE Boredom is when time is a weight burdening you, and you want to get rid of it.

SMITH Exactly, which is why it could not possibly characterize eternity. There are, however, two conjectures as to what the soul experiences in eternity. We must keep in mind that we are out of our depth here, and that these are what Plato would call no more than "likely tales," that is, human imagination's best stab at the mystery. One conjecture is dualistic. Here the soul retains its separateness and beholds, timelessly, the Glory, in keeping with Ramakrishna's dictum, "I want to taste sugar, not be sugar." In the nondualist version, what the soul beholds is so overwhelming that it commands the soul's complete attention, all 100 percent of it. With zero attention left for itself, that self drops from sight, leaving only what its attention is fixed on. As the Hindus say, "The dewdrop has slipped into the shining sea."

BENEKE This sounds like the German mystic Meister Eckhart saying that "the eye through which God sees us is the eye through which we see God."

SMITH You have it word perfect, though I am still not sure I understand what those words say. Something like what I was saying, I suppose. All the traditions make the point, though, that unless you are the rare case of a Hindu or Buddhist nonreturner, your spiritual work is not complete when you "drop the body," as Indians refer to death. Something remains to be done. Hindus and Buddhists say that *something* gets accomplished in this same world in the new bodies into which they reincarnate. The Abrahamic religions, on the other hand—Judaism, Christianity, and Islam—defer that further work on other planes: purgatory, hell, or other *bardos,* to borrow Tibetan vocabulary. The similarity that underlies these different imageries is quite apparent.

In the period immediately after death there may be a lot of confusion and bewilderment. Swedenborg thought that the first job old-timers in heaven had respecting newcomers was to convince them that they were dead. (I find the thought that heaven is that much like Stockholm rather charming, but also fanciful.) But there are also indications from psychical research—which I don't totally dismiss, though you have to step carefully. There are souls on the other side that are as confused as we are. Channelers and mediums beware! A lot of static gets mixed into the messages. Some souls may even decompose into fragmented residues. The intermediate realm between heaven and earth may be a real mess.

BENEKE Do you think channeling—spirits running through people—provides evidence of the spirit world, a realm beyond the physical?

SMITH There is no conclusive proof that convinces the Bay Area skeptics. Still, Plato took his to his *metaxy,* his "intermediate realm," which housed spirits like Eros, and Socrates's daimon, who never told him what to do but warned him what not to do. Plato took the spirit realm seriously, and I am inclined to do so also. I treat shamanism, for example, with respect. Roger Walsh's book *The Spirit of Shamanism* finesses the questions of whether the shamans' "allies" are a part of their own psyches or exist objectively apart from them. But whatever the geography of the case, in spiritual matters, space never functions as more than a metaphor for difference. Walsh too, as a professor of psychiatry, takes shamanism seriously. Wherever we choose to position them, shamanic "allies" are objectively other than the shamans' conscious minds, and they function accordingly. By the way, shamans appear in the oldest cave drawings we have, which date back about twenty thousand years, and suggest that shamanism may be humankind's oldest religion.

BENEKE The conventional way to dismiss all this is to say that consciousness is a product of the brain; you alter the brain in certain ways, and you alter consciousness. When the brain stops functioning, consciousness stops.

SMITH That could be the case, but I consider it a prejudice of minds that I have come to believe that what we can get our hands on is most real. My reaction to it is like T. S. Eliot's on reading Bertrand Russell's *A Free Man's Worship.* He said it left him with no idea where the truth lay except that it had to be in the opposite direction from the book in hand.

I find it most interesting that the science that saddled us with reductionistic materialism in its early centuries is now going beyond that position. Quantum mechanics is telling us that the universe of space, time, and matter derives from something that exceeds those matrices. Whether or not that

Primordial X is conscious, as religion holds, science cannot say. But at least materialism is now old hat.

BENEKE Noam Chomsky talks about how no one expects a cat to do algebra; similarly, there is every reason to suppose that there are fundamental laws of the universe that humans will never be able to know because of our cognitive limitations. Perhaps our ignorance is inexorable.

SMITH I was Chomsky's colleague at MIT for fifteen years, and I honor him greatly, but here *mystery* seems a more precise word than *ignorance*. In principle ignorance can be dispelled, whereas mystery cannot be, because in its case every advance that we make opens onto horizons we didn't even know existed. We are born in mystery, we live in mystery, and we die in mystery. That is not going to change.

BENEKE Let me ask an impolite question. Religion appears to some people—Freud, for example—as a form of wish fulfillment. Because people want the world to be a certain way, and because it is emotionally satisfying to believe the world is a certain way, people hold certain beliefs about God or life after death. There is evidence that where there are harsh child-rearing practices with a lot of corporal punishment, people conceive of God as very harsh and punitive. What do you make of this?

SMITH I take heart in your child-rearing example. The fact that God has been seen predominately as a loving parent suggests that harsh, punitive, corporal punishment has been the exception rather than the rule. But your question itself I don't take as impolite at all. It introduces an important issue, the appropriateness of psychologizing. Philosophers consider psychologizing a logical fallacy for being ad hominem; it diverts attention from the content of an issue to the persons who are discussing it. "Two plus two equals four" isn't untrue because the person who said it was drunk at the time. That's a crude example of psychologizing, but Freud's critique of religion and those of Marx and Nietzsche as well have the same form.

This is not to say that psychological considerations are irrelevant. We should be wary of what drunks say, and if Freud had proved that religious beliefs derive only, or even primarily, from wishful thinking and father images, I would accept his reasoning and could live with it. But he didn't come close to doing that, so I see his theories as half-truths. There are textbook cases (I won't venture how many) in which they come close to being the full truth about beliefs. But to generalize from these and turn a half-truth into the full truth is a blatant case of disciplinary imperialism. Psychology—or, in the case of Marx's "opiate of the people," sociology—colonizes religion and tailors it to fit its theories. You can see that I'm worked up on the point.

Furthermore, the psychologizing sword cuts both ways. If my beliefs simply reflect my character, yours reflect yours. If I believe because I am infantile, you disbelieve because you are counterdependent. You see why philosophers aren't fond of ad hominen arguments. They degenerate into trading insults. I come back to the idea of the world as a Rorschach blot. If you see it as consisting only of matter, then immaterial things that other people believe in will appear to you as projections. They, in turn, will see you as prey to tunnel vision and blind to half of what exists.

BENEKE Tell us about your experience with your Zen master in Kyoto.

SMITH I was drawn to Buddhism through D. T. Suzuki, whose writings held out the prospect of at least a taste of satori, the enlightenment experience, if one practiced Zen. I was in my mid-thirties, and at that stage I wanted that experience more than anything else in the world, so I entered Zen training, which led eventually to a monastery in Kyoto and *koan* training under a Zen master.

Rinzai Zen (the branch that I was in) uses *koans* [traditional Zen mental exercises] in its training. *Koans* are of different kinds, but the beginning ones are rather like shaggy-dog stories in that they involve questions—riddles, really—that make no rational sense. The one I was given was longer than most, so I won't repeat it in full, but it came down to this: How could one of the greatest Zen masters have said that dogs do not have Buddha-natures when the Buddha has said that even grass possesses it? For two months, I banged my head against that contradiction for eight hours a day. I was sitting in the cramped lotus position and reporting to my *roshi,* or Zen master, one-on-one at five o'clock each morning, what I had come up with. Precious little! It was the most frustrating assignment I had ever been given. I seemed to be getting absolutely nowhere, though I did discover as the weeks slipped by that the final word in the *koan, mu* (which translates into "no"), seemed to function more and more like the *om* mantra that I had worked with in Hinduism.

The climax came during the final eight days in the Myoshinji Monastery in the middle of a kind of final-exam period where everything else gets tabled so the monks can meditate almost around the clock. As a novice, I was permitted to sleep three and a half hours each night, but I found that grossly insufficient, and the sleep deprivation was the hardest ordeal I had ever faced. After the first night I was sleepy, after the second I was bushed, and it kept getting worse from there.

I still don't understand how Zen training works, but it seems clear that the initial *koans* force the rational mind to the end of its tether, and that sleep deprivation figures in somewhere along the line. If you can't get your mind into an altered state any other way, sleep deprivation will eventually do it for you, for deprived of dreams, the mind becomes psychotic.

Something like that happened to my mind two days before the monastic term ended. That afternoon I went storming into the *roshi* in a frenzy. Self-pity had long since become boring; that day I was in a rage. I was furious. What a way to treat human beings, I kept telling myself, and charged in to my *roshi* prepared, not just to throw in the towel, but to throw it straight at his face.

I entered the audience room with the required ritual, palms clasped together. Turning only straight corners because there are no diagonal short-cuts in Zen, I made my way to where he was sitting in his priestly robes. His short, heavy stick (for clobbering if need be) was lying in his lap. Sinking to my knees on the cushion before him, I touched my head to the floor and flexed my outstretched fingers upward, an Indian gesture that symbolizes lifting the dust from the Buddha's feet. Then I sat back on my heels, and our eyes met in a mutual glare. For some moments he said nothing, then, "How's it going?" He was one of the two *roshis* in the world then who could speak English. It sounded like a calculated taunt.

"Terrible!" I shouted.

"You think you are going to get sick, don't you?"

More taunting sarcasm, so I let him have it.

"Yes, I think I'm going to get sick!" I yelled. For several days my throat had been contracting to the point where I was having to labor to breathe.

Then something extraordinary happened. His face suddenly relaxed, its taunting, goading expression was gone, and with total matter-of-factness he said, "What is sickness? What is health? Both are distractions. Put both aside and go forward."

What I despair of conveying to you is the impact those fifteen words had on me. Without reflecting for a moment, I found myself saying to myself, "By God, he's right!" How was he able to spin me around, defuse my rage, and return me to lucidity in a twinkling? I will never comprehend. Never have I felt so instantly reborn and energized. It was as if there was a pipe connecting his *hara*—his abdomen, where the Japanese locate the self's center—to mine. I exited in the prescribed manner, not only determined to stick out the two remaining days, but knowing that I could do so.

It didn't occur to me at the time that in that climactic moment I might have passed my *koan,* and I returned to the States assuming that I had not. But when I related my story to a dharma brother (someone with whom I'd undergone spiritual training) who had trained for twelve years under my *roshi,* he said he wasn't at all sure that I had not passed it. He reminded me that the answer to the early *koans* is not a rational proposition but an experience. That, at the climactic moment in my training, I was able not just to acknowledge the identity of life's opposites theoretically, but to experience their identity. In my case the identity of sickness and health struck him as a strong foretaste of the enlightenment experience.

BENEKE Therapists talk about interventions, which require a certain timing and art where the therapist picks just the right moment to say just the right thing that leads to insight. Your *roshi* intervened in just the right way.

SMITH Apparently so. It still seems to me like genius. He knew exactly where I was, and administered exactly the light tap—ping—that changed everything.

BENEKE Your early work focused on the historical religions, ones that have written texts and cumulative histories. At a certain point you came to appreciate oral traditions as well.

SMITH I now see that in addition to the three great families of historical religions—East Asian, South Asian, and Abrahamic, or Western—there is a fourth: the primal, tribal, and exclusively oral family which is not inferior to the other three. What enabled me to honor tribal peoples as our equals is that while writing adds, it also subtracts. We tend to think that because unlettered peoples only talk and we both talk and write, we have everything they have, and something in addition. I no longer think that it's true. Writing exacts a price, which is loss of the sense of what is important.

Visualize a tribe gathered around its campfire at the close of the day. Everything its ancestors learned the hard way, through generations of trial and error, from medicinal plants to the myths that empower their lives and give them meaning, is stored in their skulls, and there only. Obviously they are going to keep reviewing what is important for them, and let what is trivial fade into oblivion.

BENEKE Tell us about your encounter with the Masai warriors in Africa.

SMITH I was in Tanzania for a conference in the late 1960s and didn't want to leave without a glimpse of big game in its natural habitat. There were no tours, so I found a fly-by-night rental joint and took off in a rickety jalopy for the Serengeti Plain. There was no road map, but that was logical because as far as I could make out there were no roads. I did encounter one road sign during the day, but I couldn't read it, besides which it had fallen over, so I couldn't tell which way its arms pointed.

A couple of hours into the desert, it suddenly dawned on me that I was completely lost. And out of gas. When we rent a car here we assume the tank to be full. Not there. They give you about enough to get out of the lot, but I didn't know that and hadn't checked. At a total standstill, I could not think of a thing to do. The car was too hot to sit in, and there were no trees to shade me from the blistering sun. Giraffes were friendly; one virtually looked over my shoulder when I had had to change a threadbare tire. There were other animals, but at that hour no lions. Dry bones were everywhere, though—portents of my impending fate. I ate my packed lunch, started rationing my last bottle of water, and tried to think of a plan of action.

None had suggested itself when two figures appeared dimly on the horizon. I started toward them, but with every step I took, they retreated. I quickened my pace, making frantic gestures of distress, and they gradually slowed their pace to allow me to catch up with them. They were disconcertingly large and wore nothing but spears taller than themselves, and flapping cloths over their shoulders to ward off the sun somewhat.

What then could I do? I was in human company but without words to communicate. *Something* had to be done, so I seized one of them by the wrist and marched him to my dysfunctional car, his companion in tow. This seemed to amuse them, and why not? What had our move to a pile of metal accomplished?

The two of them conversed and then started to leave, but I seized my hostage's wrist again. Human beings were my only lifeline, and I wasn't going to let it be severed. More laughter and conversation between them, and then one of them started off while leaving his companion with me. When he returned he had in tow a small boy who knew a few words of English, such as *hello, good-bye,* and the like. So, pointing in different directions, I said, "School, school!"

He gave no signs of comprehension, but after more conversation, he and the man who had fetched him went off, leaving my hostage with me. In about an hour, the man returned with ten adult cohorts, and the sun set that evening on as bizarre a scene (I feel sure) as the Serengeti Plain had ever staged: a white man, seated in state at the wheel of his car steering, while twelve Masai warriors pushed him across the sands. My propellers were taking the experience as a great lark. Laughing and all talking simultaneously, they sounded like a flock of happy birds. My first thought was, Who listens? then immediately, Who cares? They were having such a great time.

Six miles across the plain they delivered me to the school I had asked for, which turned out to be Olduvai Gorge, where a decade or so earlier Louis and Mary Leakey [with their son Richard] discovered the tooth that "set the human race back a million years," as the press reported their discovery. That encounter left me with a profound sense of human connectedness. There we were, as different in every way—ethnically, linguistically, culturally—as any two groups on our planet. Yet without a single word in common, we connected. They understood my predicament and responded with a will and with style.

Beware of the differences that blind us to the unity that binds us.

BOOK TWO

The Sacred Dimensions of Everyday Life

3

Two Kinds of Teaching

When I think back over the memorable teachers I had or have known, the fact that stands out most is the diversity of their styles. Bill Levi at Roosevelt College would sit cross-legged on the desk, moving nothing during the entire class hour save his lips and his mind. Meanwhile, at nearby University of Chicago, David Greene was a pacer. Fresh from his farm at eight on wintry mornings, manure still clinging to his boots as Greek poured from his mouth, he strode with a vigor that made the advancing wall seem adversary. We felt sure that sooner or later he would slam his face into it, but he never did; invariably in the nick of time he would swirl and bounce off the wall not his head but his behind, thereby gaining momentum for the return journey. Gustav Bergmann, logical positivist at the State University of Iowa, was so authoritarian that when a student dared to question something he had said he thundered, "Let's get one thing straight: from 10:00 to 11:00 A.M. on Mondays, Wednesdays, and Fridays, there is but one God, and his name is Bergmann!" His opposite was a teacher so nondirective on principle that students used to say he not only didn't believe anything, he didn't even suspect anything. I had teachers who wrestled with me socratically as evangelists wrestled with the village drunkard, and teachers who simply dished it out—very well indeed!

The surprising thing is that learning occurred in all these contexts. I conclude that there is no one way to teach; in writing here of two ways I write only of ways that have taken shape in me. Who knows who learns and under what conditions? The act remains essentially mysterious, like love, or sex, or life itself; more strange than familiar, less science than art, a word to which I shall return.

METHOD I

During its first 20 years, my teaching followed a single pattern. Questions and discussion were encouraged and were fun, but lectures were the focus.

Today, lecturers are on the defensive. Almost everything we would like students to know we can place in their hands via paperback. They can read faster than they can listen to us, and print is durable; they can go back if they miss something or forget.

All this is true, but the points don't add up to the conclusion that lectures are passé. One of my most memorable learning experiences was a course Thornton Wilder offered, once only, at the University of Chicago. The classroom was in fact an auditorium, and it was invariably packed. If there was a single question or comment from the floor I don't remember it, yet the exhilaration of those hours I shall never forget. I would leave the auditorium walking on air. In those early afternoons of autumn even Chicago was beautiful.

Plays, too, can be read faster than we can sit through an evening at the theater, but reading doesn't take the place of the performance. Moreover, lectures provide the opportunity for trying out ideas while they are in process of formation and are thus part of the teacher's laboratory. The advantage to the listener is that he or she is not presented with a finished treatise but is watching a living mind at work and being given an insight into its strategies.

Just as there is no one way to teach, so, too, there is no one way to lecture. John Dewey's lectures are said to have been rambling and dull—until the student awoke to the fact that he was witness to a powerful mind's direct involvement in the act of thinking. Minds have their own dispositions: some, like Wittgenstein's, are splitters; mine happens to be a lumper. This fact, so apparent that I suspect that it is grounded in my brain structure, makes metaphysical reticence impossible for me. And, as it affects my approach to lecturing in other ways as well, before saying more about lecturing proper I propose to indicate why a wholistic approach to my field is, in my case, the only approach possible.

Gestalt psychology has made its mark, and gestalt therapy is bidding to do so. In this age of analysis, this heyday of analytic philosophy, is there a place for wholistic, gestalt philosophy as well?

If this discipline takes its cues from the sciences, the answer seems clearly "yes." Gestalt psychology I have already mentioned; psychology abandoned atomism with its discovery that there is no area of experience, perceptual or otherwise, that is free from what positivists used to call noncognitive factors. In biology, the attempts of molecular genetics "to reach the beautiful simplicity of biological principles through concepts derived from experimental systems in which the ordered structure that is the source of this simplicity has been destroyed [are proving to be] increasingly futile," and physics, in its complete experience, "does not support the precept that all complex systems are explicable in terms of properties observable in their isolated parts [Commoner 1969]."

Turning to philosophy itself, epistemology has found element analysis ineffectual. Whether we approach knowing analytically or phenomenologically, reports agree: there is no datum unpatterned, no figure without ground, no fact without theory. Instead of a one-way process whereby through perceptual archeology irrefrangible primitive elements—Hume's impressions, Russell and Moore's sense data—are first spotted and *then* built into wholes, knowing (we now see) is polar. Part and whole are in dialogue from the start. No man looks at the world with pristine eyes; he sees it edited, and editorial policy is always forged in the widest field of vision available.

The same holds true for ethics, for doing is vectored by overview as much as knowing is. "Deeper and more fundamental than sexuality, deeper than the craving for social power, deeper even than the desire for possessions, there is a still more generalized and more universal craving in the human make-up. It is the craving for knowledge of the right direction—for orientation [Shelton 1936]."

In playing the game of life-orientation, the first rule is to capture everything in sight, for the elusive might prove to be crucial; if it is and it escapes your net, you may get rich, but you won't win. The second rule is to set what has been captured in order, to array it in pattern or design. Thus the twin principles of gestalt philosophy are: (*a*) attention to the whole, taking care to see that nothing of importance has been omitted; and (*b*) attention to the pattern of the whole's parts. Complementing clarity and consistency which are the virtues of analytic philosophy, the virtues of gestalt philosophy are scope and design.

Now back to lecturing. As a gestalt philosopher both these principles of scope and design figure in the way I approach my task. Scope enters to position the topic to be discussed within the panoply of human interests generally. Why among the myriad of things we could talk about during this hour or this semester are we giving time to this? The answer needn't take much time; indeed, no time at all if it is self-evident and acceptable. But it must be evident and acceptable to students, not just to me; that's crucial. Answers which, however evident, are *not* acceptable to students are: "because the professor happens to be working on a paper of the subject," "because this is what the instructor was taught in graduate school, so knows most about—read, is most invulnerable with respect to," "because having avoided math the student needs a course in philosophy to graduate," or "because it will help those who intend to continue in philosophy to get into graduate school."

Once the topic has been positioned in the sense of linked to an acknowledged human interest or need, the elements bearing on the topic must be positioned. Enter pattern or design.

Paintings begin with a discovery, a new and exhilarating perception. Immediately the painter faces enormous difficulties; he must force shapes and static colors to embody what he has felt and seen. The lecturer's task is analogous. He, too, must fix, articulate, and objectify what on first discovery was nebulous, fluid, and private. How, within the artifice of a class hour, can he make a subtle aspect of life or being evident? Every sentence calls for knowledge of his materials and their limitations and an unswerving eye on the effect intended. It is an old problem: how anything of the real can pass the gap between intuition and expression. The passage can be effected only by translation, not from one language into another, but from one mode of being into another, from reception into creation. Everything at the instructor's disposal—facts, concepts, anecdotes, analogies, arguments, humor—must work to enforce the intended impression to the end that at the hour's close the student feels, "that's true and important, or at least interesting." It's no good if he stops with "that's true." As Whitehead noted, "It is more important that a proposition be interesting than that it be true. The importance of truth is that it adds to interest." As irrelevancies deaden the effect, omission is of the essence.

What constitutes a masterpiece here, or (to drop hyperbole) at least an authentic work of art? When a person for whom the topic in question is vital, who as a consequence has lived with it and pondered it, summons everything he or she has discerned on the problem, distills it, compresses it, pounds it into a form that makes sense! Thoughts emerge, not in mere succession, but architecturally, in meaningful pattern—possibly, in addition, they emerge as incarnated in a life that is being lived, his or her own. That's what sent me walking out of Mandel Hall on air those Chicago afternoons. And that, now that I think of it, is the way subliminally I have sensed myself as a lecturer: traveller, pilgrim, archeologist of space and time, trying with the help of a parcel here and a fragment there to piece together the largest possible meaning for life and the world. Such meaning, though it is intelligible, exceeds the merely rational. Or if one prefers, is the highest category of the rational.

In characterizing lecturing as art, my model has been the painter rather than the actor. Not that lectures can't be dramatic performances too; they can be, as the adage that every good teacher is part ham attests. But the comparison means little to me—again, the variety in teaching styles. Writing is as different from speaking as reading is from listening, but the feelings that infuse me while writing and lecturing are much the same. Attention is fixed on content; issues of delivery and audience contact work themselves out unconsciously.

METHOD II

It will be apparent from what I have said that I haven't lost faith in the mix of lecture and discussion that is higher education's abiding rubric. I continue to teach one course each term by this format; it involves me and, given the averages, students show symptoms of satisfaction. But there has been a change. For the last eight years I have also taught a course by almost opposite canons.

This second course roots back to the summer of 1965, when I was invited to Bethel, Maine, to observe for two weeks the work of the National Training Laboratories with small groups: T- (for Training) groups, encounter groups, or human interaction laboratories as they have come to be called. By pleasant coincidence, I was to bring back from Bethel what Bethel had originally drawn from my own home base, for it was from Kurt Lewin's pioneering work at M.I.T. that the National Training Laboratories evolved. Something happened to me at Bethel, but it is also the case that I was ready for it to happen. It wasn't that I had grown disillusioned with higher education, but the question of whether it might not be better had become insistent. For however one assessed its virtues, university learning struck me—and still strikes me—as:

1. *Insufficiently experimental.* It scans less than does industry for improved ways of doing things.

2. *Too authoritarian.* Persons aged 17 to 25 years would at other times have been launched in the world. Here they continue to be subjected overwhelmingly to directives that flow down to them instead of rising from their own volitions.

3. *Too passive* in the role in which it places students. On this point clear proof is at hand. Take a word count in almost any class: who talks most, even in discussion classes and seminars? As learning requires doing, the arrangement is ideal for teachers, but one hears that it's the students who pay tuition.

4. *Too detached* from students' on-going lives, their hopes and involvements, the points where their psychic energy is most invested. It is as if the curriculum's cerebral thrust connects with the top 6 inches of the student's frame while leaving the other 60 inches idling. "It is by living, by dying, by being damned that one becomes a theologian," Luther advises us, "not by understanding, reading, and speculating." Or perhaps by both? What is clear is that academic reading, speculating, and understanding is joined very little to students' living, dying, and damnation. The most substantial recent study of American education, Charles Silberman's (1970) *Crisis in the Classroom,* concludes that reformers and innovators have an obligation to lobby for more emphasis on the education of feelings and the imagination and for a slow-down in cognitive rat-racing.

5. *Too impersonal.* Colleges used to be communities. Universities have in our time become almost the opposite: huge anticommunities like virtually every other institution in our mass, mobile, agglomerate society where rules and regulations take precedence over persons and seasoned relationships.

What encounter groups showed me first and above all else was a way to generate involvement. I hadn't been at Bethel 48 hours before my entire life seemed to sink or swim in terms of my group—my 15 strangers, none of whom I had laid eyes on two days before nor was I likely to see again 10 days thereafter. Swiftly, almost instantly, the criss-cross of human interactions—words, feelings, glances, gestures—had enmeshed me. Thought was emphatically involved, for apart from the therapeutic hour each afternoon when I deliberately turned my mind off and flung myself into the blissfully uncritical arms of impersonal nature (a lake), every waking moment was given to trying to make sense of what was happening. But not thought only; perception, too, as I tried to see what was transpiring in nuances of gesture, tone, and silence, and to feel what was happening in me at subliminal levels. My will, too, was engaged as I wrestled with whether to speak, risk, act.

New possibilities demanded consideration. How, precisely, encounter groups might ameliorate education's weaknesses, I had no idea; but it was inconceivable to me that, operating powerfully in precisely the areas of those weaknesses, they would have nothing to offer. For encounter groups are:

1. *Experimental.* This remains the case even though they have been with us in various forms since World War II. The extent to which they have caught on suggests that they tend to be useful, but they are no panacea. Their utility is neither unvarying nor established by objective criteria.

2. *Nonauthoritarian.* It is part of their definition that leaders leave them largely unstructured, let them develop in their own ways, and use whatever transpires for leaving vehicles. Part of the fascination of such groups derives from seeing what does develop when 8 to 16 lives are closeted for appreciable time while deprived of task, agenda, and assigned hierarchy.

3. *Activating.* Where nothing happens save by the group's initiative, boredom, or anxiety, the will to power and the will to play see to it that initiative is taken.

4. *Involving.*

5. *Personal.* Attention is focused on the here and now, and in encounter groups, this means people. Again, remove tasks, to which lives tend to get subordinated, and lives change from means to ends.

I shall not try here to say what encounter groups are. Let me say only that since 1965, half of my pedagogical interest has been devoted to trying to discern the potential for higher education latent in what Rogers himself considers this "most rapidly spreading social invention of the century, and probably the most potent." To the end of augmenting my understanding of group processes, and effectiveness in facilitating them, I have participated in training programs conducted by the National Training Laboratory, Tavistock Institute, and the Washington School of Psychiatry; and have led seminars and workshops each summer at Esalen Institute and other growth centers. To explore their relevance for formal education, I have in each of the past 12 semesters taught courses ranging in subject matter from "Introduction to Philosophy" to "Philosophical Anthropology" which combine encounter techniques with cognitive learning. Students are apprised of the intended mix during preregistration screening interviews; registration is closed at 16 students; and a balance of men and women is desirable. The course opens with an encounter weekend, which means that we spend 13 hours together before we open a book. My object is to get the Waring Blender of human interaction churning, then feed into it eye-dropper drips of cognitive content. After the opening weekend the class meets for a three-hour stretch each week. Typically, the first hour goes to student-directed discussion of the week's reading assignment; the second hour is mine to either lecture or continue the first hour's discussion under my direction; and the third hour continues the weekend encounter group. In mid-semester, we have a second weekend encounter, if possible off-campus and out of the city. When I can secure budget or prevail upon the good offices of my wife who works professionally with groups, I have an outside trainer conduct the weekends. This helps to reduce student-teacher distance and to get authority issues more openly onto the floor.

How has it gone? Roughly 85% of the 160 students who have been in these courses report on anonymous, postcourse checksheets that they were glad we used this approach and would recommend that it be continued. They report that compared with other humanities courses they enjoyed it more, were more interested in it, and learned more from it. I have no illusion that these statistics are clean, particularly the last one. If one esteems not only "learning that" but also "learning how" (i.e., learning how effectively to occupy a place in life as contrasted with merely knowing about life), Kierkegaard's truth as subjective transformation of oneself, and education as "the curriculum one had to run through in order to catch up with oneself," even the last statistic could be valid. I doubt, however, that students have acquired as much cerebral knowledge of subject matter in these courses as they do in others. Encounter aspects of the courses seem to fill such a vacuum in students' lives and become thereby so seductive that I find I must constantly throw the weight of my office on the side of cognitive learning to keep the course from developing into encounter group only. Being unsettled in my mind as to how cognitive learning does fare in such courses, I do not recommend casting all education in their mold. I should think it might be ideal for each university undergraduate to carry one encounter course each term, but not more. As a side benefit, a college that instituted the policy of having them do so might, I suspect, find itself reducing its psychiatric and counselling staff appreciably.

With regard to the specifics of ways in which I have tried to link group process to cognitive learning, I would happily say nothing, for I am far from satisfied with my formulae and keep devising new ones constantly. But this is the nub of the matter, so lest my statement on T-group teaching, or peer-group learning as it might better be called, end up looking like a Taoist composition around the void, I list some samples of things I have tried.

1. Have students pair with partners they know least, look into one another's eyes for two minutes without speaking, then express nonverbally how they feel

toward each other. For their next reading assign Martin Buber's (1970) *I and Thou*. Did the pairing exercise illumine experimentally what Buber means by an I-Thou relation?

2. Ask students to take 10 minutes to recall and write down their earliest childhood memory. Place the statements in the middle of the circle. Ask a student to select and read one of the statements at random. Can the group guess who wrote it? Does the discussion corroborate ontogenetic emphasis on the formative influence of early experiences as argued, say, in Erik Erikson's (1964) *Childhood and Society*?

3. Read Konrad Lorenz's (1966) *On Aggression*. Do its theses shed light on the competition and hostility that have come to light within the group's own experience?

4. Read Nietzsche's (1968) *Will to Power*. How much of the group's life—most obviously the struggles for leadership within it, but not these only—supports its central thesis?

5. The greatest anxiety I, personally, have felt in a group setting was in the initial meeting of 65 persons who were closeted for two and one-half hours with no agenda whatever. Watching every attempt to structure that chaos come to naught was an unnerving experience, but it was insightful too, for it showed me directly the way formlessness without produces formlessness within. Not knowing my place in the group, I didn't know where I stood in *any* context: who I was, how I should act, anything. Compare Heidegger's (1962) notion of *angst* in *Being and Time* as symptom of the collapse of "the worldhood of the world"; also Harry Stack-Sullivan's (1950) famous essay on "The Illusion of Personal Individuality."

6. Read the first essay in Leonard Nelson's (1949) *Socratic Method and Critical Philosophy*, and ask if the goal of encounter education is to complete Nelson's approach to philosophy with two emendations: the Socratic method becomes the *group* Socratic method with the total group replacing a single individual as midwife, and feelings as well as thoughts are intentionally brought into the picture.

7. A "low" tends to settle in on groups the last few sessions before they terminate. The impending death of the group seems to awaken presentiments of individual, personal death. The experience provides concrete, shareable data relating to Heidegger's notion of being-unto-death as a criterion of authentic living.

I stress that I have not listed these projects in order to recommend them to others. I cite them only as instances of the kinds of bridges that can be thrown from group experience to cognitive learning. It appears to be of the essence of encounter teaching that no canned rubric will work for long. I wish I could report that I feel like a veteran architect of bridges of the kind described, but the fact is the opposite. I have come to suspect that how and where to throw such bridges will be my pedagogical *koan* (Zen meditational problem resolvable in life only, not in words or formulae) till I retire.

If I have neither solved the problem of relating group process to cognitive learning nor believe that it admits of standardized solutions, why do I make of it more than a marginal issue? Others who have ventured into these waters and stayed long enough to ask questions will probably answer as I do. A new panorama has opened before me. With it has come every variety of self-doubt, fear, and suspicion: Am I simply giving students what they like, afraid to demand of them hard work and drudgery; am I playing group therapist; am I merely hungry for intimacy? But in the end I have been forced to listen to a new claim. Let me articulate that claim. *We need wisdom. To this end we need knowledge, but knowledge that is established in life—that connects with feelings, illumines choices, and is in touch with wills.* Such knowledge today's academy is not structured to elicit.

4

The Sacred Dimensions
of Everyday Life

JEFFREY KANE Let's begin with the idea that there is a spiritual dimension to reality and that it should make a difference in the way we educate children. The first question I'd like to ask you is, As you walk down the street, or as you eat your meal, or as you go to bed at night, do you see a spiritual dimension which pervades everyday existence?

HUSTON SMITH If I answer honestly and personally (it's a personal question), the answer is some days I do, and some days I don't. But let me say immediately that on the days that I don't, I feel unwell, you might say. It is as if I have the spiritual flu—something like that. When you have the flu you feel rotten, and when you have the spiritual flu the world seems drained of meaning and purpose—humdrum and prosaic. But I've lived long enough to be able to say when those days roll 'round: okay, this is the yin and yang of life—ups and downs. This is one of those dark days of the ego. Most of the time, though, meaning and purpose are discernible, often to lyrical heights. Those moments are privileged; they are gifts. Even when my happiness isn't at a rolling boil, I tend to know that there is a spiritual dimension to all things.

KANE When you think about the spiritual dimensions of reality, is it in the everydayness of the world, is it in a glass of water, or in the air that we breathe?

SMITH It's everywhere. Everything is an outpouring of the infinite that is spiritual in essence, so everything reflects that spirit. Blake is famous for having said that if the doors of perception were cleansed, we would see everything as it truly is—infinite. For him infinitude was also perfection. Limitations exist in us, not in the world.

KANE Would it be going too far to say that everything is truly sacred if we see it rightly?

SMITH Not too far at all. As the Thomists say, *esse qua esse bonum est:* "being as being is good." Of course the evil in the world tests that principle, but I think it can be defended.

KANE I remember back to C. S. Lewis, in the beginning of *The Screwtape Letters,* where he explains that the devil must consume souls because he has no being himself.

SMITH That's a good way to put it. There's another route to the same point. Heroin is horrible, but at the moment of the high, that high itself isn't bad. It's the toll it takes that is bad. Even cancer cells aren't bad in isolation. It's only the way they prey on other cells that's evil.

KANE Do you think we might actually have here a very quick first inroad to educating children? Would it be too much to say that one of the most fundamental things we need to do if we are to educate children is to help them see all things as sacred?

SMITH It would be wonderful if we could do that. Education is more your province than mine, but I've always thought that if I stop teaching university/college students I'd like to teach preschool. Somehow it's two ends of the spectrum that attract me.

KANE Incidentally, Rudolf Steiner made a point of saying that people who teach the youngest children should be the oldest teachers. Such matters aside, do you believe Emerson offered a signpost to the sacred with his contention that the invariable mark of wisdom is to see the miraculous in the common?

SMITH He's right. I wonder if tribal peoples, being closer to nature than we are, do better at that—seeing everything aglow with the sacred. That may be only a myth that we somehow need today, but I think it's more than that. Unencumbered by the busyness and humdrum of contemporary life, tribal peoples seem able to hold on to the shining world that children are heirs to.

KANE Do you think that the "doors of perception" can be cleansed through aesthetic experience—through experiences of nature, for example?

SMITH Definitely. Just this morning I wrote something on that subject because *The World's Religions* is coming out in an illustrated edition that will include the world's religious art. In writing the preface for this new edition, I found myself saying that the function of sacred art—and indeed beauty of every sort, virgin nature emphatically included—is to make easy what would otherwise be difficult. If one is viewing an icon (in a way, all sacred art is iconic), then the icon basically disappears by offering itself up to the divine. The energy of the divine pours through it into the viewer, one consequence being that the viewer's heart is expanded and becomes uplifted by a great work of art. Note that word *uplifted.* Can you imagine performing in that state a despicable act? It's often difficult for us to act compassionately, but sacred art eases the difficulty by ennobling us. So your point is well taken, including your emphasis on virgin nature.

KANE Might nature be considered the greatest of sacred art?

SMITH That's interesting. I do think of sacred art and virgin nature as two of the clearest apertures to the divine, but I've never thought of rank-ordering them. I think of Plato's statement that "beauty is the splendor of the true." I like that because it gets us beyond thinking of nature and art simply as pleasure giving. They do far more than that. They offer insight into the true nature of things.

KANE Beauty wouldn't then be simply in the eye of the beholder?

SMITH Not ultimately, though there's partial truth in the saying that when a young man falls in love with a girl, he sees something in her that others don't see. The romantic illusions that color his perception don't alter the fact that at that moment he is closer than any other human being to seeing her the way God sees her. When I hear someone say, "I don't see what he sees in her," I feel like responding, "Don't you wish you could?" I don't think it's naively romantic to think that romantic love opens a window to the inner nobility of the beloved, one that is closed to ordinary eyes.

KANE Would it be fair to say that beauty is something one is open to, rather than something that someone creates in the act of perception?

SMITH Yes, that's the case.

KANE Could we rightly look at beauty as a matter of impression, as well as expression? Normally we think of art as expression, as subjective expression.

SMITH Something of the artist figures, but the accent is on what comes to him or her. It's imprinted, as you say. I like your way of putting it.

KANE Perhaps we've reached a second education implication here, and I wonder what your thoughts are. If we are going to educate children rightly, perhaps we should spend a good deal of time in nature study and art (again to use the phrase)—as impression, attempting to open children to the beauty in the world.

SMITH I am sure that is true.

KANE There was once a teacher who taught me about Shakespeare. He said that Shakespeare pointed to various aspects of human existence and the human condition, and that he pointed beautifully with great accuracy. He (my teacher) said what we often do in school is we say, "Look how nicely he points. You see how his eye is lined up with his finger? He's pointing very directly." But this overlooks what he's pointing toward. I wonder if that isn't true as well—a flower unfolding, or a cloud passing in the sky, again, opens a door, or provides a lens into something beyond itself.

SMITH The notion of pointing, of course, suggests the Zen adage of the finger pointing at the moon. If we obsess over the finger, we overlook the moon. It's very true. Much of education falls into that trap. In higher education I am distressed by the proportion of attention that goes to methodology rather than content.

KANE When we begin to think of there being sacredness, or when we recognize this sacredness in the everyday, does knowledge have a different "shape" than we normally think of knowledge having in the West?

SMITH I think it does. My favorite book on this subject is Seyyed Hossein Nasr's *Knowledge and the Sacred*. He speaks from a traditional point of view. To fill in the background, in the hundred years of the Gifford Lectures— the most prestigious humanities lecture series in the West—Nasr is the only non-Westerner ever to have been included. His thesis is that knowledge is not so much that which discloses the sacred as that which is sacred in itself for partaking in the knowing source from which intelligence derives. Human intelligence is a reflection of the intelligence that produces everything. In knowing, we are simply extending the intelligence that comes to and constitutes us. We mimic the mind of God, so to speak. Or better, we continue and extend it.

KANE So knowing and being are intimately related?

SMITH In the end they are identical. That probably holds for all positive attributes. The closer to their source we draw, the more we find them converging.

KANE I think it is a particularly important point that, in the West, the concept of knowledge is impersonal and detached. We take out being, and say it has no place. What you are saying here is that knowledge is imbued with being. It is a direct experience. Knowledge cannot be detached as such. Would you say that knowledge of that sort is what helps you on those days when you see the sacred in the everyday?

SMITH I am sure that is the case. To linger for a moment on this issue of detached, objective knowledge, writing—whatever its virtues, and I think there are some—is especially vulnerable to becoming detached, because writing can be disconnected from the writer. There it is in print, dead and frozen. Speech, on the other hand, is not only alive, it *is* life, because it cannot be separated from the living person in one mode of his or her own being. Exclusively oral cultures are unencumbered by dead knowledge, dead facts. Libraries, on the other hand, are full of them.

KANE To quote Emerson once again, "To the wise, fact is true poetry." Would poetry present the same dilemma?

SMITH No, because poetry is art, and we've already talked about that. Poetry is a special use of language that opens onto the real. The business of the poet is truth-telling, which is why in the Celtic tradition no one could be a teacher unless he or she was a poet.

KANE Would you say if someone has learned and has become inwardly active through learning, then the knowledge gained becomes part of his or her being? Would he or she be a different person than he or she was prior?

SMITH We have to differentiate between life-giving learning and kinds that deaden the mind. I think of a TV program around mid-century (there have doubtless been others since) that featured savants, essentially. They were amazing—veritable walking encyclopedias—

KANE —what was the day of the week for January 1, Year 1, that sort of thing?

SMITH Yes, and, Who won the Oscar for best supporting actor in 1952? I was living in St. Louis at the time, and the national champion in that particular series turned out to be a St. Louisan. People knew him. He was unemployed. Couldn't get a job as a postal clerk because he couldn't pass the civil service exam. So when we talk about knowledge and learning, we have to distinguish between useless kinds and kinds that are useful—practically useful, but more important, useful in raising the stature of our lives.

KANE Please forgive me if I ask you an unfair question: If we follow this through, is it possible that we educate whole generations of savants, just in the sense that you use the term?

SMITH More than possible, I suspect. And that's what turns off kids from learning, of course—when it seems like rote memory, and what's it for? We give them hoops to jump through, keeping the destination—the purpose and the point—clearly before them.

KANE Many educators have recognized the limitations of a positivistic model of knowledge. They know that rote learning no longer works, or perhaps that it never did. The new paradigm that drives education is based upon a computer analogue wherein we storehouse individual bits of knowledge, discrete and separable. These bits can then be put into motion, as it were, through a program in critical thinking, for example. It often seems to me that we are trying to put the pieces in motion artificially without, again, reference to the content itself, without reference to being. So you might say that readers of this interview could argue, "Well, the fact of the matter is that we are teaching children how to put ideas together, how to think." But I wonder if that still doesn't miss the point.

SMITH I think it does. I've heard about this issue; I am not in close touch with what actually goes on, but I share your skepticism about teaching critical thinking in the abstract. It doesn't work because thinking never proceeds in a vacuum. So to be effective, thinking must adapt and be faithful to the context in which it works. My skepticism here ties in with my earlier skepticism about method in general. We always know more than we know how we

know it, so we get farther by attending to the "what" than to the "how." The
trouble with trying to work out a method for knowing is that it will rule out
resources that don't conform to it. Every method is, in ways, a straitjacket,
a Procrustean bed. True, we all do have methods, and when we run into
problems, it might be well to try to spot and revise if need be the course that
brought us to the problem. But to put method first is putting the cart before
the horse.

KANE If I am following you correctly, and tying it back to what you said before,
it is being that animates knowledge. It is not the method that animates
knowledge.

SMITH Yes. In the final analysis what we know derives from our entire being.
Historians of knowledge are providing us with detailed examples of breakthroughs where frontier scientists, say, simply discarded oceans of evidence
because something deep lying in them generated a "gut feeling" that the
truth lay elsewhere. Had they toed the line of the so-called scientific method,
the breakthroughs wouldn't have occurred.

KANE E. A. Burt—

SMITH —he was a dear friend of mine.

KANE —in his classic work, *The Metaphysical Foundations of Modern Scientists,*
maintained that if Copernicus had presented his thoughts to thoroughgoing
empiricists, he would have been laughed out of court.

SMITH Exactly.

KANE I wonder if this might not be a good place to familiarize some of our
readers with the modern Western mind-set that you've written about in a
good many places. At this point in our discussion, you have begun to root
out some of the assumptions that we make (one being relative to "method")
that might limit the knowledge that we gain, or perhaps again, our openness
to being. What are some of the other assumptions that have characterized
knowledge in the West and might keep us from cleansing those doors of
perception?

SMITH Science works effectively on things that impact more complicated
things—cancer cells devastating human bodies, for example. If we call this
upward causation, science is good at that. What it's not good at is downward causation—the way the superior impacts the inferior—and when it
comes to things that are superior to us, we human beings, it draws a total
blank. Because the technological spin-offs from science are so impressive,
we slip into assuming that upward causation, more from less, is the name of
the game. The universe derives (exclusively) from a dense pellet. Life derives
(exclusively) from inanimate elements. "Hydrogen is a ubiquitous substance
which, given time, gives rise to intelligence," as one scientist has put it. But
as another scientist, Stephen Jay Gould, has pointed out—one wishes that in

practice he paid more attention to his aphorism—"absence of evidence isn't evidence of absence." On balance, the wisdom traditions assure us, things proceed more by downward than upward causation. If science doesn't show this, it is because it is locked (as it should be, this being the key to its effectiveness) into a technically competent but metaphysically impoverished method—the issue of method again. The latest good book on this point is Bryan Appleyard's *Understanding the Present: Science and the Soul of Modern Man.*

KANE Does this approach to understanding create particular problems when we apply it to understanding human beings? In education, we work with children all the time, and we often have positivistic models of knowledge when we conceptualize who the children are in themselves. Do you think this is particularly problematic?

SMITH I think poor self-images cripple children—and adults as well, for that matter. Moreover, our modern Western self-image is the most impoverished human beings have ever devised. We do not think well of ourselves, Saul Bellow observes, and Marshall Salins, the anthropologist, fills in the picture: "We are the only people who think we derive from apes. Everybody else assumes that they are descended from the gods."

If I can bring this discussion back to children, there's much talk today about the wounded child within. I won't say that's all bad, but it runs the danger of encouraging self-pity. How about the struggling adult within— more attention to that, and how the fragile adult might be strengthened? I hope it's clear how our over-reliance on the scientific method has been the (indirect and unwitting) cause of our impoverished self-image. It is as if the top of science's window stops at the bridge of our nose, so that in looking through it, we see only things that are beneath our full stature.

KANE As I listen to you, I am thinking that physics, which we often think of as the most complicated, most difficult of all sciences, is, indeed, the simplest in its own way because it deals with things that are essentially lifeless. The mineral world, the physical world of atoms, I don't know if I would call the cosmos dead, but the way we view it certainly is.

SMITH You're right. The hard sciences deal so effectively with their objects because those things have no, or negligible, freedom.

KANE Science seems to lose some of its power when it turns to animate objects. I am thinking now of the Chinese notion of chi, that there is a life force which we cannot explain in terms of physics or chemistry. More power is lost when it turns to the animal kingdom. And regarding the human self, little of importance admits to scientific proof.

SMITH I think that's exactly right. To pick up with the second level where microbiology enters, R. C. Lewontin has noted that "despite the fact that we can position every atom in a protein molecule in three-dimensional space, nobody has the slightest idea of the rule that will fold them into life." Microbiologists appropriately seek that rule, but I wonder if it exists on a plane they can access.

KANE I have read of biologists who have synthesized protein compounds which, when given electrical charges, do begin to self-replicate, but then you still end up with the more primary question: Who is putting the electrical charge in to begin with? Where is it coming from? I think we're going to find in the ultimate that there are questions we ask that cannot be answered by modern science. I once found myself writing that we need to elevate our concept of science to meet the reality of the world, rather than to lower the world to meet the limitations of earth science.

SMITH I agree in principle but wonder how much the scientific method can be altered—elevated, expanded—without compromising its power. The power of science comes from its controlled experiments, and the nobler things in life can't be proved. We don't have to expect science to do everything.

KANE I know that there have been a great many people (I am thinking of Martin Heidegger, for example) who see a split between meditative thinking and calculative reason—reason being closer to science and thinking (as he uses the word) to meditation. But I can't help think that Goethe, through his understanding of art and aesthetic perception, might actually have a key to how they can both be combined. I'm not sure.

SMITH I'm not sure, either, but it is interesting. Wolfgang Goethe, Rudolf Steiner, and Emanuel Swedenborg—all three were visionaries who connected science to the human spirit in original ways. But I haven't studied them enough to say more.

KANE In another vein, can religion or ceremony bring us to the deeper dimensions of reality, or can they close us down to them?

SMITH Both, I think. Just as the world is religiously ambiguous in the sense that both theists and atheists see it as supporting their position, so too is religion itself an ambiguous enterprise. It is made up of people, and as we well know, people are a mixed bag. When they congregate in institutions, it is not surprising that we find both good and evil results. Religions do horrible things because they reinforce in-group–out-group feelings. At the same time, they nurture the transcendent urge that has compassion as its wake. In this mode it shatters existing social structures. The Book of Jonah shows the Jews expanding their theology to include even their enemies, the Ninevites. This was radical. We have to be sensitive to the two faces of religion: conservative and progressive. But that's true of almost anything. A while ago we were talking about art, but bad music, as well as good, has been written. The important thing is not to be cynical—realistic, yes, but not cynical. By functionalist criteria alone, religion would not have survived if it were not doing something right.

Connecting this to education, can religion contribute the empowering kind of knowing we have been talking about? I think it can. Why do I say that? First, because the noblest human beings that I personally have encountered have been shaped by religious traditions—His Holiness the Dalai Lama and Mother Theresa jump immediately to mind. Second, when I look at the sacred texts that inspired these people—and the commentaries that have been written on them by giants such as Shankara [Indian philosopher and theologian], Dōgen [thirteenth-century Zen master], Nagarjuna [Indian founder of the Madhyamika school of Buddhism], Augustine, and Meister Eckhart (not excepting Plato and Plotinus, who write in the same vein)— I find no alternate texts that are far beyond the public schools that we have been talking about. All I am saying is that the wisdom is there to be drawn upon and calibrated to the minds teachers seek to nurture.

KANE   Would you think that religious ceremonies have a place in educating children generally?

SMITH   I do, though in this context I don't want to get into the complicated issue of church/state and the public school. Rituals help us celebrate, and at the other end of the spectrum they help us to connect deeply with people in times of sorrow. The repetition that ritual always involves sets the present moment in a larger context and infuses it with wider meaning. It's difficult to invent rituals. The Unitarians are trying, but for the most part rituals, like myths, emerge spontaneously.

KANE   Then a myth must be what it is and cannot be made different?

SMITH   It must grow out of a deep historical experience like the Exodus, or from deep, unconscious layers of the psyche.

KANE   As I listen to you, I am wondering if ceremony doesn't provide a set moment in time for you to be silent and listen. Ceremony may be a way of blocking off the everyday—one must pay the water bill, and run to the store, and all that. Ceremony might just set apart moments of time in which you can get in touch with deep parts of one's self and the other dimensions of existence.

SMITH   That is well put. You used the word *silence*. I wondered when you said that whether you mean literal silence or an inner silence even when there is chanting and litany.

KANE   In this instance, I was using the word to mean there is no nonsense running around in your mind, in your head, you have no inner dialogue for a moment, you're actually quiet. You're receptive, rather than working daily things through.

SMITH   Sounds right. What I am not sure I had thought of before is that this apartness can come even while you are chanting or singing, for because the material is memorized, your conscious mind doesn't have to be attending.

KANE   Do you think that meditation in any of the great traditions, whether it be a Buddhist meditation, or Hasidic meditation, or Rosicrucian meditation, has any place in the education of children?

SMITH   I don't really know. Questions of age would enter, and the kind of meditation. If we think of silent meditation, I find myself saying yes. It would probably be very good to encourage even small children to sit still and shift their minds into a different gear.

As I get into the subject, I once received an invitation from a third-grade class in a parochial school in the Boston area while I was teaching at MIT. It was so cute, I remember it verbatim: "Dear Prof. Smith: We are studying religion. We do not know much about religion. Will you please come and teach us about religion?" Signed, "The Third Grade." So I went, but it turned out to be last period on a Friday afternoon, and you can imagine the blast of restless energy that met me as I stepped into the room. I heard a clear inner voice say, "Don't try to talk to these kids. Nothing you can say could possibly hold their attention. They've got to do something." So I said, "You asked me to teach you about religion, so I am going to tell you about religion in a different part of the world. In Japanese religion, they sit on the floor, so we have to move all the desks against the walls." Instant pandemonium—everybody pushing things and bumping into one another. So we got the floor cleared, and I said, "Okay, everybody on the floor. When Japanese sit religiously they sit in a special position." I demonstrated the lotus position. "Can you sit that way?" A few show-offs could. "Also they sit in silence. Can you do that?" Heads nodded vigorously. "How long?" "Fifteen minutes," a voice sang out. "Are you sure? Without making a sound?" "Five minutes." We finally settled for two, and even that was too long for them. But we were off to a great start, and they gave me a bag of jelly beans as my honorarium—

KANE   You should work with young children!

There is often a distinction made between learning by doing and learning through detachment. There are many Hasidic stories which end with the conclusion that one learns through doing. Was what you did simply a pedagogical device, or do you think that it might have illustrated that one can learn most about life's spiritual dimension by being engaged in some kind of activity, a practice?

SMITH   Perhaps the latter was involved. I find it difficult to rank-order modes of learning, because when I think back over my own experiences of learning, they have been so different—all the way from the Zen monasteries to sitting spellbound before gifted teachers who just lectured. I find if difficult to prioritize learning situations.

KANE I guess part of me likes to say one thing is more important than another, but it's important to step back. I wonder if we might now move a bit to the question of moral values. Do you see religion, or aesthetics, or beauty, or any of the things we have discussed as having an impact on the moral development of children?

SMITH All of them. Certainly, if what we were saying was true about beauty having an elevating effect—but let me be concrete. I don't think I've ever spent three or four hours in a great museum without the world looking different in a way that somehow purifies my motives. So there is beauty. As far as religion, we have to distinguish in the history of religion between three periods. In the "pre-axial" period of religion, before the rise of the great prophets and sages, around the middle of the first millennium B.C.E., religion was occupied mostly with time—death and the perishing of existence—and ethics didn't much enter. People were living in tribes and got along pretty much the way normal families do. In the post-axial period, though, populations began to be citified, which meant that a good part of one's dealings were with people who were not in one's primary group. Ethics needed bolstering, and from the golden rule to the prophets, religion shouldered the job. The modern period adds social ethics to religion's agenda, for we now realize that social structures are not like laws of nature. They are human creations, so we are responsible for them. So to beauty we must add religion with its post-axial ethics and concern with social justice. So always, if we look back, concern for face-to-face morality and its modern emphasis on justice as well have historically evolved as religious issues.

KANE To pursue this central theme here, I wonder if you see moral ideas as human-made or as human replications, or human manifestations of a higher order of law? In other words, are they subjective, circumstantial developments, or are they reflective of something higher and more universal?

SMITH Something of both, but more replicas than constructions. Morality always aims at harmony or unity, and unity is a great idea, but not only an idea. It's great because it is a mirroring or reflection of what ultimately reality is. Reality is one. In an esoteric sense, the number "one" is beyond the entire numerical sequence, not just the first in an order of integers. It is qualitatively of a different order. If it had remained that, though, it would have been finite because it would have lacked multiplicity. And since the ultimate is also infinite, it must include the multiple in some way. It is not a relation of parity, because the one has a dignity beyond the many. Still, it requires the many for it to be infinite. Multiplicity poses a problem, because for things to exist they must have centers and boundaries.

Yet something is there that doesn't love a wall. Boundaries have their downside. We have this centripetal urge, but it can be narrow and confining, so we have to live with the tension to be ourselves and also identify with others. How can we, at the same time, be ourselves and embrace others? That is one way of defining life's project. As Aldous Huxley put it, "The problem of life is to overcome the basic human disability of egoism." This is a round-about answer to your question, of whether morals are human-made, but what I want to say is that to some extent they are—there can be silly, mistaken, and even pernicious judgments that individuals and even societies fall into. But it is also the case that this is a moral universe, and through lots of trial and error, history is trying to discover what its moral laws are.

KANE   Would you say that there are certain universals that one would find through many of the world's religions?

SMITH   Yes. Two levels need to be distinguished here. The one which is the more explicit is what we should do, but beyond that is the question of the kind of person we should try to become. Now, on the first level, what we should do, there are four problem areas in human life that have to be dealt with. These are violence, wealth, the spoken word, and sex. In lower forms of life these problem areas are monitored quite adequately by instinct. Man, though, is an animal without instincts, so these problem areas can get out of hand. Moral precepts are devised to secure appropriate, life-sustaining behavior in the four areas, and they are remarkably uniform across cultures: don't murder, don't steal, don't lie, don't commit adultery. These are the basic guidelines concerning human behavior.

As for the kind of person we should try to become, the virtues point the way. In the West these are commonly identified as humility, charity, and veracity. Humility has nothing to do with low self-esteem; it is to recognize oneself as one and fully one but not more than one, just as charity is to look upon your neighbor as fully one (with all the rights and privileges pertaining thereto) just as you are one. Veracity begins with not being deceitful, but it ends in the sublime objectivity that *sees* things exactly as they are, undistorted by our subjective preferences. These are the virtues in the West. Asia, interestingly, has the same three but enters them by the back door, so to speak, by speaking of the three poisons—traits that keep the virtues from flourishing in us. The three are greed (the opposite of humility), hatred (the opposite of charity), and delusion (the opposite of veracity). To the extent that we expunge these three poisons, the virtues will flood our lives automatically. The convergence of East and West in these areas is remarkable.

KANE   If you were to look at these in an educational context, what is the meaning of what you just said for someone who now steps into a classroom filled with children?

SMITH This is your turf, and it would be presumptuous for me to pontificate. So I'll content myself with a single point. The most powerful moral influence is example. There's a saying, "What you do speaks so loud that I can't hear what you say." That's what makes it so difficult—we have to aspire to be models for our students. At the same time, what nobler goal could we set for ourselves?

5

Light

Light is a universal metaphor for God, and what science has discovered about physical light helps us to understand (more profoundly than even the spiritual giants of the past could do) why light is uniquely suited for that role. If Einstein could say at one point in his career that he wanted for the rest of his life to reflect on the nature of light, surely we can do so for a few minutes. Light is different. It is strangely different. And paradoxically different. All three of these assertions hold for God, as does a fourth. Light creates.

THE PHYSICS OF LIGHT

Uncanny as they are, the basic features of Einstein's Special Theory of Relativity have worked their way into our common stock of knowledge. The speed of light— 186,000 miles a second—is an unvarying constant, and everything else in the physical universe adjusts to it. Seated in their stalled cars at a railroad crossing, impatient drivers see the train whizzing past them, while its passengers see the cars flying past *their* windows in the opposite direction. That relativity concerns space; but physics locks space, time, and matter together like pieces of a jigsaw puzzle, so the relativity just mentioned turns up in time and matter as well. If you are hurtling through space, time (your watch) slows down. On a bicycle the slowing is unnoticeable, but if you flew a trillion miles in a fighter plane and landed at six in the evening according to your watch, the clocks in the airport you departed from would read seven. And the closer your plane came to traveling at 186,000 miles per second, the slower its clocks would run, until (if that speed were reached) the plane's clocks would stop. As for matter, the mass of an object that is in motion increases until, should it attain the speed of light, that mass would be infinite as measured by an unmoving observer.

Now let us spin all this around and look at it from light's point of view. Imagine yourself sitting on a particle. On that single "piece" (or quantum) of light you are going nowhere. You are weightless. There is neither time nor space, nor are there separated events. If from the earth it is one hundred light-years to a star, from your position on your quantum of light the star and earth are not separated at all. Moreover, it would seem as if the world were pouring out of you, you and your fellow photons, because light creates. It pumps power into the spatio-temporal world. This is most obvious in the process of photosynthesis, where the immaterial light flowing from the sun is transformed into the earth's green carpet of vegetation. Plants absorb light's immaterial energy-flow and store it in the form of chemically bonded energy. If we look beneath biochemistry at nature's foundations, we see that light's creativity "comes to light" there through its early appearance in the sequence that produces matter in its successive stages. (The phrase "comes to light" is not a pun. Everywhere in recorded history light doubles for intelligibility, comprehension, understanding, and—underlying all of these—conscious awareness. This metaphorical use of light reveals its protean power.) Situated on the cusp between the material and immaterial realms, photons (as was just noted) are not subject to our usual ways of understanding the physical universe.

Everything that was compressed into that preceding paragraph is strange, so it will not hurt to restate its content. Space? Remember that seated on light—a photon—you are going nowhere. Time? Time does not exact from photons the toll that it does elsewhere; how could it when clocks stop at the speed of light? As for matter, photons have neither the rest-mass nor the charge that material particles have. In lay language (which cannot get into *quarks* and *gluons* and other specks that sound like *Star Trek* aliens), these material particles derive from energy, which—using the word in its broadest sense—I am calling light. In addition to having rest-mass and charge, these derivative particles are also subject to time, so they are clearly material in all of those respects. Still, they are not *completely* material, for no definite position in space can be assigned to them. Atoms are more material than particles are for being locked into both space *and* time, but even they are not as "fallen" as molecules are, for isolated atoms are free to absorb and release energy to a much greater extent than atoms that have combined to form molecules, which are almost completely imprisoned in the determinism of our inanimate macro-world.

If (in some such way as I have described) light produces the physical universe, it is also responsible for its permutations. Quantum mechanics tells us that the essence of every interaction in the universe is the exchange of quanta of energy. A single quantum is the smallest packet of energy that can ever be exchanged;

Planck's Constant is its measure. It is quanta of photons that change molecules in the act of photosynthesis and that excite atoms in the retina of our eyes to enable us to see. The exchange of light maintains our universe from the level of atoms and molecules on up.

What this all comes down to is that the two great epochal changes in twentieth-century physics—relativity theory for the large and very fast, and quantum mechanics for the very small—both relate to light. Everything is created from light, and all the interactions that follow after those created things are in place proceed by way of light. As for light itself, let us hear for a final time here that it stands outside the matrices of space, time, and matter that govern all of its creations.

If you suspect that I am leading up to saying that physics tells us that light is God, you are wrong, for science cannot touch that subject. But the boost that physics has given to light as a *metaphor* for God's creative activity is dazzling. If (and I emphasize the conditional here) God were to create a physical universe, what physicists describe sounds like how God might have gone about that job.

LIGHT SUBJECTIVELY EXPERIENCED

It stands to reason that if light symbolizes clarity, lucidity, and comprehension, darkness stands for their opposites. How could it be otherwise when in the dark we grope, stagger, stumble, and fall? Our disorientation erupts into our feelings. "Nobody feels good at four in the morning," a contemporary poem begins, and there is Gerald Manley Hopkins's memorable, "I wake and feel the fell of night, not day; / Self-yeast of the spirit, a dull dough sours."

This much is obvious. Now for something uncanny—as bizarre in its own sphere as are Einstein's discoveries concerning light. The story concerns a little-known Frenchman, Jacques Lusseyran, as he tells it in his autobiography.

Lusseyran's life must surely be numbered among the most remarkable on record. The age of nineteen found him serving as a vital link in the French resistance movement in the Nazi-occupied Paris of World War II, while at the same time preparing for the École Normale Supérieure at the University of Paris. When a traitor betrayed the Volontaires de la Liberté, Lusseyran was arrested by the Gestapo and imprisoned for almost two years. When the United States Third Army arrived in April 1945, he was one of thirty survivors of a shipment of two thousand men who were on their way to Buchenwald. Stunned by their deliverance, Lusseyran tells us, the men could not at first even rejoice in their freedom.

With his freedom regained, however, something bizarre occurred. Despite the brilliance of both his academic and his wartime careers, Lusseyran was refused admission to the École Normale Supérieure because of a decree passed by the Vichy government barring "invalids." For you see, Lusseyran had been totally blind since the age of eight. While roughhousing during a school recess, one of his friends had accidentally knocked Lusseyran over, slamming the back of his head into a sharp corner of the teacher's desk. The force of the blow drove a broken rim of his spectacles into his eyes, leaving him to live out his life in total darkness.

Or so we would suppose. I would not be telling this story here were it not for Lusseyran's report that in actuality something like the opposite occurred. "Being blind was not at all as I imagined it," he tells us. "Nor was it as the people around me seemed to think. They told me that to be blind meant not to see. Yet how was I to believe them when I *saw*?"

Not at first, he admits. For a time he tried to use his eyes in their usual way and direct his attention outward, but then some instinct made him change course. In his own words,

> I began to look from an inner place to one further within, whereupon the universe redefined itself and peopled itself anew. I was aware of a radiance emanating from a place I knew nothing about, a place which might as well have been outside me as within. But radiance was there, or more precisely, light. I bathed in it as an element which blindness had suddenly brought much closer. I could feel light rising, spreading, resting on objects, giving them form, then leaving them. Or rather withdrawing or diminishing, for the opposite of light was never present. Without my eyes, light was much more stable than it had been with them.

Arthur Zajonc's *Catching the Light: The Entwined History of Mind and Life* provides a splendid, comprehensive survey of the subject of this chapter, but Lusseyran's account is the closest I have seen to a description of what Einstein's and Planck's light might feel like if we human beings could experience it directly. To what Lusseyran has already told us, I shall add only his report of the two virtues that invariably accompanied the light that reconstituted itself in him.

The first of these was joy. "I found light and joy at the same moment," he writes. "The light that shone in my head was like joy distilled, and from the time of my discovery, light and joy have never been separated in my experience." The connection was two-way. When negative emotions intruded on joy, his light became harsh, broken, jagged, and grating. In this sense, "fear, anger and impatience made me blind. The minute before I knew just where everything in the world was, but if I got angry, things got angrier than I. They mixed themselves up, turned turtle, muttered like crazy men and looked wild. I no longer knew where to put hand or foot, and everything hurt me."

The second virtue was that his intuitive powers were enhanced. "My sighted companions were nimble in bodily movements over which I hesitated. But as soon as it was a question of intangibles, it was their turn to hesitate longer than I."

It was this quantum leap in intuitive judgment that catapulted Lusseyran to leadership in the resistance movement. His ability to size up people's character and see through their dissembling was so uncannily accurate that he was put in charge of the delicate and dangerous job of recruiting, and everyone who applied to join the underground was sent to him for acceptance or rejection. His decisions were infallible, or (as he confesses) nearly so, for there was one man he admitted to the movement of whom he was not absolutely sure, and it was he who later betrayed them.

Lusseyran protested his being debarred from the École Normale Supérieure on grounds of his blindness and he was admitted. After graduating with honors, he taught in France and in the United States at Hollins College, Case Western Reserve University, and the University of Hawaii. He was tragically killed in an automobile accident in 1971.

6

The Revolution
in Western Thought

Quietly, irrevocably, something enormous has happened to Western man. His outlook on life and the world has changed so radically that in the perspective of history the twentieth century is likely to rank—with the fourth century, which witnessed the triumph of Christianity, and the seventeenth, which signaled the dawn of modern science—as one of the very few that have instigated genuinely new epochs in human thought. In this change, which is still in process, we of the current generation are playing a crucial but as yet not widely recognized part.

The dominant assumptions of an age color the thoughts, beliefs, expectations, and images of the men and women who live within it. Being always with us, these assumptions usually pass unnoticed—like the pair of glasses which, because they are so often on the wearer's nose, simply stop being observed. But this doesn't mean they have no effect. Ultimately, assumptions which underlie our outlooks on life refract the world in ways that condition our art and our institutions: the kinds of homes we live in, our sense of right and wrong, our criteria of success, what we conceive our duty to be, what we think it means to be a man or woman, how we worship our God or whether, indeed, we have a God to worship.

Thus far the odyssey of Western man has carried him through three great configurations of such basic assumptions. The first constituted the Graeco-Roman, or classical, outlook, which flourished up to the fourth century A.D. With the triumph of Christianity in the Roman Empire, this Graeco-Roman outlook was replaced by the Christian worldview which proceeded to dominate Europe until the seventeenth century. The rise of modern science inaugurated a third important way of looking at things, a way that has come to be capsuled in the phrase "the Modern Mind."

It now appears that this modern outlook, too, has run its course and is being replaced by what, in the absence of a more descriptive term, is being called simply the Post-Modern Mind. What follows is an attempt to describe this most recent sea change in Western thought. I shall begin by bringing the Christian and modern outlooks into focus; for only so can we see how and to what extent our emerging thought patterns differ from those that have directly preceded them.

From the fourth-century triumph of Christianity in the Roman Empire through the Middle Ages and the Reformation, the Western mind was above all else theistic. "God, God, God; nothing but God"—in the twentieth century one can assume such an exclamation to have come, as it did, from a theologian. In the Middle Ages it could have come from anyone. Virtually without question all life and nature were assumed to be under the surveillance of a personal God whose intentions toward man were perfect and whose power to implement these intentions was unlimited.

In such a world, life was transparently meaningful. But although men understood the purpose of their lives, it does not follow that they understood, or even presumed to be capable of understanding, the dynamics of the natural world. The Bible never expands the doctrine of creation into a cosmogony for the excellent reason that it asserts the universe to be at every point the direct product of a will whose ways are not man's ways. God says, "Let there be"—and there is. That is all. Serene in a blaze of lasting light, God comprehends nature's ways, but man sees only its surface.

Christian man lived in the world as a child lives in his father's house, accepting its construction and economics unprobed. "Can anyone understand the thunderings of God's pavilion?" Elihu asks Job. "Do you know the ordinances of the heavens, how the clouds are balanced or the lightning shines? Have you comprehended the expanse of the earth, or on what its bases were sunk when the morning stars sang together and all the sons of God shouted for joy?" To such rhetorical questions the answer seemed obvious. The leviathan of nature was not to be drawn from the great sea of mystery by the fishhook of man's paltry mind.

Not until the high Middle Ages was a Christian cosmology attempted, and then through Greek rather than biblical inspiration, following the rediscovery of Aristotle's *Physics* and *Metaphysics*. Meanwhile nature's obscurity posed no major problem; for as the cosmos was in good hands, it could be counted on to furnish a reliable context in which man might work out his salvation. The way to this salvation lay not through ordering nature to man's purposes but through aligning man's purposes to God's. And for this objective, information was at hand. As surely as God had kept the secrets of nature to himself, he had, through his divine Word and the teachings of his church, made man's duty clear. Those who hearkened to this duty would reap an eternal reward, but those who refused to do so would perish.

We can summarize the chief assumptions underlying the Christian outlook by saying they held that reality is focused in a person, that the mechanics of the physical world exceed our comprehension, and that the way to our salvation lies not in conquering nature but in following the commandments which God has revealed to us.

It was the second of these three assumptions—that the dynamics of nature exceed man's comprehension—which the sixteenth and seventeenth centuries began to question, thereby heralding the transition from the Christian to the modern outlook. The Renaissance interest in the early Greeks revived the Hellenic interest in nature. For the first time in nearly two thousand years Western man began to look intently at his environment instead of beyond it. Leonardo da Vinci is symbolic. His anatomical studies and drawings in general disclose a direction of interest that has turned eye into camera, in his case an extraordinary camera that "could stop the hawk in flight and fix the rearing horse." Once again man was attending to nature's details as a potential messenger of meaning. The rage to know God's handiwork was rivaling the rage to know God himself.

The consequence, as we know, was modern science. Under scrutiny, nature's blur was found to be provisional rather than final. With patience the structure of the universe could be brought into marvelous focus. Newton's exclamation caught the excitement perfectly: "O God, I think thy thoughts after thee!" Although nature's marvels were infinitely greater than had been supposed, man's mind was equal to them. The universe was a coherent, law-abiding system. It was intelligible!

It was not long before this discovery began to reap practical rewards. Drudgery could be relieved, health improved, goods multiplied, and leisure extended. As these benefits are considerable, working with intelligible nature began to overshadow obedience to God's will as a means to human fulfillment. God was not entirely eclipsed—that would have entailed a break with the past more violent than history allows. Rather, God was eased toward thought's periphery. Not atheism but deism, the notion that God created the world but left it to run according to its own inbuilt laws, was the Modern Mind's distinctive religious stance. God stood behind nature as its creator, but it was through nature that his ways and will were to be known.

Like the Christian outlook, the modern outlook can be summarized by identifying its three controlling presuppositions. First, that reality may be personal is less certain and less important than that it is ordered. Second, man's reason is capable of discerning this order as it manifests itself in the laws of nature. Third, the path to human fulfillment consists primarily in discovering these laws, utilizing them where this is possible and complying with them where it is not.

The reason for suspecting that this modern outlook has had its day and is yielding to a third great mutation in Western thought is that reflective men are no longer confident of any of these three postulates. The first two are the ones that concern us here. Frontier thinkers are no longer sure that reality is ordered and orderly. If it is, they are not sure that man's mind is capable of grasping its order. Combining the two doubts, we can define the Post-Modern Mind as one which, having lost the conviction that reality is personal, has come to question whether it is ordered in a way that man's reason can lay bare.

It was science which induced our forefathers to think of reality as primarily ordered rather than personal. But contemporary science has crashed through the cosmology which the seventeenth- to nineteenth-century scientists constructed as if through a sound barrier, leaving us without replacement. It is tempting to attribute this lack to the fact that evidence is pouring in faster than we can throw it into perspective. Although this is part of the problem, another part runs deeper. Basically, the absence of a new cosmology is due to the fact that physics has cut away so radically from our capacity to imagine the way things are that we do not see how the two can get back together.

If modern physics showed us a world at odds with our senses, post-modern physics is showing us one which is at odds with our imagination, where imagination is taken as imagery. We have made peace with the first of these oddities. That the table which appears motionless is in fact incredibly "alive" with electrons circling their nuclei a million billion times per second; that the chair which feels so secure beneath us is actually a near vacuum—such facts, while certainly very strange, posed no permanent problem for man's sense of order. To accommodate them, all that was necessary was to replace the earlier picture of a gross and ponderous world with a subtle world in which all was sprightly dance and airy whirl.

But the problems the new physics poses for man's sense of order cannot be resolved by refinements in scale. Instead they appear to point to a radical disjunction between the way things behave and every possible way in which we might try to visualize them. How, for example, are we to picture an electron traveling two or more different routes through space concurrently or passing from orbit to orbit without traversing the space between them at all? What kind of model can we construct of a space that is finite yet unbounded, or of light which is both wave and particle? It is such enigmas which have caused physicists like P. W. Bridgman of Harvard to suggest that "the structure of nature may eventually be such that our processes of thought do not correspond to it sufficiently to permit us to think about it at all. . . . The world fades out and eludes us. . . . We are confronted with something truly ineffable. We have reached the limit of the vision of the great pioneers of science, the vision, namely, that we live in a sympathetic world in that it is comprehensible by our minds."

This subdued and problematic stance of science toward reality is paralleled in philosophy. No one who works in philosophy today can fail to realize that the sense of the cosmos has been shaken by an encyclopedic skepticism. The clearest evidence of this is the collapse of what historically has been philosophy's central discipline: objective metaphysics, the attempt to discover what reality consists of and the most general principles which describe the way its parts are related. In this respect, the late Alfred North Whitehead marked the end of an era. His *Process and Reality: An Essay in Cosmology* is the last important attempt to construct a logical, coherent scheme of ideas that would blueprint the universe. The trend throughout the twentieth century has been away from faith in the feasibility of such undertakings. As a tendency throughout philosophy as a whole, this is a revolutionary development. For twenty-five hundred years philosophers have argued over which metaphysical system is true. For them to agree that none is, is a new departure.

The agreement represents the confluence of several philosophical streams. On one hand, it has come from the positivists who, convinced that truth comes only from science, have challenged the metaphysician's claim to extrascientific sources of insight. Their successors are the linguistic analysts, who have dominated British philosophy for the last several decades and who (insofar as they follow their pioneering genius Ludwig Wittgenstein) regard all philosophical perplexities as generated by slovenly use of language. For the analysts, "reality" and "being in general" are notions too thin and vapid to reward analysis. As a leading American proponent of this position, Professor Morton White of Harvard recently stated, "It took philosophers a long time to realize that the number of interesting things that one can say about all things in one fell swoop is very limited. Through the effort to become supremely general, you lapse into emptiness."

Equal but quite different objections to metaphysics have come from the existentialists who have dominated twentieth-century European philosophy. Heirs of Kierkegaard, Nietzsche, and Dostoevski, these philosophers have been concerned to remind their colleagues of what it means to be a human being. When we are thus reminded, they say, we see that to be human precludes in principle the kind of objective and impartial overview of things—the view of things as they are in themselves, apart from our differing perspectives—that metaphysics has always sought. To be human is to be finite, conditioned, and unique. No two persons have had their lives shaped by the same concatenation of genetic, cultural, historical, and interpersonal forces. Either these variables are inconsequential—but if we say this we are forgetting again what it means to be human, for our humanity is in fact overwhelmingly shaped by them—or the hope of rising to a God's-eye view of reality is misguided in principle.

The traditional philosopher might protest that in seeking such an overview he never expected perfection but that we ought to try to make our perspectives as objective as possible. Such a response would only lead the existentialist to press his point deeper; for his contention is not just that objectivity is impossible but that it runs so counter to our nature—to what it means to be human—that every step in its direction is a step away from our humanity. (We are speaking here of objectivity as it pertains to our lives as wholes, not to restricted spheres of endeavor within them such as science. In these latter areas objectivity can be an unqualified virtue.) If the journey held hope that in ceasing to be human we might become gods, there could be no objection. But as this is impossible, ceasing to be human can only mean becoming less than human—inhuman in the usual sense of the word. It means forfeiting through inattention the birthright that is ours: the opportunity to plumb the depths and implications of what it means to have an outlook on life which in important respects is unique and will never be duplicated.

Despite the existentialist's sharp rebuke to metaphysics and traditional philosophy in general, there is at least one important point at which he respects their aims. He agrees that it is important to transcend what is accidental and ephemeral in our outlooks and in his own way joins his colleagues of the past in attempting to do so. But the existentialist's way toward this goal does not consist in trying to climb out of his skin in order to rise to Olympian heights from which things can be seen with complete objectivity and detachment. Rather it consists in centering on his own inwardness until he finds within it what he is compelled to accept and can never get away from. In this way he, too, arrives at what he judges to be necessary and eternal. But necessary and eternal for him. What is necessary and eternal for everyone is so impossible for a man to know that he wastes time making the attempt.

With this last insistence the existentialist establishes contact with the metaphysical skepticism of his analytic colleagues across the English Channel. Existentialism (and its frequent but not invariable partner, phenomenology) and analytic philosophy are the two dominant movements in twentieth-century philosophy. In temperament, interest, and method they stand at opposite poles of the philosophical spectrum. They are, in fact, opposites in every sense but one. Both are creatures of the Post-Modern Mind, the mind which doubts that reality has an absolute order which man's understanding can comprehend.

Turning from philosophy to theology, we recall that the Modern Mind did not rule out the possibility of God; it merely referred the question to its highest court of appeal—namely, reality's pattern as disclosed by reason. If the world order entails the notions of providence and a creator, God exists; otherwise not. This approach made the attempt to prove God's existence through reason and nature the major theological thrust of the modern period. "Let us," wrote Bishop Joseph Butler in his famous *The Analogy of Religion,* "compare the known constitution and course of things . . . with what religion teaches us to believe and expect; and see whether they are not analogous and of a piece. . . . It will, I think be found that they are very much so." An enterprising Franciscan named Ramon Llull went even further. He invented a kind of primitive computer which, with the turning of cranks, pulling of levers, and revolving of wheels, would sort the theological subjects and predicates fed into it in such a way as to demonstrate the truths of the Trinity and the Incarnation by force of sheer logic working on self-evident propositions. Rationalism had entered theology as early as the Middle Ages, but as long as the Christian outlook prevailed, final confidence was reserved for the direct pronouncements of God himself as given in Scripture. In the modern period, God's existence came to stand or fall on whether reason, surveying the order of nature, endorsed it. It was as if Christendom and God himself awaited the verdict of science and the philosophers.

This hardly describes the current theological situation. Scientists and philosophers have ceased to issue pronouncements of any sort about ultimates. Post-modern theology builds on its own foundations. Instead of attempting to justify faith by appeals to the objective world, it points out that as such appeals indicate nothing about reality one way or the other, the way is wide open for free decision—or what Kierkegaard called the leap of faith. One hears little these days of the proofs for the existence of God which seemed so important to the modern world. Instead one hears repeated insistence that however admirably reason is fitted to deal with life's practical problems, it can only end with a confession of ignorance when confronted with questions of ultimate concern. In the famous dictum of Karl Barth, who has influenced twentieth-century theology more than anyone else, there is no straight line from the mind of man to God. "What we say breaks apart constantly . . . producing paradoxes which are held together in seeming unity only by agile and arduous running to and fro on our part." From our own shores Reinhold Niebuhr echoed this conviction. "Life is full of contradictions and incongruities. We live our lives in various realms of meaning which do not cohere rationally."

Instead of "These are the compelling reasons, grounded in the nature of things, why you should believe in God," the approach of the church to the world today tends to be, "This community of faith invites you to share in its venture of trust and commitment." The stance is most evident in Protestant and Orthodox Christianity and Judaism, but even Roman Catholic thought, notwithstanding the powerful rationalism it took over from the Greeks, has not remained untouched by the post-modern perspective. It has become more attentive to the extent to which personal and subjective factors provide the disposition to faith without which theological arguments prove nothing.

It is difficult to assess the mood which accompanies this theological revolution. On one hand, there seems to be a heightened sense of faith's precariousness: as Jesus walked on the water, so must the contemporary man of faith walk on the sea of nothingness, confident even in the absence of rational supports. But vigor is present too. Having labored in the shadow of rationalism during the modern period, contemporary theology is capitalizing on its restored autonomy. Compensating for loss of rational proofs for God's existence have come two gains. One is a new realization of the validity of Pascal's "reasons of the heart" as distinct from those of the mind. The other is a recovery of the awe without which religion, as distinct from ethical philosophy piously expressed, is probably impossible. By including God within a closed system of rational explanation, modernism lost sight of the endless qualitative distinction between God and man. Post-modern theology has reinstated this distinction with great force. If God exists, the fact that our minds cannot begin to comprehend his nature makes it necessary for us to acknowledge that he is Wholly Other.

These revolutions in science, philosophy, and theology have not left the arts unaffected. The worlds of the major twentieth-century artists are many and varied, but none resembles the eighteenth-century world where mysteries seemed to be clearing by the hour. The twentieth-century worlds defy lucid and coherent exegesis. Paradoxical, devoid of sense, they are worlds into which protagonists are thrown without trace as to why—the world which the late French novelist Albert Camus proclaimed "absurd," which for his compatriot Jean-Paul Sartre was "too much," and for the Irish dramatist Samuel Beckett is a "void" in which men wait out their lives for what-they-know-not that never comes. Heroes driven by a veritable obsession to find out where they are and what their responsibility is seldom succeed. Most of Franz Kafka is ambiguous, but his parable, "Before the Law," closes with as clear a countermand to the modern vision of an ordered reality as can be imagined. "The world-order is based on a lie."

Objective morality has gone the way of cosmic order. Even where it has not been moralistic, most Western art of the past has been created against the backdrop of a frame of objective values which the artist shared. As our century has progressed, it has become increasingly difficult to find such a framework standing back of the arts.

A single example will illustrate the point. One searches in vain for an artistic frame of reference prior to the twentieth century in which matricide might be regarded as a moral act. Yet in Sartre's play *The Flies,* it is the first authentic deed the protagonist Orestes performs. Whereas his previous actions have been detached, unthinking, or in conformity with the habit patterns that surround him, this one is freely chosen in the light of full self-consciousness and acceptance of its consequences. As such, it is the first act which is genuinely his. "I have done my deed, Electra," he exults, adding, "and that deed was good." Being his, the deed supplies his life with the identity which until then it had lacked. From that moment forward, Orestes ceases to be a free-floating form; his acquisition of a past he can never escape roots his life into reality. Note the extent to which this analysis relativizes the moral standard. No act is right or wrong in itself. Everything depends on its relation to the agent, whether it is chosen freely and with full acceptance of its consequences or is done abstractedly, in imitation of the acts of others, or in self-deception.

We move beyond morality into art proper when we note that the traditional distinction between the sublime and the banal, too, has blurred. As long as reality was conceived as a great chain of being—a hierarchy of worth descending from God as its crown through angels, men, animals, and plants to inanimate objects at the base—it could be reasonably argued that great art should attend to great subjects: scenes from the Gospels, major battles, or distinguished lords and ladies. With cubism and surrealism, the distinction between trivial and important disappears. Alarm clocks, driftwood, pieces of broken glass become appropriate subjects for the most monumental paintings. In Samuel Beckett and the contemporary French antinovelists, the most mundane items—miscellaneous contents of a pocket, a wastebasket, the random excursions of a runaway dog—are treated with the same care as love, duty, or the question of human destiny.

One is tempted to push the question a final step and ask whether the dissolution of cosmic order, moral order, and the hierarchic order of subject matter is reflected in the very forms of contemporary art. Critic Russel Nye thinks that at least as far as the twentieth-century novel is concerned, the answer is yes. "If there is a discernible trend in the form of the modern novel," he writes, "it is toward the concept of the novel as a series of moments, rather than as a planned progression of events or incidents, moving toward a defined terminal end. Recent novelists tend to explore rather than arrange or synthesize their materials; often their arrangement is random rather than sequential. In the older tradition, a novel was a formal structure composed of actions and reactions which were finished by the end of the story, which did have an end. The modern novel often has no such finality." Aaron Copland characterizes the music of our young composers as a disrelation of unrelated tones. Notes are strewn about like *membra disjecta;* there is an end to continuity in the old sense and an end of thematic relationships."

When Nietzsche's eyesight became too poor to read books, he began at last to read himself. The act was prophetic of the century that has followed. As reality has blurred, the gaze of post-modern man has turned increasingly upon himself.

Anthropological philosophy has replaced metaphysics. In the wake of Kierkegaard and Nietzsche, attention has turned from objective reality to the individual human personality struggling for self-realization. "Being" remains interesting only as it relates to man. As its order, if it has one, is unknown to us, being cannot be described as it is in itself; but if it is believed to be mysteriously wonderful, as some existentialists think, we should remain open to it. If it is the blind, meaningless enemy, as others suspect, we should maintain our freedom against it.

Even theology, for all its renewed theocentrism, keeps one eye steadily on man, as when the German theologian Rudoph Bultmann relates faith to the achievement of authentic selfhood. It is in art, however, that the shift from outer to inner has been most evident. If the twentieth century began by abolishing the distinction between sublime and banal subject matter, it has gone on to dispense with subject matter altogether. Although the tide may have begun to turn, the purest art is still widely felt to be entirely abstract and free of pictorial representation. It is as if the artist had taken the scientist seriously and responded, "If what I see as nature doesn't represent the way things really are, why should I credit this appearance with its former importance. Better to turn to what I am sure of: my own intuitions and the purely formal values inherent in the relations of colors, shapes, and masses."

I have argued that the distinctive feature of the contemporary mind as evidenced by frontier thinking in science, philosophy, theology, and the arts is its acceptance of reality as unordered in any objective way that man's mind can discern. This acceptance separates the Post-Modern Mind from both the Modern Mind, which assumed that reality is objectively ordered, and the Christian mind, which assumed it to be regulated by an inscrutable but beneficent will.

It remains only to add my personal suspicion that the change from the vision of reality as ordered to unordered has brought Western man to as sharp a fork in history as he has faced. Either it is possible for man to live indefinitely with his world out of focus or it is not. I suspect that it is not, that a will-to-order and orientation is rather fundamental in the human makeup. If so, the post-modern period, like all the intellectual epochs that preceded it, will turn out to be a transition to a still different perspective.

7

Empirical Metaphysics

PART I

My initiation into the entheogens took place in 1961 under the auspices of the
Center for Personality Research at Harvard University as part of a project
directed by Professor Timothy Leary to determine if a certain class of virtually
nonaddictive mind-altering chemicals—mescaline, psilocybin, and LSD—
could facilitate behavior change in desirable directions. Such changes are not
easy to gauge. Subjective reports are notoriously unreliable, but two populations
do lend themselves to statistical measurement. Six months after an entheogen
experience, is a paroled prisoner still on the streets or back behind bars, and is
the recovered alcoholic still off the bottle? Such were the kinds of questions that
the study hoped to answer, but it was necessary to start from scratch, for this
was the first concerted effort to study these substances scientifically. (At one
point Freud had hopes for cocaine, but he soon abandoned them, and besides,
cocaine falls into a different class of drugs because it is addictive.) Accordingly,
the first step was to get some idea of the range and kinds of experiences the
drugs occasion when given in a supportive atmosphere. Volunteers were
solicited to establish a data bank of phenomenological reports. Subjects were
screened to rule out those with psychological problems, and precise doses of
one of the three drugs being investigated were administered. A physician or
psychiatrist was invariably present, with an antidote ready should it be needed.
Every effort was made to keep the sessions unstressful. Flowers and music were

encouraged, and subjects were invited to surround themselves with meaningful artifacts—family photos, candles, icons, incense—if they chose to do so. Often the "laboratory" was the subject's own living room, and family and friends were welcome to be present. A follow-up report was required in which the subject was asked to describe the experience and retrospective feelings about it.

What follows is the report I turned in.

———

New Year's Day, 1961. Eleanor (who now answers to the name Kendra) and I reached the home of Dr. Timothy Leary in Newton, Massachusetts, about 12:30 P.M. Present in addition to Leary were Dr. George Alexander, psychiatrist, and Frank Barron, on sabbatical from the department of psychology at the University of California, Santa Cruz.

After coffee and pleasantries, Tim sprinkled some capsules of mescaline onto the coffee table and invited us to be his guest. One, he said, was a mild dose, two an average dose, and three a large dose. I took one; Eleanor, more venturesome, took two. After about half an hour, when nothing seemed to be happening, I too took a second capsule.

After what I estimate to have been about an hour, I noticed mounting tension in my body that turned into tremors in my legs. I went into the large living room and lay down on its couch. The tremors turned into twitches, though they were seldom visible.

It would be impossible for me to fix the time when I passed into the visionary state, for the transition was imperceptible. From here on time becomes irrelevant. With great effort I might be able to reconstruct the order in which my thoughts, all heavily laden with feelings, occurred, but there seems to be no point in trying to do so.

The world into which I was ushered was strange, weird, uncanny, significant, and terrifying beyond belief. Two things struck me especially. First, the mescaline acted as a psychological prism. It was as if the layers of the mind, most of whose contents our conscious mind screens out to smelt the remainder down into a single band we can cope with, were now revealed in their completeness—spread out as if by spectroscope into about five distinguishable layers. And the odd thing was that I could to some degree be aware of them all simultaneously, and could move back and forth among them at will, shifting my attention to now this one, now another one. Thus, I could hear distinctly the quiet conversation of Tim and Dr. Alexander in the adjoining study, and follow their discussion and even participate in it imaginatively. But this leads to the second marked feature. Though the five bands of consciousness—I say five roughly; they were not sharply divided and I made no attempt to count them—were all real, they were not of equal importance. I was experiencing the metaphysical theory known as emanationism, in which, beginning with the clear, unbroken Light of the Void, that light then fractures into multiple forms and declines in intensity as it devolves through descending levels of reality. My friends in the study were present in one band of this spectrum, but it was far more restricted than higher bands that were in view. Bergson's notion of the brain as a reducing valve struck me as accurate.

Along with "psychological prism," another phrase occurred to me: empirical metaphysics. Plotinus's emanation theory, and its more detailed Vedantic counterpart, had hitherto been only conceptual theories for me. Now I was *seeing* them, with their descending bands spread out before me. I found myself amused, thinking how duped historians of philosophy had been in crediting the originators of such worldviews with being speculative geniuses. Had they had experiences such as mine, they need have been no more than hack reporters. But beyond accounting for the origin of these philosophies, my experience supported their truth. As in Plato's myth of the cave, what I was now seeing struck me with the force of the sun, in comparison with which everyday experience reveals only flickering shadows in a dim cavern.

How could these layers upon layers, these worlds within worlds, these paradoxes in which I could be both myself *and* my world and an episode could be both momentary *and* eternal—how could such things be put into words? I realized how utterly impossible it would be for me to describe such things tomorrow, or even right then to Tim or Eleanor. There came the clearest realization I have ever had as to what literary genius consists of: a near-miraculous talent for using words to transport readers from the everyday world to things analogous to what I was now experiencing.

It should not be assumed from what I have written that the experience was pleasurable. The accurate words are significance and terror. In *The Idea of the Holy,* Rudolf Otto describes awe as a distinctive blend of fear and fascination, and I was experiencing at peak level that paradoxical mix. The experience was momentous because it showed me range upon range of reality that previously I had only believed existed and tried without much success to imagine. Whence, then, the terror? In part, from my sense of the utter freedom of the psyche and its dominion over the body. I was aware of my body, laid out on the couch as if on an undertaker's slab, cool and slightly moist. But I also had the sense that it would reactivate only if my spirit chose to reenter it. Should it so choose? There seemed to be no clear reason for it to do so. Moreover, could it reconnect if I willed it to? We have it on good authority that no man can see God and live—the sight would be too much for the body to withstand, like plugging a toaster into a power line. I thought of trying to get up and walk across the floor. I suspected that I could do so, but I didn't want to risk forcing this intensity of experience into my physical frame. It might shatter the frame.

Years later when I came upon Rilke's *Duino Elegies* I realized that he must have been sensing something like what I was experiencing when he wrote,

> *... Beauty is nothing*
> *but the beginning of terror, which we still are just able to endure,*
> *and we are so awed because it serenely disdains*
> *to annihilate us.*
> (Stephen Mitchell's translation)

Later, after the peak had passed and I had walked a few steps, I said to Tim, "I hope you know what you're playing around with here. I realize I'm still under the influence and that things probably look different from your side, but it looks to me like you're taking an awful chance in these experiments. Objective tests might reveal that my heart has been beating normally this afternoon, but there *is* such a thing as people being frightened to death. I feel like I'm in an operating room, having barely squeaked through an ordeal in which for two hours my life hung in the balance."

I have said nothing about the visual. Where it was important, it was abstract. Lights such as never were on land or sea. And space—not three or four dimensions but more like twelve. When I focused visually on my physical surroundings, I tended to be uninterested. Shapes and colors, however intensified, had little to contribute to the problem that obsessed me, which was what this experience implied for the understanding of life and reality. So I regarded the visual as largely an intrusive distraction and tended to keep my eyes closed. Only twice did physical forms command my attention. Once was when Dr. Alexander induced me to look at the pattern a lampshade was throwing on a taupe rug. That *was* extraordinary; the shapes stood out like three-dimensional blocks. They also undulated like writhing serpents. The other time was involuntary, when the Christmas tree, its lights unlit, suddenly jumped out at me. It had been in my visual field much of the afternoon, but this was transfiguration. Had I not been in the room throughout, I would have said that someone had re-trimmed the tree, increasing its tinsel tenfold. Where before there was a tree with decorations, now there were decorations with a clotheshorse of a tree to support them.

Interactions with Eleanor, who had dived inward and was reliving important phases of her childhood, form a happy but separate and essentially personal story. Around 10:30 P.M. we drove back to our incomparable, never-more-precious children who were sleeping as if the world was as it had always been, which it definitely was not for us. Neither of us fell asleep until about five, whereupon we slept until around nine. I was definitely into the cold that had been coming on, but my head was clear.

PART II

The Good Friday Experiment

Mention has already been made of the Good Friday Experiment, in which—
to test the power of entheogens to occasion mystical experiences in a religious
setting—Walter Pahnke conducted a study in which theological professors and
students were, in 1962, given psilocybin preceding the traditional Good Friday
service at Boston University. The project was the research topic for the doctoral
degree he received from Harvard University.

In addition to the detailed report of the experiment that appeared in Pahnke's
doctoral dissertation, there have been a number of journalistic accounts of it and
a study of the long-term consequences of that day for its subjects. However, one
significant incident that occurred during the experiment had not appeared in
the reports, and as I was party to it, Thomas Roberts, Professor of Educational
Psychology at Northern Illinois University, interviewed me about it to read
it into the record. Robert Jesse of the Council on Spiritual Practices was in
attendance.

———

THOMAS ROBERTS This is October First, 1996. Huston Smith will be telling us
    about an event that happened in the Good Friday Experiment in 1962.
HUSTON SMITH Just keep me on course.
ROBERTS O.K.
SMITH The basic facts of the experiment have been recorded elsewhere and
    are fairly well known, but I will summarize them briefly. In the early sixties,
    Walter Pahnke, a medical doctor with strong interests in mysticism, wanted
    to augment his medical knowledge with a doctorate in religion. He had heard
    that the entheogens often occasion mystical experiences, so he decided to
    make that issue the subject of his research. He obtained the support of Howard
    Thurman, Dean of Marsh Chapel at Boston University, for his project, and also
    that of Walter Houston Clark who taught psychology of religion at Andover
    Newton Theological Seminary and shared Wally's interest in the entheogens.

    Clark procured twenty volunteer subjects, mostly students from his semi-
    nary. Ten more volunteers, of whom I was one, were recruited as guides.
    Howard Thurman's two-and-a-half-hour 1962 Good Friday service at Boston
    University would be piped down to a small chapel in the basement of the
    building where the volunteers would participate in it. Fifteen of us would
    receive, double blind, a dose of psilocybin, and the remaining fifteen a placebo:
    nicotinic acid, which produces a tingling sensation that could make its recip-
    ients think they had gotten the real thing. The day after the experiment we
    would write reports of our experiences, and Pahnke would have them scored

by independent raters on a scale of from zero to three for the degree to which each subject's experience included the seven traits of mystical experience that W. T. Stace lists in his classic study, *Mysticism and Philosophy*. There was one borderline case, but apart from that, the experiences of those who received psilocybin were dramatically more mystical than those in the control group. I was one of those who received the psilocybin, and I will say a word about my experience before I proceed to the student that you asked about.

The experiment was powerful for me, and it left a permanent mark on my experienced worldview. (I say "experienced worldview" to distinguish it from what I think and believe the world is like.) For as long as I can remember I have believed in God, and I have experienced his presence both within the world and when the world was transcendentally eclipsed. But until the Good Friday Experiment, I had had no direct personal encounter with God of the sort that *bhakti yogis*, Pentecostals, and born-again Christians describe. The Good Friday Experiment changed that, presumably because the service focused on God as incarnate in Christ.

For me, the climax of the service came during a solo that was sung by a soprano whose voice (as it came to me through the prism of psilocybin) I can only describe as angelic. What she sang was no more than a simple hymn, but it entered my soul so deeply that its opening and closing verses have stayed with me ever since.

> *My times are in Thy hands, my God, I wish them there;*
> *My life, my friends, my soul, I leave entirely in Thy care. . . .*
>
> *My times are in Thy hands, I'll always trust in Thee;*
> *And after death at Thy right hand I shall forever be.*

In broad daylight those lines are not at all remarkable, but in the context of the experiment they said everything. The last three measures of each stanza ascended to a dominant seventh which the concluding tonic chord then resolved. This is as trite a way to end a melody as exists, but the context changed that totally. My mother was a music teacher, and she instilled in me an acute sensitivity to harmonic resonances. When that acquisition and my Christian nurturance converged on the Good Friday story under psilocybin, the gestalt transformed a routine musical progression into the most powerful cosmic homecoming I have ever experienced.

ROBERTS Are there other memories of the afternoon that come to mind?

SMITH I come back to the hubbub that erupted at times in our chapel. I was too deep into my own experience to be distracted by it, but I was peripherally aware of it and realized in retrospect that an observer would have found us a pretty unruly bunch. Half of us were enraptured, while the other half (as

I learned from several of them the next day) felt left out and were not above acting out their resentment in derisive laughter and incredulous hoots over the way the rest of us were behaving.

I also recall a short exchange with one of our number in the foyer to the chapel just before the service began. I was already feeling my psilocybin, and sensing—wrongly, it turned out—that he was as well, I said to him from the depths of my being, "It's true, isn't it?" By "it," I meant the religious outlook, God and all that follows from God's reality. He didn't respond and told me when we next met that he had gotten only the placebo and hadn't a clue as to what I was talking about. So I was dead wrong in inferring from our eye contact that our minds were in sync.

ROBERTS Anything else?

SMITH Only the gratitude I feel toward Wally for having mounted the experiment—as you know, it's a poignant gratitude for he died nine years later in a tragic scuba diving accident. I have explained how it enlarged my understanding of God by affording me the only powerful experience I have had of his personal nature. I had known and firmly believed that God is love and that none of love's nuances could be absent from his infinite nature; but that God loves *me,* and I *him,* in the concrete way that human beings love individuals, each most wanting from the other what the other most wants to give and with everything that might distract from that holy relationship excluded from view—*that* relation with God I had never before had. It's the theistic mode that doesn't come naturally to me, but I have to say for it that its carryover topped those of my other entheogenic epiphanies. From somewhere between six weeks and three months (I should judge) I really *was* a better person—even at this remove, I remain confident of that. I slowed down a bit and was somewhat more considerate. I was able to some extent to prolong the realization that life really is a miracle, every moment of it, and that the only appropriate way to respond to the gift that we have been given is to be mindful of that gift at every moment and to be caring toward everyone we meet.

ROBERTS Thank you, Huston.

SMITH You are welcome.

BOOK THREE

I Never Met a Religion
I Didn't Like

8

My Three Other Religions

To describe my encounters with the world's religions, I might adapt Will Rogers's famous *bon mot* thus: I never met a religion I did not like. When people hear that I practiced Hinduism unconditionally for ten years, then Buddhism for ten years, and then Islam for another ten years—all the while remaining a Christian and regularly attending a Methodist church—they assume I had a checklist and went down it checking off the major religions one by one. To the contrary. When I discovered Hinduism and saw its beauty and profundity, I intended to practice it, a faithful devotee, forever. But then when I encountered Buddhism and later Islam, and was dazzled by their heady possibilities, I had to try them on for size. They fit. The proper response to a great work of art is to enter into it as though there were nothing else in the world. The proper response to a major spiritual tradition, if you can truly see it, may be to practice it. With each new religion I entered into, I descended (or ascended?) into hidden layers within myself that, until then, I had not known were even there.

Three giants are striding the earth. One is a natural scientist, the second is a sociologist, and the third is a psychologist. That metaphor has teased my thoughts for a long time. The natural scientist is Western civilization, which since Aristotle would apprehend "reality" by studying and measuring objective, physical phenomena. The sociologist is China, which emphasizes social arrangements: like a pebble dropped into a pond, relationships in the Chinese worldview eddy out in concentric circles—from the individual to the family to the community to the cosmos—which reflect each other in the social order. India has been the psychologist, viewing the world through the lens of "the soul": the human psyche in Hinduism and Buddhism is an immense ocean, next to which moderns like

Freud seem Sunday bathers hugging the shore. Swami Satprakashananda first introduced me to Hindu psychology, and to that saintly man let me return.

I. HINDUISM

Satprakashananda was perhaps the only person I know who was truly a saint. The trouble with saints is that, in their even-handed goodness, they are difficult to evoke—unlike villains, whose dramatic treacheries give the writer a free ride. (Literature—for instance, Shakespeare—would have a dull time of it without scoundrels and ruthless bastards.)

Growing up as I had, I thought I knew something about piety; meeting Swami Satprakashananda, I realized I hadn't scratched the surface. He woke at six each morning and chanted the Vedas for four hours. Only then would he be ready for breakfast and to start the day. Through him I came to see that religious life went beyond beautiful thoughts and good deeds. The noble ideas that I read about in sacred books had in him become reflex action. What is different about him, I kept asking myself, different in the deep inner recesses of his psyche, that goodness and insight flow out of him so effortlessly?

I gained a clue one Thursday, during our weekly private tutorial, when Swami asked me, "Last night, when you were sleeping but not dreaming, was your mind aware?"

> *Me:* "Obviously not."
>
> *Swami:* "Oh, but you were."
>
> *Me:* "If I was aware, I was not aware of being aware." Case closed.

He waved my objection aside. He said that in sleep, when we are not dreaming, the mind remains active and alert. But just as dreams are instantly forgotten, even less can this subterranean level of the mind's operation be retained in waking memory. Yet it is then, in dreamless sleep, that the mind is closest to divinity, and were it not for our nightly immersion in that deeper mental reality, we might go crazy. (I thought of Swami's remark later, when I met Eustace Burnett, the never-sleeper, in England.)

For years Swami and I went round and round on this point, without my yielding an inch. Then I went for my semiannual dental checkup, where my dentist condemned my wisdom teeth: "Having them out will be less a problem for you than the problem that keeping them in will cause me." For the extraction I received a general anesthesia, and in the recovery room when I awoke I exclaimed, "It is so beautiful!" I had not dreamed, but obviously my mind had been aware, aware of something beautiful. My daughter Kim had a similar experience under anesthesia: upon waking she exclaimed to the nurse, "I love you!"

Being a private person, she was embarrassed to have felt propelled by whatever had happened under the anesthesia to make that statement, aloud in a public hospital setting, to whoever was there. In a lecture I described such mind-below-thought experiences, and afterward a woman in the audience told about coming to consciousness after a concussion, practically singing, "I am so happy! I am so happy!" Beauty—love—joy: these are attributes theologians use to describe the indescribable God. After my experience at the dentist, I wrote to Swami that he had been right after all.

I once asked an Indian philosopher the difference between philosophy as practiced in India and as practiced in America. "In the West you philosophize from the waking state, as though the waking state were all-important," he said. "In India we recognize four states of mind—waking, dreaming, dreamless sleep, and even a nirvanic level below that—and our philosophy tries to reflect all four." All right, I thought, but let's have some proof; show me somebody who utilized all four states and then show what difference it made. When I later read *The Gospel of Sri Ramakrishna,* about the founder of the Vedanta order, I saw that Ramakrishna had relied upon all four states of mind, and that by doing so he half-erased the difference between God and man.

Sri Ramakrishna was the great saint, and possibly more than a saint, of nineteenth-century India. He was not a great intellectual; in fact, he was illiterate. But he seemed to have access to parts of his psyche that ordinarily people never do, and this gave him extraordinary power. When he was dying, the doctor touched his throat where the cancer was, which caused him excruciating pain. Ramakrishna told the doctor to wait a moment; he shifted his consciousness and then felt no pain at all. (The next day, however, when he heard two boatmen violently arguing, he felt *their* pain so intensely he could not stop howling.)

The novelist Christopher Isherwood thought Ramakrishna shows what it's like when divinity puts on human form and walks among us on earth. When two pundits questioned Ramakrishna and then announced he was "the godhead," he replied humorously, "At least it's not a mental disease." Perhaps Ramakrishna was some sort of avatar, but what I cherish him for is his human example, showing how to appreciate different religions and to empathize with different people. My finding something valuable in what everyone says, even students espousing seeming nonsense, is but the palest reflection of the way Ramakrishna dismantled the wall separating mind from mind and person from person. And every religion he thought was a valid path to God, worth practicing. Sri Ramakrishna, in effect, wrote *The World's Religions,* except, being illiterate, he wrote it with his life.

To return to Swami Satprakashananda, I recall an evening at the Vedanta Center when he made a huge vat of rice pudding, stirring the pot for hours. During a break, a woman picked up a spoon and tasted the concoction. Now, in

Hindu tradition, food that's being prepared for a *puja*, or offering, may not be tasted by anyone, not even the cook, until after it's presented to the deity. Swami saw the woman tasting it, scooted over and dumped the whole vat down the sink. The woman felt offended and said so: "I am incensed. I should walk out of here and never come back. I won't, though, because you are the holiest person I've ever met." He was the holiest person I had ever met. And he was mundane compared with Indian mystics like Sri Ramakrishna. What was the country like that could produce such spiritual paragons? During the 1950s I was practically on fire to go see for myself.

Hardly anyone I knew had been to India, but in 1957, thanks to Mr. Danforth's generosity, I was on my way there. Upon arriving, on the long ride in from the Delhi airport, I inhaled India, rising from a half million cooking fires in the dusty evening air, and I was intoxicated, hooked. Over many visits over many years, I would ask myself: "What is it that made this place, these people, so different?" while at the same time thinking, "I know them. I've always known them. A part of me has been here before." I was able to return to India when I was teaching and leading students on their academic year abroad. It was always an adventure. A student might knock on my door at dawn to tell me that he was staying in India and could I please inform the university and his parents. The students showed genuine curiosity about much of India; I was ten times as eager to see *all of it*. At the southernmost tip of India, for example, lies an entirely underground temple that held services at 4 A.M. The first morning I was turned away as an infidel; the second morning, turned away as improperly attired; the third morning, I wore a dhoti and was admitted. I was not to be deterred; I had to explore everything in India, both the visible and the hidden.

In that spirit I made a pilgrimage to Vrindivan, the legendary birthplace of Krishna, the incarnation of the god Vishnu. There under a tree was a well-dressed gentleman in a suit lecturing to a group, obviously about Krishna. Our eyes connected, and I thought here was my chance to find our whether Krishna had been an actual person, or a myth shrouded in the early mists of prehistoric time.

 Me: Good morning, good sir. Can you tell me when Krishna lived?

The Pandit: Most certainly. A long time ago.

 Me: I suspected as much. But exactly how long?

The Pandit: Longer—longer ago.

 Me: In which century would that be?

The Pandit: I shall tell you. A longest time ago.

The pandit was right. In India there is a sense of time that does not ticktock in tune with modern clocks, just as there is a knowledge that is not gained through science and empirical experiments. In the modern West knowledge is of objective, finite particulars in historical time. India recognizes that kind of useful information: it calls it "lower knowledge." Higher knowledge (*paravidya*) proceeds differently, or rather it doesn't proceed at all but enters history full-blown on the morning of a new creation. New epochs begin when a soul, waiting in the wings, as it were—Krishna, Jesus, the Buddha, Ramakrishna—is born, and born already wise, to impart the wisdom particularly suited to the coming era.

Christ said, "I am the Truth," but Hinduism has *truths* (plural). Coming from my Christian background, I was surprised that the single destination of sanctity could admit of so many different avenues leading to it. For each different type of person, Hinduism prescribes a different path (yoga). Here I will simply refer to four of the principal ones. (1) *Jnana* yoga tries to achieve holiness through knowledge, by which is meant not factual information but understanding or vision. (2) For *bhakti* yogis, feelings are more real than thoughts, so they approach the divine through love and devotion. (3) In *karma* yoga, salvation comes through work, but work done not for gain but for its own (or God's) sake. And finally there is (4) *royal* or *raja* yoga, comprising meditation and inward exploration. Can the four yogas ever meet, be fully combined? Probably not in the same person. Imagine Socrates and Saint Francis and Gandhi and Siddhartha Gautama meeting at some ethereal pub: they might agree on some common goal, but to reach it they would head off in different directions.

All paths are equally valid, but to my thinking one was more so. For if you don't have *jnana*, knowledge or vision, how can you even understand what yoga is, what a path is? When I made this argument, in India in 1969, my daughter Kim objected. Kim loved India for its over-the-top riot of feeling and sensory overload. In India her emotions reveled in the street dramas and extravagant displays and Technicolor texture of life. When I extolled the *jnana* yogi (which I am), I was unintentionally discounting the *bhakti* yogi, who understands through feeling and compassion, as Kim does.

Her reaction startled me. A memory, long forgotten and walled off, came back into consciousness. "Kim, if there is one thing in my life I regret," I said to her, "it was leaving you and Karen and Gael when I went on Mr. Danforth's trip in 1957." When I received Danforth's letter, I had been terribly torn: Do I seize this opportunity and feel guilty? Or do I stay home and resent my children? Everyone told Kendra and me not to pass up such a once-in-a-lifetime chance. I arranged for another professor and his family to move into my house in St. Louis to look after our daughters, and for those seven months the two families lived amicably together. Kim would brag that her mommy and daddy were explorers, going all around the world. She was seven at the time, though, and what she really felt but could not express was: her parents had died. Now in that Indian hotel with Kim, I realized that though I may have done the right thing intellectually (*jnana*), it was the wrong thing emotionally (*bhakti*). Understanding the four yogas allowed me finally to see that. And that understanding allowed me, in that hotel room, to apologize. When I asked her forgiveness, Kim broke down and cried. And cried. And cried. And I cried with her.

Our family, though small in number, has all four kinds of yogis in it. (There's the *jnana* papa and the *raja* mother and the various yogini daughters.) One reason family dynamics can be difficult is that the members assume they are talking to one another, but with all of them having such fundamentally different perspectives, the words sail past each other. The intimate conversation between husband and wife or brother and sister can be as mutually incomprehensible as different foreign languages. We need the different and complementary perspectives of the various yogas—and, ideally, of all religions—not only to reach God, but to reach each other.

II. BUDDHISM

Out of the Great Mother, out of the cradle of India, sprang a second world religion besides Hinduism. That religion is, of course, Buddhism. In mid-twentieth-century America few Americans stumbled into Hinduism; you had to be lucky; you had to bump into someone like Swami Satprakashananda, and there weren't many like him. By contrast, if you had any curiosity about spiritual possibilities, you did not have to search for Buddhism. It would tap you on the shoulder and say, "Hey you!"

In the 1950s Alan Watts was putting his popular introductions to Buddhism on everyone's bookshelf. Huxley commented to me about Alan Watts, "What a curious character. Half philosopher, half racetrack operator." Watts was the guru of Zen who advised everyone to meditate but did not bother to do it himself. He was, however, an excellent companion to go drinking with. And if I got tipsy, it was not from the alcohol. Watts's description of Buddhist awakening, of becoming a bodhisattva, made me drunk with the possibility of awakening myself. Siddhartha Gautama had said there is a Buddha in every grain of sand, and I reasoned that if this was true of every grain of sand, there might be a Buddha in Huston Smith, too. I would have traded my soul—except that Buddhism lacks the concept of a soul—for *satori*, for a glimpse of enlightenment. Some friends accused me of whoring after the Infinite. Well, what better whoredom is there?

Alan Watts was not, however, the man who opened the door of Buddhism for me. Watts's books were popularizations of a greater figure, and it was that man who plunged me into a decade-long search for *bodhicitta*, the mind of openness and clarity. A poem by Muriel Rukeyser records my meeting with that man, which took place, of all places, on television.

FRAGILE

I think of the image brought into my room
Of the sage and the thin young man who flickers and asks.
He is asking about the moment when the Buddha
Offers the lotus, a flower held out as declaration.
"Isn't that fragile?" he [the young man] asks. The sage answers:
"I speak to you. You speak to me. Is that fragile?"

In that flickering TV image the young man is me and the sage is Daisetsu T. Suzuki. On public television I interviewed well-known figures like Eleanor Roosevelt about the direction our society was heading. The producers decided the series should include a token Asian, some wise man from the East. I proposed D. T. Suzuki, who had introduced Zen to America. I was nervous. Suzuki was ancient, and TV production then was arduous and exhausting, shot under klieg lights as hot as the Sahara. Suzuki's companion, a Mrs. Okamura, astutely brought a futon to the studio, and in breaks between filming he would take catnaps. The old man astonished me: such an impromptu rendering of wisdom before a TV camera. I felt the curtains of truth parting, and I could imagine generations hence watching this show enthralled. At the end of that long hot day, however, the head cameraman apologized: they had forgotten to put film in the camera. Would we mind doing the whole thing over? This time, tired and fatigued, Daisetsu's brilliance was less, but, if anything, his grace and good manners were even greater. I recalled a Chinese phrase from my childhood: "Your courtesy exceeds all permissible bounds." That day I determined to go to Japan, to learn what had produced such a gentle sage.

I was to visit Japan and Daisetsu Suzuki many times there. Particularly unforgettable to me was our final visit. There he was, when I got off the train, looking impossibly ancient, sunning himself on the grass, talking with an old friend, another relic of time. Mrs. Okamura explained that the two old men were deaf and each could not hear a word the other said but they enjoyed one another's company nonetheless. Mrs. Okamura told how when they had been schoolboys together, they had daydreamed about their future:

Friend: Daisetsu, what shall you do when you come to manhood?
Daisetsu: My peculiar desire is to spread Buddhism in the West. And you?
Friend: I shall become a businessman. I shall prosper. I shall grow rich. And I will use that money to help you spread Buddhism in the West.

Their youthful dreams came to fruition, and that fruition is: me. Me and thousands of people like me who have benefited from Buddhism's coming to the

West. I am as old now as Daisetsu was then: why don't I sit deaf and content in the sun, in the company of a friend, needing nothing more, happy in *satori*?

For in Buddhism you don't have to go to heaven to realize lasting happiness. Under our neurotic frets—this is one of the first things I learned from Daisetsu Suzuki—everyone is already enlightened. Everyone is, underneath, at heart, innately a Buddha. "If everybody's a Buddha," I have heard people object, though, "why is there so much suffering and misery and war and torture." It's undeniable: people suffer, and unjustly. Yet from the heart of the combat zone we sometimes get reports of *something else*. A former student of mine was caring for his gravely ill wife day and night, until he was so exhausted that he did not know if he was coming or going. Then, in a grocery store of all places, under the neon glare, he had the uncanny sensation that everything would be all right—indeed, that it already was. The child fiddling with the cereal boxes, a pregnant woman choosing between toothpaste brands, the carts in the aisles, the light and the air—all were exactly as they should be.

My daughter Kimberly had a similar experience. When her first husband informed her, out of the blue, that he was leaving her, she was devastated. In the night she lay awake feeling shocked beyond thought. But then she felt something like a pillar of light descending through the back of her head and down her spine, and she was filled with peace. She thought, It is all right. Hospice workers report that at the very instant of death, on most people's faces a look of sweet repose comes. In Buddhism that luminous peace already exists within, even if obscured, as on a cloudy day the sun is there behind the clouds. You need go nowhere to find it, but, inspired by Suzuki, I made up my mind to travel to Japan, to see whether I might find it there.

With China closed to foreigners, Japan became my adopted native country. Over the course of my ten visits there Japan would advance from a black-and-white impoverished economy into rainbow prosperity: only unchanging was how I always felt happy there. Polite courtesy, reminiscent of Suzuki's, smoothed the jagged edges of every human exchange. In America people on the subways or streets look harried or hurried, as though they wished to be elsewhere; I was in a hurry, too. In Japan, I became lighthearted and content simply to live. I wonder why. For my purpose in being in Japan was anything but aimless or indolent.

I had not come to admire the cherry trees in springtime or be served sake by geishas. With *satori* in mind, I had gone to Japan to meet that stranger, my own mind. I had arranged to undergo Zen training and to do so in Kyoto at *Myoshinji sodo* ("The Monastery of the Temple of the Marvelous Mind"), which was famous, or infamous, for its strictness and discipline. I didn't have much choice; its *roshi* was one of only two Zen masters in Japan who then spoke English. A marine drill sergeant might have learned a thing or two at *Myoshinji sodo*. I was told not to distract myself by reading or writing, which was almost as habitual with me as breathing. "Suppose I have to write my mother on a matter of utter emergency?" I asked. If I must, I was told, do it in the *banjo*, or squat toilet. Literary sensibility evidently ranked low in the scheme of things here.

The *roshi* at *Myoshinji sodo* did not want spiritual sightseers, which he suspected I must be. He was training thirty monks fifteen hours a day to achieve a rarefied state of mind, and here was a Western religious tourist (he assumed) who would demand exceptions to be made in his case. In my initial interview, Goto Roshi in effect dismissed me by saying that everyone there practiced sitting in the lotus position, knowing full well that Westerners could not. As it happened, though, I could.

The previous summer, in anticipation, I had trained my long legs little by little to stretch into the shape of pretzels. When I first tried the lotus position, my knees jutted up about a foot from the floor. My desk had eight-inch legs, so I rammed a knee into the space between the floor and where the bottom drawer began. After a week of tendon stretching, I wedged a thin pamphlet over my knee to force it down farther. After a few weeks the pamphlet became a phone book. I even demonstrated the lotus position on television, which elicited this letter from one viewer:

> Dear Professor Smith,
> *This will not be long, for I can't write well in this position.*
> I have my right foot in my left pocket, and my left foot pretzelled and resting on my right thigh.
> My question is: how do I unwind? I am eagerly awaiting your next program.

I remembered that viewer's letter at *Myoshinji*. I had never practiced the lotus position for longer than half an hour, but at the monastery we sat for hours at a stretch (or not stretched). My legs were in physical agony. The physical pain slowly abated over two months—and was nothing compared with my mental agony when I began the study of *koans*.

Koans are Zen riddles that you do not solve so much as step through, as through Alice's looking glass, into Mad Hatterish conundrums designed to stun rational sense and in its place induce wordless insight. Perfect, simply perfect, for driving a professor of philosophy insane. The most famous *koan* is, What is the sound of one hand clapping? (Don't try hitting one hand in the air. Do, and you'll hear the sound of one hand clapping—the *roshi*'s against the side of your head.) My *koan* concerned a monk who asked Joshu (a famous master in Tang-dynasty China), "Does a dog have a Buddha-nature?" Joshu's answer seemed to imply no. The conundrum: since the Buddha said that even the grass has Buddha-nature, how can a dog *not* have it?

Every day I came up with another ingenious answer; every day the *roshi* frowned and shook his head no; every day the bell would ring and I would be told to come back tomorrow. I turned the *koan* upside down; I pulled it inside out; I unpacked each word and repacked its meaning. Finally I thought, I've got it. The key word was *have*. A dog does not *have* Buddha-nature, not the way I have a shirt or an ice-cream cone. Rather Buddha-nature has, or is momentarily taking the shape of, that dog. But the *roshi* did not even hear out my ingenious solution. Halfway through my explanation he roared at me, "You have the philosopher's disease!" Then he softened a bit: "There's nothing wrong with philosophy. I myself have a master's degree in it from one of our better universities. Philosophy works only with reason, though, and there's nothing wrong with reason, either. Your reasoning is fine, but your experience is limited. Enlarge your experience, and your philosophy will be different." *Ding-a-ling-a-ling* sounded the little bell— signal that the interview was over. I had my impossible assignment: to think of how to think the way I do not think.

If a *koan* is mentally exhausting, try it on sleep deprivation. It all but pushed me over the edge. At the end of my stay at *Myoshinji* there was something like a final-exam period, when the monks meditated virtually around the clock. Since I was a novice, I was permitted the sybaritic luxury of three and a half hours' sleep a night, which was grossly insufficient. That prolonged sleep deprivation was the hardest ordeal I've ever endured. After the first night I was simply sleepy. By the third night I was a zombie. From then on it got worse. The *koans* force the rational mind to the end of its tether, and then sleep deprivation kicks in. Since you are not sleeping and hence not dreaming, you in effect dream or lapse into quasi-hallucinations while you are awake, a kind of a temporary psychosis. I was in that altered state during my last days at *Myoshinji*.

And in that state I stormed into the *roshi*'s room. Self-pity had become boring; fury was the order of the day. What a way to treat human beings, I raged to myself. I wouldn't just throw in the towel, I'd smack it across the *roshi*'s face. However, a certain decorum prevailed as I entered his audience room. I clasped palms together and bowed reverentially; as I approached him I touched my head to the tatami floor mat and flexed my outreached fingers upward to symbolize lifting the dust off the Buddha's feet. Then our eyes met in a mutual glare. For a few moments he said nothing, and then he growled, "How's it going?" It sounded like a taunt.

"Terrible!" I shouted.

"You think you are going to get sick, don't you?" More taunting sarcasm, so I let him have it.

"Yes, I think I'm going to get sick! Sick because of you!" For several days my throat had begun to contract and I was having to labor to breathe.

And then, curiously, his face relaxed. His smirking expression disappeared, and with total matter-of-factness he said, "What is sickness? What is health? Put aside both and go forward."

I despair of ever conveying the uncanny impact those twelve words had on me. I thought, He's right. He is right! Sickness and health suddenly seemed beside the point of what it means to be human; compared to that more abiding reality, health and sickness were two sides of the same coin. Buddhism speaks of the "Great No's," such as "no birth, no death" and "no coming, no going." There is something within us that is not born and does not die and that comes from nowhere and goes no place. Somehow after the *roshi's* few words I found myself unexpectedly in a state of total peace. I did my prescribed bow to the floor and exited the room, not only determined to complete the two remaining days, but confident that I could do so. Since then I have often been sick, but off it goes to the side, and I go forward.

When I had been sitting contorted for hours in the lotus position, that month seemed to drag on forever; now all too quickly it was over. It was time to say good-bye. Ritual governed all aspects of life at *Myoshinji sodo,* so I knew my farewell interview with Goto Roshi would be a ceremonious and formal affair. I was wrong. Roshi met me at the doorway to his tiny house, not in his usual priestly robes, but dressed casually. He could have been anybody and I somebody who just chanced to drop by. In his miniature living room he pulled back a short hanging curtain and introduced me to a shriveled-up woman working at a tiny stove. "This is *Oksan,* who takes care of my food." Then through another sawed-off curtain, he gestured to a futon on which a thin coverlet was spread. "This is my bedroom, and this is my television where I watch sumo wrestling. Do you watch sumo wrestling? Oh, too bad. It's wonderful!" He led me out the back door, where empty beer bottles were stacked. "And here are the remnants of the beer I drink while watching sumo wrestling." I got it: he was knocking the teacher off his pedestal. But then he proceeded to knock Zen off its pedestal. *Koans* can be a useful exercise, he said, but they are not Zen. And sitting in meditation, he went on—that is not Zen. Then why had I been torturing myself with *koans* and body aerobics, I wondered, and what the hell, then, was Zen?

"You will be flying home tomorrow," he said. "Don't overlook how many people will help you to get home—ticketing agents, pilots, cabin attendants, those who prepare your meals." He bowed and placed his palms together, demonstrating *gassho,* the gesture of gratitude. Straightening up, he pointed to the beam that supported the corner of the house. Another *gassho.* He glanced up at the ceiling that kept the house dry and executed yet another *gassho.* Then he did a *gassho* to me. "Make your whole life unceasing gratitude," he said. "What is Zen? Simple, simple, so simple. Infinite gratitude toward all things past; infinite service to all things present; infinite responsibility to all things future. Have a safe journey home." And he gave me a wonderful smile. "I am glad you came."

Such was my initiation into Buddhism. Each new Buddhist country I visited was like another classroom, a deeper immersion into dharma studies. In Thailand the saffron-robed monks sallied forth at dawn with their begging bowls, and Huston Smith with his begging bowl went with them. In America we would have thanked and chatted with the benefactors who put food in our bowls. Here the monks, holding out their bowls, did not look up at the women; the women, giving us our food, did not look directly at the monks. It was Goto Roshi's pure gratitude on one side and pure generosity on the other. Does a dog have Buddha-nature? Our bodies, in those moments, experienced the nature of generosity and gratitude, and we felt more alive.

In Burma, Kendra and I went on retreat with the Vipassana master U Ba Khin. The body is its own spiritual journey. When we meditated on the body, wherever Kendra focused her attention, her skin would turn red at exactly that point. During the retreat she became ill with diarrhea and vomiting, but U Ba Khin pronounced that a good sign. He hinted at possessing extraordinary powers. I gave no credence to his claim that he could cure the sick, but when U Ba Khin boasted of having a student who could go into *samadi* (that deep trance supposedly bordering on enlightenment) at will I was intrigued. U Ba Khin summoned the student—a successful businessman who used meditation to cure his horrendous migraines—and told him to go into *samadi*. U Ba Khin then invited me: "Go ahead. You can stick him with a needle now." No thank you. However, I clapped my hands loudly next to his ears, and he stirred no more than a statue, and when Kendra took his pulse, it was thirty beats per minute. The man became a celebrated meditation teacher—S. N. Goenka. Later in India, Goenka told Kendra he was planning a ten-day retreat, and he planned not to sleep at all during ten days. I was moving into things undreamed of at the University of Chicago philosophy department.

The Chinese had sealed off Tibet from foreigners, so in 1964 I traveled to the Tibetan areas of northern India to learn of their form of Buddhism. Arriving at a Tibetan monastery in the Himalayas, I was ushered into the abbot's bungalow, and a hot bowl of Tibetan tea was placed in my hands. In my travels I have encountered only two objectionable foods—poi in Hawaii, which would make excellent wallpaper paste, and Tibetan tea. I took a big gulp before its rancid yak-butter and rock-salt taste registered. A woman missionary in Africa, when served a soup made from a live monkey thrown into a pot of boiling water, prayed, "Lord, I'll put it down, if you'll keep it down." I could see myself throwing up over the gorgeous Tibetan carpets on the floor.

I retired early, in preparation for a four-day festival that would begin at three in the morning. Three A.M. came ungodly early, and as I listened to the lamas' monotonous chanting, it was still dark outside. I was tired from my travels, and—what I'm getting around to is . . . I fell asleep. Only to be jolted awake: the monotonous monotone had changed into beautiful tonal chords. I thought I was still dreaming, surrounded by an angelic choir. The choir then stopped singing, leaving it all to a cantor. It was stranger than any dream: a first, a third, and a barely audible fifth chord came from his single larynx! Nobody in the music department at MIT, I thought, is going to believe this. I borrowed an old German tape recorder, to prove to skeptics back at MIT that the human voice can sound more than one tone at a time. As a result a new term would enter the vocabulary of musicology: *multiphonic chanting.* A second result of the scratchy tape I made is that the Grateful Dead came to hear about these monks and sponsored them on several world tours. Indeed, multiphonic chanting became something of a fad; popular courses were given in it (Kendra took one), and the choir at St. John the Divine in New York began to sing it.

What those lamas did, however, has a significance that goes beyond singing. They took from the outskirts of awareness overtones ordinarily too faint to be heard and made them conscious. This is what worship is intended to do: move the sacred—in this case, sacred sound—from the periphery to the center. I asked one lama, "What's it like to sing like that?" He answered that at first it was quite ordinary, what anyone experiences when singing. Then, as the resonant chords take on a life of their own, it felt as though not he but a deity was creating the music and he was just riding the waves of it. As the chanting climaxed, in that crescendo all distinction between lama, deity, and chords collapsed and all sound was holy sound.

As I was leaving the monastery, the monks said that I should go to Dharamsala and meet the Dalai Lama. No. I would not intrude upon that busy man just to boast that I had shaken his hand. But the monks, it turned out, had already arranged the interview. I was determined to limit the meeting to ten minutes, knowing that the Dalai Lama had more important things to do. Thus it came about that a few days later I did shake his hand (a firm, warm handshake it was), and I expressed my sympathy for the Tibetan people and proposed that he visit America. He said that I was the first person to make that suggestion. I could not but be impressed: here was someone raised like a king and venerated like a god, yet he exhibited not the faintest trace of egotism. We conversed through a translator, but after ten minutes as I rose to leave, he mumbled to himself in English, "I must decide what is important. Decide now." Then he said to me, Please, would I sit down again, and could I stay longer?

It was due to a misunderstanding. On my calling card was Massachusetts Institute of Technology, and since I taught at MIT, the Dalai Lama assumed I must be a scientist. Since his arrival in the modern world only a few short years before, the new scientific theories he was hearing about, from DNA to the big bang, had intrigued him. Did they disprove Buddhism, or did they validate it? Surely a professor from MIT could answer his questions. Fortunately I had recently heard the Harvard astrophysicist Harlow Shapley lecture on the big bang, on how the universe expands and contracts—which suggests there may have been more than one big bang. The Dalai Lama concurred: "It's bang bang bang." From my explanation of DNA, he concluded that DNA was compatible with Buddhist reincarnation. "But if the words of the Buddha and the finding of modern science contradict each other," the Dalai Lama added, "the former has to go." He was not setting science above religion but expressing his conviction that the two are allies, different roads to one reality. In *The Universe in a Single Atom: The Convergence of Science and Spirituality* he would later write: "When I count my teachers of science, I include Huston Smith among them." I wish that he had had that day a better, a more MIT-ish, MIT teacher.

That quiet afternoon in Dharamsala began a lifelong friendship. Among many cherished memories I particularly remember the time I arranged for him to speak at Syracuse. Someone in the audience asked him, "What should I do with my uncontrollable anger?" and the Dalai Lama sang out in English, "Control it." Another questioner kept goading him to assert Buddhism's superiority over Christianity. The Dalai Lama finally stopped the pest: "If I say anything against the Lord Jesus, the Buddha will scold me." Later, in Bodh Gaya, my student Phil Novak (later my coauthor of *Buddhism: A Concise Introduction*) asked the Dalai Lama to explain how rebirth works. Phil knew the usual metaphors of one candle flame lit from another or the apple seed that grows into a new apple tree, but he was still perplexed, saying, "We're not candles or trees, we're human beings." After reflecting a moment, the Dalai Lama answered, "Yes, something that might be called a self does continue from lifetime to lifetime, but it is so different from what we usually mean by *self* that it is better not to speak of it."

As I listened, I was reminded of the story of the man who asked the Buddha, "Is there no self?" When the Buddha gave no answer, the man exclaimed, "So there is a self!" to which again the Buddha made no reply. Later the Buddha's attendant asked him, "You always say there is no self. Why did you not answer the man?" The Buddha explained that the man had not wanted to heal himself or to help anyone but merely to form a theory. Helping and healing—not hypothesis and beliefs—were the Buddha's concerns as they have been the Dalai Lama's. Listening to him in Bodh Gaya, I felt I was not only at the place of the Buddha but almost in his presence as well.

Back then my academic colleagues considered my interest in Buddhism odd and obsolete, as if I'd taken up, say, blacksmithing. Today every other person I know is, if not a Buddhist himself, someone whose sister or first cousin is. Why has Buddhism become so popular in America? The short answer: because it appeals to one's own experience, not dogma, and because it offers practical help. I used to wonder why Buddhism had no key poetic text the way Hinduism has the Bhagavad Gita and Taoism the Tao Te Ching. Then I realized that Buddhism deals less in poetic metaphors than in practical methods. And the starting point of those methods (as well as their end point) is your own mind.

Meditation is Buddhism's way of introducing you to your own mind. My good friend Heng Sure, a modern Buddhist hero, decided to go on a silent meditation walk, and the walk lasted three years. Heng Sure (an American who assumed a Chinese Buddhist name) undertook a pilgrimage on foot without speaking, walking from Los Angeles to Ukiah in northern California. It required three years because he did it in the traditional manner, taking three steps then bowing, taking three more steps then bowing, on and on, inching into the near and far. He thus inched through the Watts ghetto, where menacing youth shouted at him, "Look at the crazy honky!" and past the mansions of Beverly Hills, whose owners told him to grow up and get a job. With his vow of silence, he could not respond; he could only observe his reactions through the double mirror of his own and others' eyes.

Recently I asked Heng Sure what he learned from those three years. "Not much," he answered. "Perhaps just this: When I feel some urge, it does not push me immediately into action. I experience an extra split second of inner distance, and in that split second I can decide whether to act or not." Heng Sure's answer was modest, but isn't that the definition of freedom? We are free when we are not the slave of our impulses, but rather their master. Taking inward distance, we thus become the authors of our own dramas rather than characters in them.

When I think of freedom, or of the mind and its power, I think of the Dalai Lama at the precise moment he left Tibet. Behind him were the mountains of his homeland and everything he knew, now forever closed to him; before him lay the unknown horizon, where everything would be unaccustomed and unfamiliar. In his perilous escape he could bring with him nothing but his thoughts; he had nothing to offer the unknown world except his thoughts. Thoughts are intangible, ephemeral—as delicate as the flower the Buddha held out to his disciple. Yet from that flower, or rather from the Dalai Lama's thoughts, almost inconceivably, has arisen a whole new world of Buddhism in the West. As Daisetsu Suzuki said to me, "Is that fragile?"

III. ISLAM

I had sought out Hinduism and Buddhism, but it felt like Islam came in search of me. Of course I had taught it in my college courses, and I admired Muhammad as a great religious reformer who, among other achievements, improved the status of women in his time. The Holy Qur'an (or Koran) is, however, a difficult book for non-Muslims. I remember first reading it on a family vacation just as we were passing the Great Salt Lake in Utah. If you dove into the lake, its heavy salt content would practically bounce you back out of it. So, too, my attempts that summer to dive into the Holy Qur'an were rebuffed. Little did I suspect then that I would embark on a decade-long, deeply personal involvement with Islam. It came about in this way.

In 1974 I was preparing to lead a group of students on a study year abroad. As soon as I arrived in Japan, I was to lecture on Shinto, and, a drawback, I knew nothing about Shinto. I noticed an unread book on my shelf, *On the Trail of Buddhism,* and—I can't resist peeking into any book—lo and behold, it had a chapter on Buddhism's ally in Japan, Shinto. To boast, in Japan I gave a brilliant lecture on Shinto. I simply parroted what the book's author, someone named Frithjof Schuon, had said. Later in India I chanced upon another volume by this Schuon called *Language of the Self,* which I thought equally brilliant. Still later I found Schuon's *Understanding Islam* to be the best introduction to the subject and his *Transcendent Unity of Religions* one of the best spiritual books I ever read. Wherever I ventured in the world's religions, Frithjof Schuon had been there before me. Who was he? I must meet him, I decided, if he is alive, whoever he is, wherever he might be.

He was indeed alive, and I tracked him down in Switzerland. When I met him there, he looked every inch a figure of mystery and romance. He wore flowing robes, and upon entering his presence, you kissed the ring on his finger. That is, if you could gain access to his presence, for he would not talk to just anyone. I had to first pass an interview with an attendant—the keeper of the gates, as it were—who had to approve of my position on matters important to Schuon. Did I, the attendant asked, believe in evolution? I sensed that if you accepted evolution, and not Majestic Divinity, as the key to explaining life, you would be bidden a polite adieu. In fact I do believe in evolution: the fossil record is a wondrous three-and-a-half-million-year story of man in the making. But on the technicality that evolutionary theory has not yet adequately explained consciousness, I answered a resounding, "Me? Evolution? Absolutely not!" I was then ushered into my audience with Frithjof Schuon.

The Romantic poets (Shelley, even Yeats) had fantasized about a fraternity of hidden adepts who practiced in secret throughout the world. Schuon headed such a secret order of Sufi adepts, and I had dreamed of belonging to something like it, before I even knew it existed. At our first meeting Schuon inquired what my own religious order was. When I answered Protestant, he shook his finger at me, pronouncing, "No. Christianity knows only two legitimate traditions, the Roman Catholic and the Eastern Orthodox." (Later, I was told, because of me Schuon came to accept Protestantism as a valid tradition as well.) The world overflows with glorious expressions of spirituality, he explained; but if you wanted to be in his fraternity, his *tariqa,* he urged you to become a Muslim.

Nothing on earth is easier than to become a Muslim. Want to inscribe yourself among the faithful? Then do as Schuon had me do and as millions of others have done: simply make a declaration of intent and swear belief in Allah (God). Schuon gave me my new initiate's name. I gasped. The Arabic syllables as they rolled off the tongue sounded so sonorous, charged with mystery, and as for their actual meaning—what insight Schuon had: of all possible names it was the name that I would have chosen for myself. What is it? In Schuon's *tariqa* one must not reveal his initiate name to outsiders, but upon hearing it, I knew a great adventure had begun.

Frithjof Schuon opened the doors of Islam for me. I had been searching in the wrong places and looking in the wrong way. I thought Muhammad was a kind of avatar, somewhat like Jesus or the Buddha, but he is not that kind of incarnation. In fact Islam does have an "avatar": the Qur'an itself. But I had been reading the Qur'an in the wrong way. Admittedly it is not a book one curls up in bed with. Schuon unlocked the Qur'an by explaining that, while the Bible is history with theology thrown in, the Qur'an is theology ornamented with arabesques of history. The Bible moves you through historical time; the Qur'an intrudes you into the atemporal terrain of canonical truth. Once I absorbed that fact, the Qur'an spoke to me more poetically than poetry. In the Qur'an, God or Allah—referring to himself as "We"—talks directly and intimately to you. Muslims cannot understand how Christians can prize a book in which God is so inaccessible, talked about only in the third person.

To understand how Muslims communicate with God has grown my perspective, has enlarged my sense of the sacred. To learn what the Sufis mean by reality has made my own reality richer. Sufis, the mystics of Islam, do not want to hear about God at gossipy second hand. Most mystics don't want to read religious wisdom; they want to be it. A postcard of a beautiful lake is not a beautiful lake, and Sufis may be defined as those who dance in the lake. What drew me to the Sufis was in fact their dancing, how they pray not merely with their minds but with their bodies. I made a pilgrimage to Konya, where the poet Rumi and his fellow Sufis had whirled their bodies into prayers to God. And later I learned to dance that way myself.

In Tehran, an Iranian professor whom I had known in Boston arranged for me to attend a *majlis*, a Sufi gathering. The *majlis* took place not in a temple or shrine but in the basement of a house in an alley. Through a nondescript door I descended a narrow staircase into a dark, secretive world. Sufis have needed to exercise caution and shroud their activities from public view. They (and mystics in Christianity, too) have at times courted martyrdom by making their identity with the Divine too explicit. Thus the mystical Al-Hallaj wrote:

I saw my Lord with the eye of the heart. I said: "Who are you?"

He answered: "You."

In that basement *majlis* the dancing whirled till "I" and "you" blurred in dizzying embrace.

Forty of us arranged ourselves in the basement in concentric circles. A faint light seeped through the transom, leaving us shadowy silhouettes in the haunted dimness. Chanting began, which gradually turned to wailing. One by one we rose to our feet, half hypnotized by the wail-like chanting, which seemed to come from a collective voice at once ours and not ours. Sometimes each danced in his own sphere, shuffling from foot to foot. Then, unpremeditated, we would be holding hands, at other times locking arms around one another's shoulders, as the tempo speeded up, as the pace became ever more frenzied. Individual identities, self-consciousnesses, fell away into whirling together in a semitrance. Of the forty men there only I, trained to be the intellectual observer, was not to pass over into a bliss beyond knowing. Surrounded by ecstatics, I hovered between two worlds, on the shoreline, while every face I looked at was in a transport of ecstasy. Rumi, when dancing, was called to prayer, and he answered, "I am already praying." So, too, the whirling men in that basement: they dizzied and spun themselves into a sense of the divine. After how long I cannot say, the wailing began to subside; the whirling circles fragmented back into individual bodies. The men regrouped into two lines facing each other. Silently a scroll of white paper was unfurled between them, and on it generous portions of couscous topped with raisins were dished out. Those who had to work the next day departed after they finished their meal, but the old men lingered until dawn, and I lingered with them, to bathe in the lingering glow of the *majlis*.

Ecstasy is only one mood and Sufism only one mode of Islam, and neither exhausted its appeal for me. Islam is a true path, coherent and communal and supportive, in a world that is too often none of these. The five pillars of Islam—from the affirmation of faith to the daily prayers, from Ramadan to the giving of alms—were pillars that supported and gave structure to my life for ten years. I never undertook the *hajj*, or pilgrimage to Mecca, which in any case is optional, depending on one's finances and health. I did observe Ramadan, fasting from sunup to sundown, eating in the middle of the night, until, out of sync with Kendra and the girls, it caused too much havoc in my household. I reluctantly excused myself from fasting during Ramadan on the authority of the Prophet, who declared that married life is half of holiness. Otherwise I was to be counted, by both conduct and inclination, among the faithful.

I especially valued the call to prayer five times a day, which I answered—I was going to say "religiously"—every day for twenty years. Praying at regular intervals imposed rhythm and structure on my activities, which can otherwise become diffuse and scatter in all directions. Jesus said to pray ceaselessly, but to pray all the time you probably need to be a saint, preferably one with a trust fund. In the Qur'an, Muhammad records a humorous dream in which he is the negotiator between Moses and God as they barter over how often one must pray. God at first says fifty times a day; Moses tells Muhammad to negotiate a lower figure. God reduces it to forty times, then twenty, then ten, and Moses still objects.

When Muhammad finally gets it down to five times a day, he tells Moses: accept it, or you go talk to Him. Five times a day may be perfect. Those moments become like holy beads upon which consciousness through time, from our first arising to our at last lying down to sleep, is threaded. Osteoporosis today prevents me from performing the prostrations, but prayers in Arabic I can still do.

In the Qur'an, Allah is merciful, but he is also "ruler of the Day of Judgment." His goodness tempers his power, but his power compels our goodness, so that we don't behave like the spoiled child of an overly indulgent parent. My friend Virginia Gray Henry told me a funny story in which her merely referring to Allah's judgment dissolved all obstacles. Gray had been married to an Egyptian and lived for thirty years in Cairo, to which she returned after years away. Her taxi driver from the airport charged her an astronomical fare, which, with her knowledge of the city, she knew was exorbitant, but he would not back down. "All right," Gray said in impeccable Arabic, "I see you are stubborn and the hour is late and I am tired, so I will pay that amount. But remember this night, for on the Day of Judgment Allah will remember it." Hearing the invocation of Allah and the Day of Judgment, the cab driver broke down, begged her forgiveness, and refused to take any money at all.

On my bookshelf sits an old translation of the Qur'an by a Victorian convert to Islam, the delightfully named Marmaduke Pickthall. Traveling from gray England to the sunny Mideast, Pickthall became lighthearted, and he met, he said, for the first time truly happy people. Islam was for Pickthall—as it is to me— a mecca of order, meaning, beauty, and understanding. Today, however, when my countrymen look to the Middle East (especially since 9/11), they often look with eyes of fear and foreboding. In the West today no religion is more misunderstood than Islam; on both sides religion has gotten hijacked by politics. When I think how the Islam I saw by the light of spirituality is now obscured by the dark of ideology, my heart becomes heavy indeed.

I am at the end of my professional career, giving only an occasional talk. I won't be teaching any more students at MIT or Syracuse or Berkeley about Islam. Yet for one last time let me be the teacher and teach one last thing—a verse from the Qur'an: "If We [Allah is speaking] wished, We could have made you one people, but as it is, We have made you many. It is better this way. Therefore, vie among yourselves in good works." Elsewhere the Prophet tells us that in Paradise upon arrival all you do is say one word, over and over: *Peace—peace—peace.*

Peace.

9

Explaining Fundamentalism

Although Huston Smith's talk ranges from metaphysics to comparative religion, since the tragic events of September 11, 2001, one of his most impassioned topics has been what he calls "the hijacking of religion." Under that combustible phrase falls the explosive topic of "fundamentalism." When I approached him about the possibility of this interview, he immediately agreed out of his deep conviction that we must seek out the root causes for the dark side of religion and its exploitation by militants. In this exchange he reveals his deep desire to "set the record straight" on the true nature of the religious adventure. (Phil Cousineau, winter 2005)

PHIL COUSINEAU I'd like to begin at the beginning, in the spirit of the great Italian scholar of mythology, Roberto Calasso, who wrote in his ambrosial book, *The Marriage of Cadmus and Harmony*, "And where did it all begin?" Calasso uses that question as a kind of musical reprise throughout his book because he believes it is central to mythological and philosophical thinking. As someone born to evangelical Christian missionary parents, in Soochow, China, in 1919, you have been immersed in religion all your life. I can't help wondering if you can recall your first encounter with fundamentalism?

HUSTON SMITH Let me see if I can recall. Yes, I have it. Missionaries had furloughs every seven years, and one summer when I was fourteen years old our extended family rented cabins around a lake in Michigan for three weeks. I can remember that after dark when we kids went swimming, skinny-dipping I suspect, we could hear the adults arguing at the top of their voices over whether the words in the Bible were all literally true. My father and one of my uncles who was a pastor had been to seminary and argued the negative, but another of my uncles who was an insurance salesman argued vehemently for literal accuracy of the Bible's every word and refused to back down. As far as I can remember, the heated debate about the inerrancy of the Bible was the centerpiece of their conversation every evening in those three weeks.

PC The poignancy of your anecdote brings to mind the roots of the dark side of fundamentalism, the manner in which religion has been cleaved down the middle, dividing the "right side from the wrong side." Can you tell us the origins of Christian fundamentalism, and then later we will delve into its other versions?

HS Good. We'll have to hone in on this. It's appropriate to start with Christianity, and we can narrow this to Protestant Christianity, actually, for Catholics are not Bible-centered and have the Pope to adjudicate disputes. And you do well to have us begin at the beginning, for as T. S. Eliot says in his poem, "East Coker," "In my beginning is my end." But come to think of it, there's something that precedes historical origins—definitions. Origins of what? So let me speak to that first.

"Fundamental" is a good word; it derives from the same root as foundation. Every structure—whether it is a building, a structure of thought or a life—has to be founded on something, hopefully something solid. But now comes the "ism"—fundamentalism—and immediately our guard goes up, or should. I'm tempted to generalize and turn this into an aphorism: "Beware the 'isms'—they turn into schisms." So "fundamentalism" takes what is intrinsically an indispensable necessity and turns it into a doctrine, which is likely to be disputable. This small detour sets the stage for your question of fundamentalism's origins.

PC I see it more as a meander through the labyrinth. It seems that the one thread through the debate about the root cause of fundamentalism is the specter of being threatened, cornered, even shamed by modernity.

HS Exactly. I like your phrase, "the specter of being threatened." In the case of Christianity, the specter emerged around the end of the last century. Why then? Because churches felt *threatened*, as you say. This is worth coming down hard on for the point will thread its way through the rest of the interview. The underlying cause of fundamentalism is this sense of being threatened.

The threats that produced fundamentalism a century or so ago were basically two. The first was Darwinism, which was getting a grip on the public mind, and the second was the so-called Higher Criticism, which showed that the Bible was spliced together from a number of documents. Christians started to convene conferences to consider what they should do about these threats.

Were churches mistaken in feeling threatened by these developments? Yes and no—no regarding details, but yes in the underlying principles. Regarding Darwinism, from the very start Christians had recognized that our time is not God's time—"a thousand years in our sight is but a day in the sight of the Lord," etc. . . . So, as the six days of creation were metaphorical, not literal, there was nothing to fear from the fossil record that showed that it took billions of years for human beings to come into existence. However, there is no way to derive the foundational component of the human self—the *imago dei* (image of God), the Buddha-nature, the Atman, and the Uncarved Block, whatever the idiom—from natural selection working with chance variations. So if Darwinism claimed to tell the whole story, it did threaten Christianity.

As for the Higher Criticism: yes, scriptures are pieced together from fragments—knowledge of history and the languages involved show that that is so. But these are secular tools and they cannot do justice to the transcendental world that religions derive from and are the custodians of. As the Jesus Seminar demonstrates, there is no way to get Christ's divinity from its secular tools.

To consider these threats a number of conferences were convened. The most important of these was the one that met at Niagara Falls in 1895. It issued a statement that listed five things a person needed to believe if he/she was a Christian: (1) The verbal inerrancy of the Bible. Its every word is literally true. (2) The Divinity of Jesus Christ. (3) The Virgin Birth. (4) Substitutional atonement, i.e., Christ redeemed us from our sins through his death and resurrection. (5) The physical resurrection of Christ and his bodily return at the end of time.

Drawing on what I said earlier, I would say that the second and fourth of these are relatively uncontroversial among Christians, but that is not the case with the other three. In any case, this Niagara statement was widely circulated. A decade later it was expanded and collated into twelve tracts which also circulated widely. Three wealthy men had these papers bound, and distributed 300,000 copies of the volume free of charge—they continue to be available through an organization in Los Angeles. After another decade the Christian Fundamentalists Association was formed and the word *fundamentalism* was solidly ensconced in Christian minds.

Though it was ensconced in religious circles and vocabulary, it took the 1925 Scopes Trial in Dayton, Tennessee, to bring the word to national and even international attention. William Jennings Bryan, the flamboyant three-time Democratic candidate for President, was the chief prosecutor, and Clarence Darrow, John Scope's defendant, branded Bryan a fundamentalist. A mid-20th-century play, *Inherit the Wind,* was a huge success and ingrained the event into the public consciousness—but it turned history upside down. The play, which became a film starring Spencer Tracy and Frederic March, was brilliant theater but atrocious history. As historian Edward Larson shows in his book, *Summer of the Gods*, it *hijacked* history and religion to make them serve secular ideology.

The whole affair is a fascinating study in American social history, but more important for our interview, it bears directly on our understanding of fundamentalism. For the media's handling of the Scopes Trial shows how hostile to religion our public consciousness has become.

PC You have pointed out that fundamentalism had an upside and a downside. The upside is its attempt to hold on to the enduring truths of Christianity, but in doing that it latched on to its particular understanding of what those truths are and pronounced other understandings anathema. This defensive posture has splintered Christendom into warring, "us versus them" factions. Karen Armstrong suggests in *The Battle for God* that there is a kind of seething cauldron of resentment in all the different guises of fundamentalism.

HS Yes. She points out that there are actually two fundamentalisms today, religious fundamentalism and the equally dogmatic fundamentalism of today's secular culture. Call it conservatives vs. liberals—this is the inevitable downside of isms. It causes a lot of mischief, but then, it's probably inevitable, for when has everybody been of the same mind? Moreover, aren't differences not only the human lot, but the source of novelty, creativity, in history?

PC Yes, of course, but doesn't it depend on how those differences are interpreted or tolerated? I remember our old friend, the mythologist Joseph Campbell, describing a fundamentalist's version of religious tolerance as: "You worship God in your way and I'll worship Him in *His*." This kind of self-righteousness brings us back to what James Hillman frequently calls "the sin of literalism." It's a way of interpreting one's holy books that concretizes their psychological truths, and rules out their symbolic and mythological dimensions. It may even border on what your mentor, Aldous Huxley, called "the idolatrous worship of the word," which ties in with "the inerrancy of the Bible" that the Niagara Falls convention listed as one of the required beliefs of a Christian. Are Campbell and Hillman right in thinking that symbolism and mythology are important to an in-depth understanding of religion?

HS Important? They're indispensable, for they are religion's "technical language." I need to explain what I mean by that.

Science has shown us that there are three great levels of size, which give us, in effect, three worlds. There's the *micro-world,* where size is measured in pico-meters. Next comes the *macro-world,* where distance is measured in inches, yards, and miles. Finally there's the *mega-world,* where distance is measured in light-years.

Now: neither the micro- nor the mega-worlds can be consistently described in everyday language—try to do so, and you land in paradoxes of the kind that plague cartographers when they try to map our three-dimensional planet onto the two-dimensional pages of geography books—Greenland always balloons absurdly. Scientists can, however, access those worlds by using their technical language, which is mathematics.

Now comes the clincher. If you can't describe the micro- and mega-worlds in ordinary language, what chance is there to describe God and other spiritual things in such language, for they are at least as different from our world as are those flanking worlds for the sufficient reason that God *encompasses* those worlds. To conclude this point, which has the force of a syllogism: though spiritual realities cannot be described in everyday language, they can be described in religion's technical language, which is metaphor, symbolism, and myth—"and Jesus spoke to them in parables." Campbell and Hillman have it exactly right.

PC If I hear you correctly, mythology and mathematics are technical languages that access realms that cannot be described in everyday languages. So mythology is to religion what mathematics is to physics.

HS Well put.

PC The word *myth* is indelibly linked with Joseph Campbell, who devoted his career to puncturing the stereotype that myths wear the cloak of falsehood. For him, myths were the masks of the gods, transcendent metaphors for the mysteries that reflect the timeless realities of the soul.

HS I'm so glad you mention Joe Campbell. I'm inclined to say he singlehandedly rescued "myth" from the thieves that had stripped it of its rightful meaning. When Joe entered the scene, myth carried the stigma of being false. I was personally bruised by that stigma, for it came close to earning me the only failing grade I would have received in my student career. In a graduate seminar on logical positivism I was indiscreet enough to quote approvingly in my term paper Reinhold Niebuhr's comment that "myth isn't history, it's truer than history." My instructor, who was himself a logical positivist, wrote in the margin of my paper, "That isn't even wrong; it's meaningless. To be judged true or false an assertion must be meaningful, and the statement you cite has no meaning." Of course you and I and Joe are not being blinded by logical positivism, which with all its pretensions had a pretty short history, so we can readily understand what Niebuhr was driving at. Myth is *truer* than history because it addresses things that are more deep-lying, more enduring than history. In a word that ties in with this interview, myth addresses issues that are more "fundamental" than the pitter-patter of daily discourse.

PC I want to tighten the screws on our conversation, Huston, and move into the hotly disputed territory of *radical* fundamentalism that pervades the headlines today. I'll move toward my question by way of two authors. Teilhard de Chardin once remarked, "Once upon a time everything seemed fixed and solid. Now everything in the universe has begun to slide under our feet."

HS "Everything that's nailed down is coming loose," was the way the early 20th-century play *Green Pastures* put it.

PC Yes. Karen Armstrong describes the situation as a besieged mentality that arises out of a sense of deep fear. Can you help us make some sense of the terror we are living with in these fearsome and perilous times?

HS Yes, Karen Armstrong is very good—I'm inclined to regard her as the best all-round religious reporter today. The underlying cause of fundamentalism, as we have seen, is fear, the fear that derives from the sense of insecurity, of being threatened. People are scared; the world is scary.

PC But, Huston, not all fearful people become violent. Not all besieged people strike out. Is it possible to determine the "tipping point," to use Malcolm Gladwell's phrase, where the victimized decides to become a suicide bomber rather than walk down the nonviolent path, as espoused by Gandhi or Nelson Mandela?

HS I'm going to use a startling phrase to begin my answer. It's when they become patriotic. I chose that provocative idea to begin my answer to make you sit bolt upright. And now that I have your full attention I will explain what I mean.

It comes down to the difference between individuals and groups. I've already mentioned Reinhold Niebuhr, and his most durable book has proved to be *Moral Man and Immoral Society*. I have heard that there was a moment when John F. Kennedy, Che Guevara, and Fidel Castro were reading that book at the same time, but I know of no way to verify that hearsay. The thesis of Niebuhr's book is that individuals can sacrifice themselves but groups cannot. Saints can practice the Sermon on the Mount (turn the other cheek, and the like), but there never has been, nor can there ever be, a pacifist *religion*. Pockets of pacifists, such as the Amish and Quakers—but not an entire religion.

The first instance of a suicide bomber in the Bible is Samson. Chained between pillars of a temple, he used his legendary strength to pull them in on him and brought the roof crashing down on his head. He would rather die than feel helpless—a victim. Wars are simply the Samson story writ large.

PC What I'm searching for here is another perspective on the pandemic violence among those with intransigent intellectual and moral convictions, one that might give us a handle on how to allay the violence perpetrated in the name of God.

HS Another perspective. Yes. My mind flashes to George Lakoff, whose DON'T THINK OF A PINK ELEPHANT has catapulted him onto the front pages. In the normal course of events, it would never occur to anyone to think of a pink elephant; but tell them not to, and its impossible for people *not* to think of one. Lakoff's answer for what you are looking for, another perspective, is "reframing." Reframing an issue gives us another way of looking at it, another perspective on the matter. So how can we reframe the "us versus them" conflicts that currently have the world in flames.

PC   Precisely. A new frame of reference might even help us understand the various degrees of intolerance in ourselves.

HS   My suggestion is that we approach our opponents in a "what can we do for you" attitude instead of in a "what can we do you for" stance. Instead of saying to our opponents, in effect, "We know what you want, and we're not going to give it to you," we might ask them, "What would you like from us?" It takes vision and courage to make that shift.

Those are precious commodities and always in short supply, but they are not completely out of reach. It doesn't follow from reframing the question that we must give the opponent what he wants—that would have to be weighed. But it would provide the new perspective on the conflicts that are currently on the brink of doing us in. And it brings us to the ultimate reason *Parabola* has mounted this interview. Fundamentalism isn't an academic matter. Information can help, but only if it crests into the question, "What can we do about this problem?"

PC   What about other forms of fundamentalism at work in the world today?

HS   Thanks for the reminder; it would have been a serious oversight. First, Islam. We're at war with Iraq, and as nations never have impartial views of their enemies, it's important that we try to see what the present war that we initiated is doing to Islam. It has turned Islam over to the fundamentalist extremists.

It's well to remind ourselves that until the West stumbled onto the scientific method—which gave Western colonial imperialists the power to carve Asia up and divide its pieces among themselves—Islam was the dominant power in the world, not only militarily, but in science, art, and philosophy. And now, thanks to colonialism, they are at the bottom of the heap. That's humiliating for a proud people, and it's a breeding ground for extremists. They are swamping the liberal Muslims in every Islamic country who want Islam to get back into the swim of the modern world and modernize by broadening the curriculum of the schools, and learning technology, learning how to manufacture things, and learning how to negotiate.

Judaism presents a very different picture. If we define fundamentalism as accepting the inerrancy of scripture, all Jews who have not become secular are fundamentalists in believing that the Torah is the word of God. But they are saved from dogmatism (which comes close to being another definition of fundamentalism) by the Talmud. The Torah is the word of God, but the question remains of how it is to be understood—interpreted. In the Talmud, the rabbis' interpretations of what God says in the Torah's margins is open-ended; it will never shut down. This saves Jews from being dogmatic. So yes, divisiveness enters Judaism when it becomes politicized, as it is in Israel today where the Orthodox have full control of Parliament. Should buses be allowed to run on the Sabbath? It's on questions like these that the battle lines get drawn.

PC I'd like to end with an admonition from Joseph Brodsky, the great Russian poet of "existential terror." He wrote, "No matter how abominable your condition may be, try not to blame anything or anybody: history, the state, superiors, race, parents, the phase of the moon, childhood, toilet training, etc."

Huston, the endless blame games of history appear to lead to a constriction of the mythic imagination, which is lethal to the vitality of the authentic religious life. In other words, Brodsky, as well as other spiritual leaders like His Holiness, the Dalai Lama, remind us not to let our grievances rationalize our desire for vengeance, which only turns our hearts to stone.

HS: Yes, yes. We must recognize "hijacked religion." Religion is the sitting duck, if I may mix my metaphors, because the primary commitment of politicians is not to religion, but the use of religion for political proposes. What really breeds violence is political differences. We live in a politically divided world in which each half shouts: "We are on God's side." The flip side of that is believing your opponents are the devil, the evil axis, the empire of evil. The rhetoric is exactly the same. The vicious circle of religious or political blame games leads to the dehumanizing of entire peoples, when, in fact, authentic religion is the search for the *deeply real* and is the greatest humanizing force we have.

10

What They Have that We Lack

On Native American Religion

My title derives from the justly famous tribute to the Native Americans by John Collier, one-time United States Commissioner of Indian Affairs, which begins, "They had what the world has lost . . ." The losses that Collier mentions are "reverence and passion for human personality, and for the earth and its web of life." Accepting them as genuine losses, I shall build on them to target three other losses our civilization has suffered. We are less clear in our values, which is to say less sure as to what is important in life. We are less able to see the infinite in the finite, the transcendent in the immanent. And we have lost our way metaphysically. Because my meditation on these three impoverishments is offered as a tribute to Joseph Brown, I shall begin with the story of how we met, for the circumstances were so bizarre as to suggest that more than chance was at work.

The year was 1970, and my wife and I were passing through Stockholm, where the first beanbag chair we had seen caught our eyes and we bought it. On our way back to our hotel, swaying from a strap in a crowded subway, I felt foolish carrying our shapeless purchase over my shoulder like Santa's pack and was remarking to my wife that I was glad we were abroad and incognito when a face emerged from the crowd and ventured, softly, "Would you be Huston Smith?" It was Joseph Brown, who had recognized me from my filmed lectures on *The Religions of Man,* which he had showed to his classes. Things moved rapidly, and before we parted we had accepted Joseph and his wife Eleanita's invitation to have supper with them the following day, the last before our flight left Sweden.

It was an unforgettable evening. The Browns were in Stockholm for Joseph to complete his doctoral dissertation under Ake Hultkrantz, the world's foremost authority on the Native Americans, and their apartment walls were covered with larger-than-life photographs of archetypal Indian faces. What was remarkable, though, was how rapidly our conversation plunged to things that matter most. When they learned that our next stop was to be London, Joseph directed me to Martin Lings of the British Museum, who proved to be an important link to the Traditionalist outlook of René Guénon, A. K. Coomaraswamy, and Frithjof Schuon that was beginning to impress me as true. And on the strength of the friendship that was forged that evening, Joseph became my teacher in showing me the enduring importance of the Native Americans and other primal peoples in the religious odyssey of humankind.

From the many things I have learned from Native Americans, I turn to the first of the three virtues I see them as having retained, and we let partially slip. I say *partially* because I do not want to romanticize or traffic in disjunctions. Trade-offs are involved at every point.

I. KNOWING WHAT IS IMPORTANT

I am not an anthropologist, and as my professional schooling occurred before midcentury, I was taught to think that myths are childish in comparison with systematically articulated metaphysics, and that "primitive" religions—the adjective explicitly intended to be pejorative—were and remain inferior to the historical ones, which command written texts and a cumulative tradition. Meeting Joseph Brown rescued me from those prejudices. That shortly after meeting him I moved from the Massachusetts Institute of Technology to Syracuse University solidified the change in my thinking, for I then found myself within five miles of the Iroquois Long House. It was not without amazement that I came to know the residents of the Onondaga Reservation—Chief Shenandoah, Audrey Shenandoah, and Oren Lyons among them. Reading Joseph Brown's writings paralleled my visits to their reservation, and together the two shattered mental stockades, permitting new insights to erupt.

The insight that concerns me in this first section of my remarks is the loss that writing inflicts. Before I met Joseph, A. K. Coomaraswamy's *The Bugbear of Literacy* had already shown me that education cannot be equated with book learning; the great civilizations of the past were not dependent on the ability to read and write. Craftsmen—the builders of temples, mosques, and churches; the sculptors of Konorak and of Chartres—were not literate, and oral tradition carried poetry and sacred knowledge for millennia before books appeared. Coomaraswamy also brought out the toll writing takes on our memories. Literate peoples grow lax in recall; they do not require much from their memories, for books and manuals are at hand to fill in the blanks. Lacking those resources, unlettered peoples make libraries of their minds. Their memories are legendary.

As I say, those two validations of orality—both memory and learning flourish in its precincts—were in place before I met Joseph Brown; but it was not until I came to the Native Americans through him that I realized that I needed to add a chapter on the primal religions to *The Religions of Man,* now titled *The World's Religions.* It was while writing that chapter that it dawned on me that orality (which I shall use here to mean exclusive orality; speech that is not supplemented by writing) carries with it another blessing that is, if anything, more important than having a rich memory. Functioning something like a gyroscope, orality keeps life on keel by ensuring that priorities and proportionalities are not lost sight of. Somewhere in his writings Frithjof Schuon defines intelligence exactly this way, as the sense of priorities and proportionalities. By this definition, primal peoples can be ignorant of many things, but they are rarely stupid.

Imagine a tribe, gathered around its campfire at the close of the day. Everything that its ancestors learned arduously through trial and error, from which herbs heal to stirring legends that give meaning and orientation to their lives, is preserved in their collective memory, and there only. It stands to reason that trivia would not long survive in that confine, for it would preempt space that was needed for the things that needed to be remembered.

A library lacks this winnowing device. Natural selection, the survival of the fittest, doesn't enter its workings, for space permits virtually everything to survive, important or not. Where a page is a page, a book a book, the issue of quality scarcely arises.

To personalize this point: I happen to enjoy the services of one of the great library systems in the world, that of the University of California. Thinking back to the guided tour that brought me into its orbit, I find that I still remember the statement with which the leader of the tour welcomed us. "When you enter this library looking for a book," she said, "think: it's here. It may take us a while to locate it, but it's here." As I learned how the immense holdings of the local library locked into compatible libraries around the world through Internet and interlibrary loan, I found myself believing her.

I do not discount the help and pleasure that accrued from having recorded human history at one's fingertips. It is the trade-off it entails that the Native Americans have taught me. When I step out of the elevator onto a floor of my university's library, I am greeted in effect by arrows directing me to its numerous corridors: history here, chemistry there, a bewildering array. There is no arrow that reads, "importance," much less "wisdom." It's more like, "Good luck, folks. From here on out you're on your own."

The burden this places on individuals is enormous; whether it is supportable remains to be seen.

We are inundated by information today, to the point of drowning in it. When the British Broadcasting Company first went on the air, the newsroom policy on a no-news day was simply to say there was no news and play classical music. Is there a newsroom in the world that has the restraint to honor such a policy today? Alvin Toffler warned us in *Future Shock* a quarter century ago that information overload was already "pressing the limits of human adaptability," but all he offered by way of counsel was that we develop a consciousness that is capable of adapting to changes that look like they are going to keep on accelerating.

That advice is no match for the problem we face, and it may take a breakdown of sorts to drive that fact home. More than any other breakthrough, it is the computer that has increased the quantity of information that can be saved, retrieved, and transferred. It was assumed that this increase would raise our industrial efficiency, but the country is still waiting for the big payoff that electronic boosters keep promising. Many experts are now concluding that for all their power, computers may be costing U.S. companies tens of billions of dollars a year in downtime, maintenance and training costs, useless game playing, and—the relevant point here—information overload. As Yale economist and Nobel laureate Robert Solow has noted, "You can see the computer age everywhere but in the productivity statistics." From 1950 to 1973, when computers were still a novelty, the U.S. economy enjoyed one of the greatest economic booms in its history. Since then, as computers have taken over nearly every desk in the land, the rate of productivity growth has mysteriously plummeted. Many experts believe that computers may be more the cause of the problem than the key to its solution.

If information overload can impair industrial efficiency, what about life efficiency; which is to say, the ability to avoid squandering life on frivolous ends? The great orienting myths that primal peoples rehearse endlessly, and carry constantly in their hearts and heads, protect them from this danger.

Something that Claude Lévi-Strauss observed relates to this. For an anthropologist, he took surprisingly little interest in what myths meant to the peoples who lived by them. Deeming science the noblest human pursuit, he wanted to parallel what Noam Chomsky was doing in linguistics and put anthropology, too, in the service of science's efforts to discover how the mind works. Artificial intelligence, he believed, was on the right track in assuming that the mind works like a computer—through binary, on-off flip-flops—and Lévi-Strauss saw himself as corroborating that hypothesis by showing (as in *The Raw and the Cooked*) that myths proceed binarily, from a forked starting point. In the course of his investigations, though, he picked up something that is important. The primitive mind, he reported, assumes that you do not understand anything unless you understand everything, whereas science proceeds in the opposite manner, from part to whole. Lévi-Strauss considered the scientific approach superior to the mythic, whereas I find them complementary and equally important.

II. SYMBOLIC MINDS

The item I wrote just before turning to this tribute to Joseph chanced to be the Foreword to a collection of excerpts from Emanuel Swedenborg's writings, and as I was already thinking ahead to the present piece when I came upon this passage, I was struck by its relevance to this second point I shall be making.

> I have learned from heaven [Swedenborg wrote] that the earliest people had direct revelation, because their more inward reaches were turned toward heaven; and that, as a result, there was a union of the Lord with the human race then. But as time passed, there was not this kind of direct revelation but an indirect one through correspondences. All their divine worship consisted of correspondences, so we call the churches of that era representative churches. They knew what correspondence was and what representation was, and they knew that everything on earth was responsive to spiritual things in heaven and portrayed them. So natural things served as means of thinking spiritually. . . . The earliest people saw some image of and reference to the Lord's kingdom in absolutely everything—in mountains, hills, plains, and valleys, in gardens, groves, and forests, in rivers and lakes, in fields, and crops, in all kinds of trees, in all kinds of animals as well, in the luminaries of the sky.

Swedenborg proceeds to confirm this way of seeing the world by citing his own visionary experience.

> I have been taught by an abundance of experience that there is not the slightest thing in the natural world, in its three kingdoms, that does not portray something in the spiritual world or that does not have something there to which it is responsive.

From there he continues:

> After knowledge of correspondences and representations had been forgotten, the Word was written, in which all the words and their meanings were correspondences, containing in this way a spiritual or inner meaning.

Paraphrasing these three stages into which Swedenborg divides religion: In the first stage, nature is transparent to the divine and is seen as divine without remainder, so no divinity apart from it is sought. Presumably this first stage is something like the natural religion of early childhood, when (as a poet has said) "heaven and a splendorous earth were one," before the child's clear eye is clouded over by ideas and opinions, preconceptions and abstractions. In the second stage, nature loses this transparency, but remains (we might say) translucent. Divinity continues to shine through mountains, groves, and springs, but those objects now *exist*—"stand out apart from" their source—in having acquired a certain objectivity of their own. This distancing obscures their connectedness with their divine source, and that connectedness needs to be recovered through symbolism: Swedenborg's representations and correspondences. If we take light as our example, at some level of their awareness, people in this second stage recognize that its power to enable us to discern things by seeing them is a prolongation of the divine intelligence. Water tokens the divine purity and nurturance, flowers its beauty, and so forth, world without end.

The first stage requires no mental processing. In the second, some mediation is needed, but correspondences (which serve that function) are so obvious that little articulation is called for. In Swedenborg's third stage, this ceases to be the case. Opaqueness—the fall into matter—has proceeded to the point where language and thought are needed to state explicitly what earlier intelligence took for granted: that rocks and trees are not self-subsistent in the way optics by itself presents them. It now needs to be *said* that nature carries the signature of the divine—not only nature as a whole, but its parts, each of which betokens one of the ninety-nine beautiful names of Allah, as Muslims put the matter.

Generalizing from this threefold division, it seems appropriate to credit primal peoples with prolonging the second period into our own more materialistic age. To invoke Coomaraswamy again, when he came to the United States to become director of the Oriental Section of Boston's Museum of Fine Arts, the traditional lore of the American Indians deeply moved him, for he saw in these much-persecuted remnants of the indigenous population of the continent an organic intelligence that was still able to read the open book of nature as others read their written scriptures. His South Asian heritage led him to associate the Native Americans' metaphysical insight—their capacity to see the world and everything within it as a living revelation of the Great Spirit—with Vedic times in his own heritage. Without exaggeration, he felt, he could speak of their wisdom as belonging to an earlier *yuga* that somehow had persisted into these later times, an extension that carried a message of hope to a forgetful and much-tormented world. The recognition that every plant, every insect, stones even, participate in the *dharma* and need to be treated, not as spoils for human appetites, but as companions in terms both of origin and ultimate destiny, conditioned all the Native Americans' ideas of what is right and wrong. What a happier world this would be, Coomaraswamy concluded, if such ideas had not been marginalized.

III. METAPHYSICAL ACCURACY

"Strictly speaking," Frithjof Schuon has written, "there is but one sole philosophy, the *Sophia Perennis*; it is also—envisaged in its integrality—the only religion." *Philosophy* here refers to descriptions of reality's deep structure, among which (Truth being one) there can be only one accurate account, which other accounts (insofar as they are accurate) embellish but do not contradict. As for religion, it refers to the methods for conforming one's life to reality's structure. Ken Wilber has recently said that belief in the *Sophia Perennis* (or Great Chain of Being as he calls it) has been "so overwhelmingly widespread that it is either the single greatest intellectual error ever to appear in human history, or it is the most accurate reflection of reality yet to appear."

Modernity has departed from this sole true philosophy, and the difference between it and the science-oriented alternative with which modernity replaced it can be stated simply. Whereas traditional philosophy proceeds from the premise that the less derives from the more—from what is greater than itself in every respect, primacy, power, and worth being foremost—modernity sees the more (as it climaxes qualitatively in the human species) as deriving from the less.

I have already credited Joseph Brown for introducing me to the Native Americans and the distinctive outlook of primal peoples generally, and here I can credit him more pointedly. In one way or another many anthropologists have dealt with the two preceding resources of primal peoples, but Brown stands alone in detailing, in his important study, *The Sacred Pipe,* the way in which Native American religion embodies the *Sophia Perennis* in its own distinctive idiom.

In briefest capsule: The Native American outlook conforms to the Great Chain of Being in seeing the whole of things as an ontological hierarchy in which lesser things derive in graded sequence from the Great Spirit, which is its version of the *ens perfectissimum.* In *Creek Mary's Blood,* the sequel to *Bury My Heart at Wounded Knee,* Dee Brown gives us a glimpse of the initial cut that the Native Americans enter—that between the sacred and the profane—by writing that:

> In those days there were always two levels in the world of the Cheyennes. We did not consider the world of hunting or hide curing or arrow or moccasin making, or any of those things as the real world. The real world was a place of magic, of dreams wherein we became spirits.

Subsequent divisions in the real and sacred world vary according to which tribe we are speaking of. The Tewa, for instance, have five sacred realms, whereas the Plains Indians that Brown worked with most will content themselves with three. When we add the everyday world to these three, we come up with the minimum number of "links" in the Great Chain of Being that peoples have found it necessary to posit. In *Forgotten Truth,* I call them the terrestrial, the intermediate, the celestial, and the infinite; and in *The Sacred Pipe,* Brown tells us how the Oglala Sioux describe them. Mounting from the mundane into the sacred world, the Oglala find its lowest echelon populated by myriad spirits, some good, some bad. Human beings can access this realm from time to time, as Dee Brown points out, but its natural population consists of discarnates of various stripes. Shamans enter into working relationships with those spirits, enlisting good ones as allies to do battle with those of evil intent.

Above this spirit world, which is something of a mélange, stands the Great Spirit, *Wakan-Tanka*, who can be apprehended in two modes: as Father and as Grandfather. In the context of world religions generally, this division corresponds to the division between, on the one hand, God who has personal attributes and can therefore be known; and on the other hand, God in his absolute, infinite nature, which the human mind cannot concretely grasp. Definitively, Brown describes the difference between the two as follows:

> *Wakan-Tanka* as grandfather is the Great Spirit independent of manifestation, unqualified, unlimited, identical to the Christian Godhead, or to the Hindu *Brahma-Nirguna*. *Wakan-Tanka* as father is the great Spirit considered in relation to His manifestation, either as Creator, Preserver, or Destroyer, identical to the Christian God, or to the Hindu *Brahma-Saguna*.

Going back to Mary Dee's report, the mundane hunting and hide curing that she cites are those activities after the symbolic mind has dimmed, for when that mind is in full force, all activities are (to continue with the vocabulary of the Oglala Sioux) *wakan* (holy, sacred). They are sacred in "corresponding"— Swedenborg's word—with the other world and thereby perforating the line between the two. "This world" acquires its own reality only to the degree that its ties to the other world are forgotten. Joseph Brown quotes Black Elk as saying, "Any man who is attached to the senses and to the things of this world lives in ignorance."

CODA

Having begun with an anecdote, I shall conclude with one as well, my favorite in my well-stocked repertoire relating to Joseph Brown.

Joseph was accompanying Black Elk on a mission to Denver, and a long winter's bus ride landed them there well around midnight. Hotels were filled, and the only available shelter from the bitter cold was little more than a flophouse. Entering their room, Black Elk glanced at its dingy furnishings, took one breath of its foul air, and announced: "This requires a sweat!" Chairs were upturned, blankets stripped from the beds to cover them, and the electric heater impressed for the sacred fire. The men peeled down to their breechcloths, and the purging bath began.

It is an allegory, this midnight scene. In dismal, uninviting circumstances, two men, ethnically diverse, saw what needed to be done and instantly did it.

11

Three Ways of Relating to the World. Three Geographies. Three Religious Traditions

I

Inescapably, human beings are involved in three basic encounters: with nature, with other people, and with themselves. Roughly these may be identified as humankind's natural, social, and psychological problems.

The great surviving cultural traditions are also three: the East Asian, the Indian, and the Western. It helps us to understand and relate the unique perspectives of these three traditions in their religious as well as other dimensions if we think of each as having attended to one problem more diligently than to the other two. The decision to do so represents each tradition's fundamental option, the main direction each has chosen in its ceaseless pursuit of salvation and the real. Thus, though in one sense the language of the human spirit can be regarded as a universal language in that wherever it is spoken it must attend to some extent to all three human problems, it is equally the case that this language has been spoken in different accents, each bespeaking a unique symphony of emphases and orientations which has constituted its culture's religious self-identity.

Specifically, the religions of the West (Judaism, Christianity, and Islam) have accented the problem of humanity's relation to nature; those of East Asia (Confucianism, Taoism, and Shinto) have stressed the social problem; and those of India (Hinduism, Buddhism, and Jainism) have attended primarily to the psychological issue.

That is my thesis. Now for the supporting evidence.

II

I begin with the West: with Judaism, Christianity, and Islam, which, despite their important differences, can be grouped together on grounds of their family resemblances. All were semitically originated, all share a common theological vocabulary (while using it to say different things at times), and all stand in a single historical tradition inasmuch as Christianity claims to be the fulfillment of Judaism and Islam the fulfillment of Judaism and Christianity.

It may sound surprising to suggest that these religions are notable for their interest in nature, for we have been more conscious of their supernatural than of their naturalistic components. This, though, is because we tend to compare them with other strands of Western culture, rather than with other religions. Compared with Western science, Western philosophy, or even Western art, Western religions *are* more otherworldly. But when they are compared with other religions, their distinguishing feature is seen to lie in their higher regard for nature and the greater extent to which they have come to grips with it.

Initial evidence for this appears in the principal discoveries that the West came up with, the three most important of which are modern science, the idea of progress, and the concept of the individual and its rights. On examination, each of these turns out to be directly related to one of nature's matrices: space, time, and matter. Science obviously focuses on matter. Scrutinize the material world and one notices invariant sequences which, abstracted from, become the laws of nature. The idea of progress, for its part, is obviously related to time. Ponder the mystery of time long enough and one becomes aware, first, of the novelty that it can introduce into experience, and from there it is but a step to the realization that the new might be better than the old. Finally, the individual relates to space. What ultimately distinguished human beings from one another is the fact that they occupy different bodies, which is to say, different regions of space. The connection also turns up in the adage that the frontier (with its wide open spaces) is the breeding ground of individualism.

That the West's great discoveries mesh with nature in these ways seems clear, but if we push on to ask what inclined the West toward nature in the first place, we are on trickier ground. This may not be due only to the fact that questions of origins root back into the twilight zone of protohistory where evidence is too scanty to allow for confident conclusions. Such questions may have no final, empirical answers. That this is consonant with theories that trace religious differences to divine revelation—theories which, though this is not commonly recognized, are as prominent in Hinduism as in the West—does not displease me; but the inherent mystery of origins, if such it be, may have a human explanation as well. For if freedom is real, the innovators who first pressed their faiths in different directions may simply have chosen differently, in which case the differences would have no empirical cause. What I am reaching for is a balance between total explanation and none. I shall cite influences that may have encouraged early Westerners to look expectantly toward nature without presuming that they dissolve the mystery that resides in all great historical, as in all great personal, happenings.

1. *Matter.* "Christianity," as Archbishop Temple used to contend, "is the most avowedly materialistic of all the great religions." Denis de Rougemont concurs: "Compared with the religions of the East, Christianity might be called materialism." Judaism and Islam should be ranked beside Christianity in these judgments, but thus enlarged they stand.

Obviously there have been anti-matter eddies in the Western stream—Manichaeanism, Gnosticism, Docetism, Neo-Platonism, Plotinus, and others. But they never take over. The first three are explicitly condemned as heretical, and Plotinus and the Neo-Platonists are bypassed in favor of Aristotle's and Aquinas's acceptance of matter as altogether real. Moreover, and equally instructive for our thesis, the inspiration for the matter-disparaging outlooks usually comes from the East, often from India herself. For India, matter is a barbarian, spoiling everything it touches. By contrast, the West respects matter and takes it seriously, meshing nature and spirit wherever possible. Time and again she seems on the verge of slipping into the view that spirit is good and matter bad, but always she recovers. The Judeo-Christian Bible opens with the assertion that "God created the heavens *and the earth*," and before the chapter concludes it has God surveying all that He created, earth included, "and behold, it was very good." Good, moreover, not only for beholding, but as a field for endeavour; for in the center of that crucial opening chapter of Genesis humanity is commissioned to "have dominion . . . over all the earth," a commission later assumed to have been accepted and fulfilled: "Thou madest him to have dominion over the works of thy hands; thou has put all things under his feet" (Psalm 8:6). The Incarnation pays matter its highest conceivable compliment—it can become divine. The Kingdom of Heaven, from Jewish and early Christian apocalypticism right down to the social gospel, is to come *on earth.* Even in death the West will not desert the body. If there is to be life after death it, too, must be in some sense physical: hence, "I believe . . . in the resurrection of the body." Throughout the entire sequence runs the effort to maintain a sense of kinship between humanity and nature which totemism had earlier pointed up. Paul sees the entire cosmos as locked with people in their fallen condition, groaning and travailing as it awaits its redemption with and through theirs. An earthquake forms the backdrop for the crucifixion. "Nature also mourns for a lost good."

It is unlikely that such a high regard for matter would have emerged in regions where nature confronted humanity as a holy terror. But in the parts of the Near East that cradled the Western religions, nature's guise was beneficent.

Ancient historians have christened the arc that begins with the Nile, moves up the Palestinian corridor, across Syria, and down the Tigris and Euphrates valleys "the Fertile Crescent," and it may even be no accident that the Garden of Eden story comes from this region, for nature here was in a most favorable mood—rich and joyous and treating humanity as a friend. To the Jews, Canaan seemed veritably to flow with milk and honey. There were problems to be met, challenges to equal; but their proportions were such as to coax rather than to discourage inquiry and advances. Matter appeared as a plausible matrix within which to continue the quest for human fulfillment.

India early ceased to think so, but China didn't. China resembles the West in seeking life's solution within a material context of some sort. But this isn't enough to define naturalism. A thoroughgoing naturalism requires not only that matter but that time as well be taken seriously, and Chinese religion implicates itself in time no more than does Indian.

2. *Time.* To take time seriously is to be conscious of (a) the directional character of history, (b) the radical novelty it can introduce, (c) the uniqueness of every event, and (d) the potential decisiveness of some. Indian and Chinese religions stress none of these points. The Indian view of time is cyclical, reducing all that occurs to the anonymous insignificance of an ephemeral passage through illusion, while the Chinese tend not to generalize about time any more than about other things. For the East, time is a placid, silent pool in which ripples come and go. For the West, time is an arrow or river: it has origin, direction, destination, and is irreversible. It is not difficult to see why. Judaism, the foundational religion of the West, was instigated by a concrete historical happening—the Exodus—as those of India and China were not. In addition, the basic concepts of Judaism were forged while the Jews, being either displaced persons or oppressed, were a people in waiting—first to cross over into the promised land, then to return to Jerusalem, then for the coming of the Messiah who was to deliver them.

This built into Judaism a future-oriented character which was unique until duplicated by Christianity which too is grounded in unique historical occurrences—the Incarnation and the Resurrection—and looks toward the future, in its case to the return of Christ and the coming of his kingdom on earth. The idea of progress, which arose in the West, and independently in the West only, is the secular offshoot of this Messianism, while the equally Western-originated Marxist vision of a classless society is its giant heretical facsimile.

3. *Space.* The third property of nature is space, which has religious overtones because of its relation to individuality.

What distinguishes two persons most irrevocably is the fact that they are spatially discrete by virtue of occupying different bodies. It may be no accident, therefore, that the tradition which values individuality most and sees humanity's destiny to consist not in transcending the ego but in continuing and developing it, is the tradition in which space occasioned fewest problems because it was most plentiful. A recent report from India reads:

> Too many people everywhere! Three servants for my simple hotel room. Seven or eight men, one of whom is working, in every tiny shop. The roadway invaded by a crowd moving in all directions, so that the passage of wheeled traffic is always obstructed. The pavements thick with sleepers at night. And I saw five people on one bicycle!

In such an everlasting swarm, there simply may not have been room for individuality to rise to its possibilities. The ideal breeding ground for individualism, as was earlier noted, is the frontier, and among the world's faiths it is Christianity that has been preeminently the frontier religion, moving first into the desolate swamps and forests of Northern Europe, and then across the waters into the Americas. The West's high estimate of the individual may be partly child of this fact. In the East everything participates in everything and nothing ever gets really detached from anything, neither a son from his father nor what is dead from what is alive; what is most prized in persons is the essence of their humanity which is shared in common with others. The West, by contrast, considers differences and distinctions to be virtues; the infinite worth which attaches to each individual derives in part precisely from the fact that everyone is unique and irreplaceable. This is part of the meaning of Kierkegaard's description of Christians as "joyful heirs to the finite"; they not only accept the finite, they rejoice in it. In death no less than in life, the West resists the East's temptation to merge the soul with the Absolute, insisting instead that it retains its identity through all eternity. The theological correlative of this concept of an individual soul is the concept of a personal God which again contrasts with Eastern, more impersonal, alternatives.

Western religion has involved itself more deeply, confidently, and expectantly in space, time, and matter, all three, than have those of India and China. Using "natural theology" in this special sense, we can identify it as the West's distinctive theological contribution.

III

East Asia, on the other hand, concentrated on social ethics; so much so, indeed, that it is often asked whether her basic philosophy—Confucianism—is rightly considered a religion at all.

At least two facts suggest that East Asia may have turned in this direction because nature looked less promising. The first of these is the Mongoloid physiognomy which bears marks of having originated under conditions of severe cold, probably in Siberia and eastern Central Asia where high winds were matched by temperatures which fell below minus 80°F. Such conditions were a far cry from the mild and sunny climes of the Mediterranean. They were so fierce that to this day the Mongoloid carries their impact on their faces. "There is no question," writes Walter Fairservis, "that the Mongoloid face is better equipped for cold weather than any other." It has more protective fat, and its most exposed surface area, the nose, is reduced by the forward extrusion of the cheekbones and a retreat of the nose itself. Its eyes are protected by an extension vertically of the eye orbits and the whole area padded with fat, while the epicanthic fold which extends from the nose area over the upper eye narrows the slit of the eye and, with the fatty padding, acts as a kind of snow goggle against glare as well as an eye shield against the cold. Breathing through the nasal passages is facilitated by the retraction of the nose area into the face, while the banking up of nasal passages with fat provides maximum heat for the air on its way to the lungs. Face hair, which is a handicap in extreme cold because the beard stores breath moisture as ice which freezes the face, is reduced more than in any other human type.

The other conspicuous fact is China's rivers. Chinese culture, like that of the West, is riverine in origin. But whereas the Nile, and the Tigris and Euphrates after their first cataclysmic floods, were well-mannered and orderly, China's rivers were unmanageable. The soil in the great treeless mountain ranges where the Yellow River and Yangtze rise washes badly, feeding into the rivers enormous quantities of yellow silt. The Yangtze dumps 400 million tons of this silt into the China Sea every year, while in the Yellow River it reaches 46% by weight and gives the river its name. Building up the riverbeds, this silt causes the rivers to flood inordinately. A single breach in the dikes, which in places have been built to heights of fifty feet to contain the elevated waters, can inundate hundreds of square miles and cut millions of farmers off from their sustenance. As resultant sedimentation can be as much as six feet deep, years may elapse before flood-ravaged lands can be cultivated again. I was myself living as a boy but twelve miles from the Yangtze during the catastrophic floods of 1932 which inundated an area equal to Missouri, Kansas, and Iowa combined and cost a million lives. The record of the Yellow River is even worse. Not without reason has it been called "China's Sorrow." "More than . . . any other great river, the Yellow River presents human-kind with a seemingly insoluble problem. Rulers of China have always faced but never conquered it." Very early in China the rivers came to be symbolized by the dragon, which was also for centuries China's national emblem.

One stands in awe of dragons; one doesn't expect to tame them. We should be prepared to find, then, in China, a certain deference toward nature. There is a kind of naturalism in Chinese thought, but it is the naturalism of the artist, the nature lover, or the romanticist, rather than that of the scientist—the naturalism of a Wordsworth or a Thoreau rather than of a Galileo or a Bacon. Nature in China is something to be appreciated, intuited, communed with, or reverenced;

there is no sustained notion that it might be mastered. A passage from the *Tao Tê Ching* puts the point in a nutshell:

> Those who would take over the earth
> And shape it to their will
> Never, I notice, succeed.
> The earth is like a vessel so sacred
> That at the mere approach of the profane
> It is marred
> And when they reach out their fingers it is gone.

Chinese science, as a consequence, doesn't develop. For a field of constructive endeavour the Chinese turned instead to society. They may have been lured in this direction by the fact that their population was racially homogeneous and so presented no surface discouragements to the natural wish for a harmonious society. But there were also factors which *forced* them to attend to the social problem. One was the crowded conditions under which they lived. Another may have been the joint family system under which several generations and relatives as distant as third cousins might be grouped in a single household—three of Confucius' five famous relationships are concerned with the family. China's rivers may also have figured here, for from the beginnings of Chinese civilization they required vast, cooperative dike-building projects to keep them in their channels. Finally, China's basic outlook was forged in the social furnace of her "Time of Troubles," those five convulsive centuries between 700 and 200 B.C. during which the Chou Dynasty was in decay, centuries which culminated in the endemic violence of the "Warring Kingdoms" in which anarchy was the order of the day. In this context the burning question facing every responsible thinker was the one which, on a smaller scale but under vaguely similar circumstances, faced Plato as well: How to save Athens?

The solution as it finally emerged gathered together many strands but bore the distinctive stamp of Confucius' genius. It amounted to nothing less than the attempt to "Emily Post" an entire way of life in which human relationships were always the focus of attention. Subtle differences in relationship were delineated and prescribed to a degree paralleled in tribes, but in no other civilization—witness the complex vocabulary for distinguishing paternal from maternal uncles, aunts, cousins, and in-laws, and for expressing fine distinctions in seniority. The prescriptions were enforced externally by sensitizing individuals to the way they were regarded by others—"face" in the peculiarly oriental sense of that word—and internally by deliberate self-examination. Interests of family and community were given precedent over those of the individual, and tested ways of the past honored—by ancestor worship and filial piety—above innovation and experiment.

The content of the life-pattern thus secured centered in the ideal of the *chün-*

tzŭ, or gentleman in the best sense of the term; the person who is completely poised, competent, confident, and adequate to every social occasion; the one of perfect address, who is always at ease within and therefore can put others at their ease. This attitude toward others is that of *jen,* usually translated as "benevolence," or simply "goodness." But the matter isn't left thus generalized. What *jen* requires in specific instances is carefully prescribed by the delineation of "graded love"—that is, love for others according to one's relationship to them, the five most important relationships being those between father and son, elder brother and younger brother, husband and wife, friend and friend, ruler and subject. The sum of the conduct befitting these relationships is *li,* meaning propriety, but significantly ritual as well, since it amounts to the ritualization of the entire social process, from the way the emperor opens the doors of the Temple of Heaven on great ceremonial occasions right down to the way one entertains the humblest guest and serves tea. With scholars placed at the top of the social scale and soldiers excluded from it altogether, learning was revered and violence despised. A system of local and Imperial examinations, which made learning the prime qualification for public office, opened the door to social mobility—the poorest peasant's son might aspire to high public office—and produced the closest approximation to Plato's vision of the philosopher-king as this planet has seen. Age was respected, courtesy raised to the level of an art, and beauty admired to the point where the facility of an alphabet was rejected in favor of calligraphy, the most handsome, as well as most difficult, form of written expression ever evolved.

If cross-cultural comparisons are difficult, cross-cultural evaluations are even more so. It is easy to say that China attended to social relationships more carefully than to science or psychology, and more carefully than did India or the West. But did China thereby achieve more in this regard? No judgment on this question can at this point pretend to be objective; too much depends on whether one favors dynamism, passion, tumult, creativity, and the individual (the West), or quiet, conservative good order. Avoiding comparisons, let me simply say that I find China's social achievement impressive. Chinese culture has a flavor all its own. It is a compound of subtlety, brilliance, and reticence that produces an effect that can be described only as good taste. Traditionally the Chinese have exalted the life of reasonable enjoyment and despised the destructive. As a consequence they have been able to unite an immense area of fertility and to create—if we multiply duration by size of population included—the most extensive civilization ever achieved, one which at its height included one-third of the human race. The political structure of this civilization alone, the Chinese Empire, lasted under various dynasties for 2133 years (from 221 B.C. to A.D. 1912)—a period that makes the empires of Alexander the Great and Caesar look insignificant. Its power of assimilation was equally impressive. Having the most open frontier of all great civilizations, China was subject to wave after wave of invasions by cavalried barbarians who were always ready to fall on the earth-bound agriculturalists. Always at their gates were the very Tartars whose one long-range raid inflicted a mortal wound on the Roman Empire. But what the Chinese could not exclude they absorbed. Each wave of invasion tends quickly to lose its identity. As the great sinologist Arthur Waley has remarked, there is scarcely a barbarian conqueror who came in purely for profit who within twenty years was not attempting to write a copy of Chinese verse which his master, who is also his conquered slave, might say was not wholly unworthy of a gentleman. And already the conqueror is hoping to be mistaken for Chinese. Here is a cultural furnace with enough heat to effect a real melting pot. There is no evidence that these barbarians were ever as impressed with what they found in Europe.

IV

Turning to the third great tradition, the Indian, we find neither the natural nor the social environment inviting India's primary attention. Geographically India today is a land of fierce extremes, running from the icy peaks of the Himalayas to the steaming jungles of Cape Cormorin. In summer, wrote Rudyard Kipling, "there is neither sky, sun, nor horizon. Nothing but a brown-purple haze of heat. It is as though the earth were dying of apoplexy." During this furnace season, millions of Indian villagers lie gasping in their mud huts. Wells dry up and fields blow away. When the monsoon rains come in the fall, the torrential downpours drown the arid land in surging floods. Only in the winter months does India appear comfortably livable and nature kind. We cannot, however, assume that nature was always this harsh. It is possible that with fruit that dripped from the trees and climate that demanded virtually no clothing, there was a time during which nature in India was so easygoing that nature didn't challenge humanity in its direction at all.

What is clear is that for one reason or another India bracketed nature. China in doing so turned its attention to society. But here India found itself facing the most devilish of all social problems, ethnic diversity. India is one of the greatest ethnographic museums in the world. An English anthropologist has likened India to "a deep net into which various races and peoples of Asia have drifted and been caught." The three main color divisions—yellow, black, and white—are represented, and these in turn have been further divided into seven distinct racial types. No Indian ingenuity was equal to this problem. Caste was in part an attempt to deal with it, but instead of caste's solving the problem, in the end the problem took over caste, turning it into a device for perpetuating social distance. Relatively early, India abandoned hope of solving life's problem on the social plane. Instead India turned inward, centering her attention on the psychological problem. Nature? No; even at its best it drags us toward senility and death and leaves us with regrets. Society? No; as long as people are people there will be inequities and blockages on this front. But the individual—to the Indian the individual looked promising. If only we could discover who we truly are, might we not win through to an inner freedom beyond the opposites which block both nature and society? The following lines from the *Katha Upansihad* will be recognized at once as typical of the Indian theme:

> ... The senses turn outward. Accordingly, man looks toward what is without, and sees not what is within. [The wise man] shuts his eyes to what is without, and beholds the self.

For the Indian, the senses are false witnesses.

> The world is not what it appears to be. Behind this surface life, where we experience the play of life and death, there is a deeper life which knows no death; behind our apparent consciousness, which gives us the knowledge of objects and things ... there is ... pure ... consciousness. ... Truth ... is experienced only by those who turn their gaze inward.

As this conviction spreads, "such intellectual energy as had formerly been devoted to the study and development of a machinery for the mastery of the ... forces of the cosmos ... was ... diverted inward. ... The cosmic energy was being taken at its fountain head ... all secondary, merely derivative streams of energy ... being left behind. In Indian thought ... the whole outer world was dwindling in importance."

India became, as a consequence, the world's religious psychologist. One evidence of India's preoccupation in this area is found in the elaborateness of its psychological vocabulary. Coomaraswamy, while curator of the Oriental Museum in Boston, used to say that for every psychological term in English there are four in Greek and forty in Sanskrit. Mrs. Rhys Davids lists twenty Pali words whose subtle distinctions of meaning are obscured by single, indiscriminate English rendition as "desire" or "desires."

What India actually discovered of importance in psychology is, of course, a moot question. Elsewhere I have suggested eight specific insights which are remarkably contemporary to have been discovered in India over two thousand years ago. Here I shall confine myself to a single point and several supporting testimonials. The point concerns the subconscious which breaks upon the West in the nineteenth century but in India before Christ, with (in my judgment) two continuing advantages in India's favor: first, India's delineation of several layers of subconsciousness, not just one; and second, her greater awareness of the creative potentialities of the subconscious along with pathological ones. As for tributes, I shall content myself with three. It was the *Upanishads*' analysis of the self which caused Schopenhauer to stamp them "the product of the highest human wisdom," and Count Keyserling to say that Hinduism at its best has spoken the only relevant truth about the way to self-realization in the full sense of the word. The third tribute is the more impressive because it comes from the leader of the Barthian-grounded school which insists that religious truth is contained fully and exclusively in the Christian revelation. Despite this conviction, Hendrick Kraemer grants that "the wisdom of the East possesses a greater psychological virtuosity in analyzing man, in order to teach him to manage and master himself by spiritual and other kinds of training. As is well known, Eastern wisdom and spiritual experience meet here with the great discoveries in psychology and psychotherapy since Freud."

Neither China nor the West has given a fraction of India's attention to the mind. Historically, India rightly deserves the title of the world's religious psychologist.

V

We have suggested that each of the three great religious traditions has shown a unique specialization—the West in "religious naturalism," China in social ethics, and India in religious psychology. It remains to point out the inevitable price of specialization: ineptness in the subjects neglected. "Nothing fails like success." In the end all three traditions are brought to disaster or its brink because each succeeded so well on one front that it felt safe in neglecting the other two.

China and India have both neglected nature, the injunction to "have dominion." Consequently science has not developed, and the standard of living remains intolerably low. In China the problem periodically proved too much even for social genius. Between dynasties there was regularly a long period of civil strife which can always be correlated with population pressure on cultivated land which failed to increase productivity because improvement of agricultural technique was negligible. As for India, its only scientific contributions to the world at large have been in pure mathematics, where India was dealing not with the outer world but with the resources of the mind. In addition to ineptness toward nature, India adds social clumsiness, vividly illustrated by the present state of the caste system, and China adds psychological naïveté.

Occasionally we catch glimpses in China of an interest in the mind and what it can do, as in the quietistic movement in the Chou Dynasty, the *Tao Tê Ching*'s esoteric rendering of the idea of *te,* Mencius's passage on "the dawn breath," and Chu Hsi's discussion of "silent sitting." But the interest is never systematically pursued, and it usually takes a social turn: the mind is being inspected not for itself but for what it can contribute to social stability. One gets the impression that when China does get around to psychology, it is only social psychology that really interests it. East Asia's deficiencies in this field are seen most clearly in its failure to recognize the danger of repression. The Chinese scheme had no place for emotional carthasis, spontaneity, and unrepression. Consequently, negative emotions got dammed up until eventually the dam gave way and the emotions came forth in terrifying form; Mao's Cultural Revolution of 1966–76 is the twentieth century's glaring instance of this. The pattern carried over to Japan where, as Robert Guillain has pointed out, a youth "received a Spartan training which developed his aggressive instincts and, at the same time, screwed down over his violent nature a sort of lid of blind obedience and perfect politeness. This made him an explosive creature, ready to burst like a bomb."

The deficiencies of the West have been in psychology and sociology. Psychologically the West has been until recently merely inconspicuous, but in sociology one wonders if the West has not been delinquent. At least four facts must be faced as evidences of the West's ineptitude in social relations and lack of perceptiveness as to the forces that make for social cohesion and group harmony.

1. The first comes to light in simply comparing Europe's political map with those of China and India. Whereas Chinese civilization had the power to expand, uniting more and more people in a common heritage, and whereas Indian civilization could at least hold its own, the record of the West has been one of continuous secession. After the union of the Northern and Southern Kingdoms in Egypt, there is no further fusion in the Fertile Crescent. Instead, fission sets in. The Hebrews divide into Israel and Judah. "The fatal danger of Greece," writes Gilbert Murray, "was disunion as many see it in Europe now." The Christian Church splits into East and West, the Western Church into Roman Catholic and Protestant, and Protestantism splinters. The Medieval Empire shatters into nations, and the process continues. Norway, Denmark, and Sweden, originally a Scandinavian unit, divide. Belgium and Holland, once united in the Netherlands, are apart. The British Isles have been plagued with separatist movements. The United States has had its Civil War and continuing North-South animosity. What has enfeebled and discredited us in our own day, writes Arnold Toynbee, "is the atrocious fratricidal warfare, within the bosom of our Western Society, since 1914. . . . We Westerners have fought among ourselves another bout of wars that have been as savage, destructive and discreditable as our earlier wars of religion." Western history since the Middle Ages is one long story of inability to inspire embracing loyalties strong enough to outweigh provincial attachments.

2. Western religion appears to have shared in this social ineptitude. The only large-scale persecuting religions have been those of the West—Judaism, Christianity, and Islam. Since the Middle Ages, Christianity has been divisive by itself. To continue with Toynbee: "For 400 years and more, from the outbreak of the struggle between the Papacy and Frederick II in the thirteenth century down to the end of the Catholic-Protestant Western wars of religion in the seventeenth century, the Christian Church in the Western World was a force that made not

for gentleness and peace and concord, but for violence and dissension. . . . Before the end of the seventeenth century, the hatred, strife and atrocities inflicted on the Western World by Christian *odium theologicum* had become a scandal and menace to the Western Civilization."

3. The West has invented the two things which, combined, most endanger the world's future: total war and religious nationalism.

4. Eventually (one almost says inevitably) there emerges in Europe a social theory—or more accurately a religion, albeit a heretical one—which pushes the Western emphasis to its logical extreme. Paralleling the West's temptation to reduce psychology to physiology, Marx reduces sociology to economics. In the end, were one to believe him, there *is* no social problem. Once the material problem is solved, the social problem will automatically take care of itself and the state will wither away.

VI

We have suggested that each of the world's three great religious traditions has exercised a noteworthy influence on one of the basic human problems, but seems to have tended insufficiently to the other two. It would appear that an adequate civilization must strike all three notes as a chord. In developing this chord of a fully adequate world culture, each of the three great traditions appears to have something of importance to contribute. Perhaps each has something to learn as well.

EPILOGUE

Not often in discussions as general as this does one stumble upon evidence so clear-cut as to stand as independent verification for an entire thesis. But since completing the above, a point has occurred to me which seems to come close to this.

What is truth? The question didn't arise in our discussion. But if one does raise it, one finds the three civilizations answering along the lines we would expect. For the West, truth is essentially correspondence with a state of affairs that exists independently in nature or history (past nature). A Chinese, on the other hand, will feel that the primary objects to which assertions refer, and are responsible, are the feelings of persons involved. Hence the normality of white lies and keeping one's mouth shut when appropriate. India has a third criterion: to India truth is essentially spiritual pragmatism. One can generate little interest in India over whether Hindu myths are "true" in our Western sense—whether Krishna really lived, for example. The accounts are true to the needs of the human spirit. What could be more important?

12

Shinto

A Japanese Sense of the Sacred

All life-forms look out upon the world from a center of individual identity, and this holds for collectivities as well as for individuals. For the Japanese people Shinto constitutes their identity while Buddhism opens them to the world—most directly to the peoples of China and Korea, but beyond those to India and all Asia. Thus while Buddhism is centrifugal, Shinto is centripetal; at heart it is reverence and love for things Japanese. Spatially this reverential love is directed towards the land, the Japanese islands. Temporally it focuses on a genealogy which, beginning at home and in neighborhoods with family and clan, moves through the myths of the imperial family to the Sun Goddess Amaterasu, symbol of the metaphysical reality from which all things proceed.

Actually, the land too is included in this lineage, for the *Nihonji* reports that the islands of Japan arose from drippings from a jeweled spear that Izanagi and Izanami plunged into the briny sea. By virtue of that miraculous origination, nature in these islands is sanctuary, a truth that finds expression in *tori-i* placed to frame sacred landscapes, and in the designation of notable natural objects— mountains, groves, springs—as *kami*. One of the most treasured objects in my own home, the gift of a Japanese professor who visited me while I was teaching at the Massachusetts Institute of Technology, is a *kakimono* whose handsome inscription reads 天地有情 (The universe is spiritual). I treasure it for its beauty, but even more for its message as a corrective to the lifeless, mechanistic cosmology that scientism has foisted on the West.

Returning to the human side of the sacred genealogy, we notice that veneration mounts as we travel backwards in time: ancestors are more esteemed than the living, age is exalted over youth, and parents are more respected than children. As this "reverse time orientation" runs counter to the modern myth of progress, historians of religion have saddled it with the epithet "ancestor worship," the implication being that in East Asia human progenitors double for the divine, taking its place and serving as its substitute. Asians see the matter differently. Rather than standing in for the divine, ancestors constitute a bridge to it. There is something metaphysically sound in this institution that, as the world and its spinnings derive from divinity, those who stood closer to creation were closer to the Creator as well and more bathed in its light. Whether they were actually better than we are—whether "there were giants on the earth in those days" (to quote the biblical version of this myth) that were morally as well as physically our superiors—we cannot know, but to think that there were, buttresses our sense of the sacred. For if the heroism of patriarchs derived from their proximity to the point of origin, two things are accomplished in a single stroke: the origin is honored by being credited for their heroism, while we for our part are accorded noble pedigree. We derive not from some primordial ooze but from the gods themselves. The notion strengthens us for the nobility that is required of us, for if our nature is noble we feel both that we should act nobly and that we can so act. The exemplary models our ancestors provide are relevant. To be true to them is, at the same time, to be true to ourselves and true to God.

From the two preceding points, the sacred origin of the Japanese islands and the Japanese people, a Shinto ethic derives. It is an ethic of purity, sincerity, and simplicity. That two of these three words duplicate Dr. Suzuki's characterization of Zen Buddhism should not surprise us, for the degree to which Shinto and Buddhism coalesce in the lived lives of the Japanese people has already been remarked. On NBC's 1958 "Wisdom" series, Dr. Suzuki characterized Zen as consisting of simplicity, sincerity, and freedom.

Purity ties in with the sacredness of nature, as the phrase "virgin nature" attests, but in a way simplicity is fundamental. When on one occasion I mentioned to Prof. Ono Sokyo, author of *The Kami Way,* that I could find no English exposition of Shinto theology, he said that the reason was clear: Shinto has no theology. And in ethics, he added, its precepts reduce to purity and sincerity. The parsimony in these answers is reflected in Shinto sanctuaries which are virtually empty, and in the Japanese esthetic sense generally which is world renowned. Everyone has heard of at least one Japanese principle of flower arrangement: compose the flowers as they should be, then remove half of them, then half of what remain. In the tea ceremony we find the same understatement and paring back to essentials. If we see in this austerity a naturalness that derives in ways from nature, its connection with ancestors is even more apparent, for whether they were better than we are, their lives seem clearly to have been simpler, and thereby exempt from the complications and attendant ambiguities and compromises that bedevil so much of modern life.

13

The Spiritual Heritage of India

Around the middle of this century Arnold Toynbee predicted that at its close the world would still be dominated by the West but that in the twenty-first century "India will conquer her conquerors." Preempting the place that is now held by technology, religion will be restored to its earlier importance and the center of world happenings will wander back from the shores of the Atlantic to the East where civilization originated five or six thousand years ago.

The spiritual heritage of India is one of the world's standing miracles. It would rank among its greatest human achievements were it not that "achievement" isn't really the right word. It is more like a reception—the opening of a people to receive, through inspiration, the Breath of the Eternal. For the outbreathing of the Eternal is what India has taken truth to be.

We know that "Hinduism" is a label affixed by outsiders. Long ago, people to the west of the Indus River mispronounced its name and called those who lived on it or to its other side "Hindus," and in time "Hinduism" came to be used for their beliefs and practices. The Indians themselves knew no such word. There was no need for them to think of the truth by which they lived as other than the *sanatana dharma,* the Eternal Truth. It was Truth Itself—truth that had become incarnate in the tradition that sustained them.

How the incarnation was effected is itself an interesting point. In the West we tend to think of knowledge as cumulative: bits of information get joined into bodies of information that can grow indefinitely. India recognizes a kind of knowledge that fits this model, but she considers it "lower knowledge"—knowledge that is gained by reason and the senses playing over objective, finite particulars. Higher knowledge *(paravidya)* proceeds differently. Or rather, it doesn't proceed at all, for it enters history full-blown. It is futile to ask when this higher knowledge first appeared, for India has no notion of absolute beginnings—beginnings require time, and time for India is not absolute. The most we can say is that when a new cosmic cycle opens there are souls waiting in the wings, so to speak, with the higher wisdom already in store. Who these souls are is not a genetic accident: India has no place for chance or accident—the law of karma precludes it. The men and women who are born wise on the morning of a new creation are so because, though the world they enter is young, they themselves are not. Their *jivas* (individual psyches) having been held over from preceding cosmic cycles, they are already "old souls"—old chronologically to be sure, but more importantly in experience. Specifically they are yogis and yoginis who used their preceding lives to cultivate what might be regarded as a kind of "night sight"—the night vision of the spirit by which fixed stars of eternity can be seen in broad daylight. Adepts in such vision, these seers stand poised on the brink of their final liberation when the new cycle begins. Their concluding legacy to the phenomenal world is to impregnate the new cycle with reflective knowledge of the truth they have assiduously shepherded. Keeping in touch with this truth through meditation, these *rishis* (seers) transmit it orally, direct from guru to disciple, until eventually their oral tradition gets committed to writing. In India the texts that resulted were the Vedas.

If we see the Vedas in this light, as apertures through which the Infinite entered conscious human awareness in South Asia in the present cosmic cycle, what word of the Infinite do the Vedas impart?

First the warning that on this topic words are unequal to their task. They can be useful, of course, or the Vedas themselves would not have been written, but a fundamental Vedic teaching concerns the limitations of words themselves when directed towards ultimates. Sooner or later these ultimates phase beyond language entirely. *Neti, neti,* not this, not this; the map is not the terrain, the menu is not the meal—the Vedas never tire of repeating this basic point. In this kind of knowing, words do not cause understanding; at best they occasion it: from spirit to spirit communion leaps. The word *Upanishads,* denoting the culminating sections of the Vedas, makes this point in its very etymology. Deriving from roots which when conjoined mean to approach *(upa)* with utter *(ni)* firmness to loosen and destroy *(sad)* spiritual ignorance, it warns the reader right off that the topics one is about to encounter call for more than book learning. For their province is that "higher mathematics" of the human spirit where knowing merges with being. Upanishadic truth is so subtle, so abstruse, that purely objective, rational intellects are likely to miss it entirely—off such intellects it rolls like water off oil. Only when discerned in a life that is living it—a life that incarnates it in its outlook, moods, and conduct—does truth of this order become fully convincing. It is like art. There comes a time when every master musician must say to his or her pupil, "Don't bother with what I say. Just watch how I take that passage."

To be able to perform as one's teacher does, the student must become a changed person. The change begins with a change in his or her understanding—one now has some inkling of how the passage should sound—but other changes are required as well. Subtle muscular habits must be acquired and integrated, through feedback loops, with subliminal sensitivities to nuances of color and sound. The analogy helps us to see that the truths the Vedas deal with exceed language in a double sense. To the fact that the Infinite cannot be fitted into concepts which are finite by nature is joined the further fact that the knowledge in question resembles "knowing how" more than "knowing that"; it is more like knowing how to swim or ride a bicycle than like recognizing that these activities require certain movements of arms and legs. Vedantic epistemology involves yoga. To know, one must be; to deepen one's knowledge of the kind in question, one must deepen one's being.

These points must never be lost sight of, but provided they are kept in view, the mind may be given its due in the transformative process. Of the world's manifold traditions, none has held more firmly than India's to the double truth that (a) though the mind is intimately *meshed* with other components of the self, (b) it can take the lead in *changing* the self. First the student hears the truth, then he/she reasons on it. It is later, we are told, that he/she meditates on it to deepen his/her understanding and bring other components abreast of where his/her mind, as advance scout, has already proceeded.

The territory into which the mind is forever pressing is the Infinite, and if we were to look for the place where India most deserves to be credited for originality, it is perhaps here that we find it. The Chinese notion of the Tao is rich in its *sense* of the Infinite, but the Chinese were content to rest in that sense itself; they felt no compulsion to conceptualize it. The Greeks, on the other hand, tried to conceptualize everything they encountered, but this very penchant excluded them from ready access to a notion concepts could never close in on. Anaximander's Unbounded *(apeiron)* held promising possibilities, but instead of pursuing these his successors backed away from them—Greek philosophers were not about to give high marks to something that lacked determination. By the time of Aristotle, infinity had come to be associated with imperfection and lack *(Physics,* III:6–8); it meant the capacity for never-ending increase and was always potential, never completely actual. Not until the Neo-Platonists did a full-blown, positive view of the Infinite emerge in the West, and then in part, perhaps, through Indian influence. If we look at a map of the world, Europe looks like an appendage growing out of a central, Asian body or trunk, and in this matter of the Infinite, capitalized because affirmatively conceived, the appearance seems accurate. For not only did India give that notion its earliest explicit articulation; it made the notion central to its history. This no other civilization has quite done. To speak only of ourselves, the modern West has an infinite of sorts, but it is of a largely mathematical variety which is not infinite at all in the complete sense of the word. For though a mathematical infinite is unlimited in certain respects—with regard to extension or number, for example—it is clearly not inclusive in all respects: sounds, colors, and other things that make our world substantial and concrete have no place within it. India's infinite is otherwise. It includes everything, which gave the Indian outlook right off a striking amplitude. When we think inclusively about the West the phrase that comes to mind is "the Western world." The comparable phrase that comes to mind when we think of India is "the Indian universe."

I have labored this point about the infinite because, though it is abstract in itself, it carries concrete implications. Everyone agrees that India is different, but what is it that *makes* her different? When a newcomer sets out to locate the elusive, distinctive ingredient, the old-timers smile and wait. They wait for the moment they know well, all having encountered it in their turn. It is the moment when the visitor will throw up his or her hands and admit that India is indefinable, because it seems to include everything.

Which, of course, is precisely what the Infinite includes. "As above, so below"— I am suggesting that India's exceptional variety and inclusiveness derives from the fact that India saw the source of all things as Infinite in the all-inclusive and positive sense of that word: *sat,* Being in its totality, is endowed with consciousness *(chit)* and bliss *(ananda).* Philosophers know that to speak of such an Infinite requires paradoxes: because words and propositions are limited, every half truth they utter must be balanced by the other half they omit. The historical counterpart of this is the paradox of India—a whole host of paradoxes, actually, for wherever we turn, India confronts us with opposites so extreme they would have torn other civilizations apart but are here kept in creative tension. Bejewelled maharajas who receive as birthday presents their weight in precious stones from their starving subjects. Naked ascetics stretched on beds of nails, balanced by naked voluptuaries on temple friezes. Or the question of God: three hundred and thirty million deities sounds like polytheism gone haywire until we hear that nothing other than the sole, indivisible Brahman even exists. What are we to make of such paradoxes?

Swami Prabhavananada's *The Spiritual Heritage of India* (Hollywood, Calif.: Vedanta Press, 1979) integrates the variety in the Indian heritage which, left to itself, can be bewildering. Even Buddhism and Jainism, technically considered by Hindus to be unorthodox, are here shown to be authentic expressions of the basic Indian vision. Or the Six Systems of Indian Philosophy; often regarded as competitors, they are here shown to complement one another. And of course philosophy and psychology are not separated from theology as if they belonged in distinct compartments. It would be too weak to say that Indian thought as it emerges in the reading of this book is interdisciplinary. It is, rather, pre-disciplinary: in the rich and holistic way that biblical, Chinese, and early Greek thought are.

14

The Importance of the Buddha

That Arnold Toynbee should have emerged from his twelve-volume *A Study of History* listing Gautama the Buddha as one of the dozen or so "greatest bene-factors of the living generation" surprises no one, I suppose. But who was this Buddha, this "Awakened One"—one of a handful of snowflakes that deserve to be singled out from the total human snowfall for attention and gratitude?

There is no need for me to dwell here on the well-known facts of his life. Instead I shall pick up on Toynbee's point and speak to its importance. What was there about the Buddha that made him important in the past and important today? Important for Westerners today, for us who are spatially as well as tempo-rally removed from the world in which the Buddha lived.

Begin with the past. The reason usually given for the Buddha's historical im-portance is that he founded one of the world's great religions. No one doubts that he did this, but our secular and pluralistic age has contracted the word *religion* so far in the direction of individual belief and practice—"what a man does with his own solitariness," was the way Whitehead defined it—that to peg the Buddha as the founder of a religion is to miss the full scale of his achievement. It would be truer to say, with Trevor Ling, that he founded a civilization—one whose soul was indeed religion, but whose body was a body politic. As a civilization, Buddhism was a total view of the world and humanity's place in it. It created for the commu-nity of its adherents an entire universe, one that gathered into a coherent whole levels and aspects of life that the modern world divides into economics, politics, ethics, law, art, philosophy, and the like. E. F. Schumacher reminded us of this by including a chapter on "Buddhist Economics" in his *Small Is Beautiful,* but the view of Budhism as an exclusively spiritual affair persists.

The Buddha that jumps first to mind is the one iconography so effectively presents to us: the solitary Buddha seated motionless beneath the Bodhi Tree. So strong is the hold of this other-worldly Buddha that we forget his other side. We forget that no sooner had he launched his ministry than he was drawn back into the royal circles he had renounced to seek his enlightenment. For Indian monarchy was in its infancy then, trying to forge a viable alternative to the village-based Brahmanic *panchayat* (rule by five) that was fumbling with population growth and other changes that were occurring.

The greatness of the Buddha in shaping that civilization is attested by the greatness of the civilization itself. Geographically it spread beyond India to bless all of Asia, while temporally it continues residually, in southern Buddhism, right down to today. Southern Buddhism (Theravada) is usually distinguished from its northern, Mahayana counterpart doctrinally, but the difference that underlies their doctrinal disputes is that Theravada Buddhism, standing closer to original Buddhism, continued to cling to the ideal of Buddhism as a civilization, whereas Mahayana Buddhism never did so cling. I recognize that this is not the usual view of the matter, but a return to the Buddhist world last year in a visit divided between Sri Lanka in the south and Japan to the north convinced me that it is accurate. We have yet to see a history of Buddhism that presents the rise of Mahayana as Buddhism revisioning itself to accommodate to civilizations other than its own—first in India when it became clear that the Vedic tradition and its *varnashrama-dharmic* social stipulations were not going to be displaced, and then in China, whose civilization never did admit of an alternative.

This divestment process—the extraction of Buddhism's spiritual essence from the total civilization in which it was originally cast—points directly to the second question I posed for Buddhism's continuing importance. For Buddhist civilization is a thing of the past; even in Burma, Thailand, Sri Lanka, and Cambodia we see today only its debris. For the continuing importance of the Buddha's achievement we must look to Buddhism as a religion, capable of accommodating itself to civilizations in the plural. We have it on no less authority than that of Edward Thomas that the religious essence of Buddhism has never been definitely identified, so what follows will be an approximation only.

Consciousness feels like a passive medium, through which the world simply flows in to us as it is in itself, but this is far from the case. To begin with, we select from the world, seeing in the main what we choose to see; as the Tibetans say, when a pickpocket meets a saint, what the pickpocket sees are pockets. And even what we choose to see we structure by our thoughts and feelings: poor children asked to draw a penny will draw it larger than do rich children—it looms larger in their minds' eyes. In so many ways, what we take for the world's "facts" are actually psychological constructs, as the Latin *factum* ("that which is made") suggests. This much Buddhism shares with virtually all contemporary psychology.

What it adds is that at a deeper level our thoughts and feelings are themselves vectored by what the Buddha called The Three Poisons: desire (lust, greed, and grasping), aversion (fear, hatred, and anger), and ignorance. And the greatest of these is ignorance. For it is ignorance—most pointedly, ignorance concerning our true identity, who we really are—that causes us to divide the world into what we like and dislike. Thinking that we are, in the last analysis, individuals, we seek what augments our isolated selves and shun what threatens them. What we call our "self" is the amalgam of desires and aversions that we have wrapped tightly, like the elastic of a golf ball, around the core of separate identity that is its center.

This tight, constricted, golf-ball self is inevitably in for hard knocks, which is why the Buddha prefaced his teachings with "life is suffering." For a long while Western understanding of Buddhism was arrested at this first of the Buddha's Four Noble Truths; it is from this arrested position that the charges of Buddhism as life-denying and world-negating—in a word pessimistic—have been leveled. The truth, we now almost see, is more nearly the opposite. The startling claim of the Buddha, announced in the third and fourth of his Noble Truths, is that the suffering of unregenerate life is dispensable; it can be transcended. And we can see how to transcend it. There is only one kind of person I oppose, the Buddha once observed: he who says there is no way.

This is not the place to say in detail what the Buddha saw the way to be—many books do that. It will be enough here to reverse the two preceding paragraphs' "archaeology of consciousness" that exposed the root of life's routine suffering and construct from bottom up a model of the alternative self the Buddha perceived. The foundation of this reconstituted self will be an enlarged self-identification. Ideally the new self will identify with everything, greeting everything that comes its way as a reflection of an aspect of its own self. But we need not be categorical. Every step in the recommended direction will be to the good. For with each step we will find our desires and aversions relaxed; more of what comes our way will feel congruent with what we sense ourselves to be. Closer to the surface of our awareness we will see that the easing of our demands on life reduces the distortions our thoughts and feelings impose upon it. The logical terminus of this line of reasoning is clear. If we could attain the limit of expanded identity—the point where we relinquished partiality toward our finite selves entirely—there would *be* no separate self and the Buddha's key insight, *anatta* (no separate self), would be directly experienced. We should not let the negative form of the Buddhist terms for this eventuality mislead us: *nirvana* is "nothing" only in the sense of "no (demarcated) thing"; *sunyata* is "void" only in being devoid of separating distinctions. The words point toward the limitlessness of the self we would become.

Needless to say, the succinctness of this formulation is no gauge of the difficulties it presents. The practical agenda it sets before us is more than enough for a lifetime—in Buddhist symbolism innumerable lives are required. Still, the discovery of what life's true agenda is can arrive in an instant. And its arrival is decisive; it is hardly too much to say that to identify life's problem and set foot on the path indicated is more important than traversing the path's full length. For to set forth on the path is to turn one's back forever on the stance of victim. To pass from thinking of ourselves as *having* problems to seeing that we *are* the problem is to step from darkness into at least a glimmering light. Tears and labors may await us, but if we have truly effected the "Copernican revolution" in outlook we are already, in germ, ourselves the "Buddha"—from the root *bodhati*: he awakens; he understands. We can echo for ourselves the words with which the historical Buddha concluded his six-year quest: "I have been a fool, [but] I have found a path."

If this way of putting the Buddhist perspective seems contemporary in a way Buddhist civilization does not, it is why I suggested that the Buddha not only was important, but continues to be important today. In doing so I suspect I have also suggested why his life and teachings are pertinent for the contemporary West and not just Asia. That I could even attempt to summarize the Buddha's message in contemporary psychological idiom is itself proof that the high walls that separated traditions in the human past are down. In part, at least, we emphatically *can* understand what the Buddha was getting at. And because our Western scientific approaches tempt us to try to explain the more in terms of the less, with the danger that in doing so we shall lose sight of the freedom that constitutes our human opportunity, we *need* to understand what the Buddha was saying. If we succeed in understanding him, a curious prediction that has been attributed to the eighth-century Tibetan saint Padmasambhava will have been strikingly confirmed:

> When the iron bird flies,
> and horses run on wheels. . . .
> the Dharma will come to the land
> of the red man.

15

Tibetan Chanting

On a recent sojourn among Tibetan lamas, I stumbled on an extraordinary phenomenon that lends itself to rigorous inspection (by spectroscopic analysis and computer simulation). It is the capacity of certain specially trained lamas to chant in a way that makes multiple tones audible simultaneously, the capacity of single lamas to sing—solo—chords.

I shall begin my report of this phenomenon with a personal narrative, in which I recount the circumstances under which I encountered the chanting. An acoustic description, which consists of a report by scientists of what, in terms of the physics of the human voice, the lamas actually do, may be found in my article in the *American Anthropologist* 69, no. 2 (April 1967), "Unique Vocal Abilities of Certain Tibetan Lamas." After my personal narrative, I shall discuss hermeneutics, in which I try to assess the meaning this kind of chanting assumes in the context of Tibetan Buddhism.

NARRATIVE

Debarred from Tibet proper because I am a United States citizen, I spent the autumn of 1964 among lamas currently in exile in north India. A chance meeting with a high lama of the Gelugpa sect on a bus to Dalhousie led to admission to Gyütü Monastery on the outskirts of that Punjab hill station. The original Gyütü, in Lhasa, boasted some 800 lamas; its reconstituted, exilic version houses one-tenth that number in refugee quarters that the Indian government provides as partial compensation for work on high roads in the Himalayan foothills performed by Tibetan laypersons.

It happened that I had entered the monastery on the eve of the annual four-day *puja* commemorating the arrival in Tibet of two renowned statues, one from Nepal, the other from China, important symbols of the Indian and Chinese civilizations on which Tibet has drawn and whose features it has blended uniquely. The ceremonies began at three o'clock the following morning in the "ceremonial hall," which—we were in refugee quarters—was in fact no more than a large tent. I mention this detail because the immediate impulse of the first musicologist who heard my recording of the chanting I am about to describe was to credit what he heard to resonances awakened by "the thick walls of those Tibetan fortress monasteries." In actuality, the acoustics of the "hall" contributed nothing to what he was hearing.

Some eighty lamas, richly robed, seated themselves on cushions on the dirt floor in six rows running the length of the tent, three on each side of the center, all facing the center. I was end man on one of the back rows, near the altar. For the opening hour the chanting was monotonous. A guttural, gravelly, low-pitched, unvarying drone, it reminded me of the chanting in Japanese monasteries and recalled the fact that Tibetan Vajrayana and Japanese Shingon are subbranches of the same Buddhist limb. The darkness of the early hour combined with the monotony of the drone to make me sleepy, and I was on the verge of dozing off when I was brought to my senses abruptly by what sounded like an angelic choir. The boring monotone had given way to rich, full-chorded harmony. If the accompanying bells and cymbals had begun to simulate the tones of the King's Chapel organ, I would hardly have been more astonished. My first thought was: they're singing in parts. This thought was striking enough, for I had always known harmony as a Western art form, the Orient having concentrated, by contrast, on melody and rhythm. But this jolt was nothing to the one that awaited me, for after several minutes of such chords the choir suddenly cut out, leaving everything to a single soloist or cantor. And he, seated perhaps ten feet to my right and two rows in front, was singing by himself what sounded like a three-tone major chord composed of a musical first, third, and fifth. Subsequent spectroscopic analysis of the recording I eventually made shows only two of these tones—the first and third—to be distinctly audible. I believe this is due to faulty recording but cannot be certain, for it is my ear and memory against what the tape actually registers.

The balance of the story is brief. The rituals lasted for 15 hours on each of the four days, punctuated by two ten-minute toilet breaks and two meager meals served in place within the tent. Most of the time the lamas were seated, bell in the thumb-groin of the right hand, diamond scepter in that of the left. Periodically, they would wave and interweave their hands in elaborate *mudras* to accompany their chants. For about ten minutes once every hour and a half, their voices would splay out from their monotone drone into the chords of which I have spoken. It was my distinct impression that when they did this, they were all doing what the cantor did: each one of them producing all of the notes in the chord. But since the evidence I brought back affords no way of proving that the lamas were not sounding different notes of the chord, the analysis that follows confines itself to the solo portions of the chanting, not the choral portions. Richly embroidered vestments and elaborate headgear were changed periodically, and each afternoon there were ceremonial processions around the inside of the tent, culminating before the altar. The entire celebration climaxed in an elaborate outdoor fire sacrifice in the late afternoon of the final day. An anonymous benefactor (a *yon bdag*, "fee master"; or *yin bdag*, "bounty master") provided each lama with a rupee (20¢) for his 60-hour vigil; in this recompense the writer was generously included.

On the day following the puja, I located in a school near Dalhousie a tape recorder and returned to the monastery to record the effects described. On returning to MIT, I took the tape to my colleague, Professor Kenneth N. Stevens, who specializes in the physics of the human voice. He had not heard, or heard of, the human voice functioning in this way, and after a spectroscopic analysis of the tape, produced, with his colleague Raymond S. Tomlinson, the explanation of the solo portion of the lamas' chant that forms the next section of this article. (As I watched them work, I thought of a line from C. P. Snow's *The Two Cultures and a Second Look:* "Greenwich Village talks precisely the same language as Chelsea, and both have about as much communication with M.I.T. as though the scientists spoke nothing but Tibetan." The MIT scientists before me weren't speaking Tibetan, but they were working on Tibetan speech.)

HERMENEUTICS

Why do the lamas go to what is apparently great trouble to achieve the chord effect? Not, we may assume, for its esthetic yield alone, any more than medieval monks perfected Gregorian chant solely for the sake of art. Music inspires as well as delights, and as lamas are not primarily musicians, we can surmise that they developed the chord primarily for its inspirational power.

To "inspire" means, of course, to "induce spirit," or if (as Buddhists believe) the Buddha-nature is in human beings from the start, to inspire is to bring it to the fore. Sound can facilitate this process, for if through language human beings reached out and took possession of the world, through it human beings also reached inward and awakened, among other things, intimations of a higher life. India has been vividly aware of language's creative power, considering it no less than metaphysical. According to legend, Brahman himself was born from the cosmic being's mouth, a notion embedded in the fact that the root of the word *Brahman* means "breath."

If the Brahmins thought sound could produce God, one is not surprised to find them believing that it could vitalize the God in human beings *(Atman)*. As prime vehicle for this power, they forged the sacred syllable (Sanskrit *mantra;* Tibetan, *gzunis snags*), literally, "tool for the mind." A mantra is not a concept, for divinity exceeds conceptualization. Nor is it a name, only designating. It might be conceived as a vocal variant of Locke's quality-less substance, around which humanity's intimations of the sacred can accumulate and adhere, but for the best mantras this image is too passive. The best mantras do not merely *accept* sacred associations, they *elicit* them. To do so, they must be natural symbols, not just conventional ones; that is, they must be ones that contain within themselves intrinsically, not just by association, features contained to greater degree in what they symbolize. AUM—the first of the two syllables on which the lamas build their chords and the paradigmatic mantra of Indian spirituality—possesses such natural symbolic qualifications in abundance. Some of these have been known since the *Mandukya Upanishad.* Compounded of the first and last syllables of the alphabet, AUM is Sanskrit's alpha and omega, the beginning and end of all that can be said. If one objects that the preceding clause should read "the beginning and end of all that can be *written,*" the Indian will not object; he or she will simply point out that orally, too, the syllable is inclusive. Correctly pronounced, it executes a glide that traverses all articulatory positions in the range of the human voice, from deep in the throat (A), through the mouth's center (U), to the closing of the lips (M). The syllable compresses, therefore, speech as well as writing: "As · all parts of a leaf are held together by a central rod, so all speech is held together by AUM" *(Chandogya Upanishad).* And insofar as thought rides on language, AUM contains it too in seed. It is the most compact, meaningful representation of the All, which is why the Indians hold that in it, as Lama Govinda wrote, "all the positive and forward-pressing forces of the human mind are united and concentrated like an 'arrow-point.'"

What the physics of sound adds to our understanding of AUM as a natural symbol is the concept of overtones. The aural impact of that syllable need not derive exclusively from the claimed fact that it glides the full length of the vocal tract; part of that impact can derive from the fact that it is a syllable with strong overtones. For overtones awaken numinous feelings: sensed without being explicitly heard, they stand in exactly the same relation to our hearing as the sacred stands to our ordinary, mundane lives. This is why gongs appear so frequently in religious observances—they were prominent in the pujas in which the chords were set. Rich in harmonics,

> the sound of the gong extends from the lowest tone of human perception to the highest, and the tone does not cease. It stays in one's ear till its sound blends into the noise of the world. In the sound of the gong there are all sounds. It is impossible to pick out the infinitely many individual tones, and therefore it is impossible to describe the experience minutely. In the sound of the gong there is all that there is; it is one.

The object of the spiritual quest is to experience life as one hears the gong, replete with overtones that tell of a "more" that can be sensed but not seen, sensed but not said, heard but not explicitly.

The lamas' chords place, as it were, a magnifying glass over the aural symbolic virtues embedded in the AUM mantra: they peak to the point of full audibility overtones that otherwise are sensed but not explicitly heard. The chords also provide a clue to why HUM, the other syllable on which the chords build, worked its way into mantric position. The human vocal cavities are such that it is impossible for them to produce vowels having separately identifiable overtones, except at low frequencies. With all their skill and effort, the lamas, to achieve their chord effects, had to begin with vowels in the region of those present in our words "boot," "good," and "law." HUM meets this requirement. It is consonant with this hypothesis, though not directly related to the lamas' chord, that the requirement is also met by "wu" and "mu," the virtual mantras of Ch'an and Zen Buddhism as embedded in the "wu" kung an and "mu" koan.

16

The Relevance of the Great Religions for the Modern World

Religion can, of course, be irrelevant and often is. No human endeavor is immaculate, and one that traffics with millions is bound to emerge a mixed bag. In this respect religion is no different from other corporate enterprises—education which quickens and represses, government which orchestrates and restricts. Religion has been revolutionary and conservative, prophetic and priestly, catalytic and incubus. It creates barriers and levels them, raises church budgets and raises the oppressed, makes peace with iniquity and redeems, in part, the world.

I

Religious relevance takes different forms according to the period in question. I propose to distinguish three great ages through which humanity has passed with an eye to what religious relevance has meant in each.

1. The first age, by far the longest, was the archaic. It lasted, roughly, up to the first millennium B.C. In this Archaic Period, during which humans were rousing out of their animal innocence, their chief spiritual problem was time. Lower animals are oblivious of time, for they possess neither foresight nor hindsight, neither anticipation nor memory. When human beings first acquired these time-binding faculties they found the implications terrifying: the future, they discovered, was contingent, and the past impermanent. Their recourse was to blink from these terrors; insofar as possible simply to turn their back on them and deny their existence by attending to their opposite. This opposite—Great Time—was in fact timeless. It consisted of momentous originating acts which their myths told them had brought order out of chaos and established the patterns for mean-

ingful activity: creation of the world itself, the first planting, the first mating, each act accomplished by the gods in epic proportions. For archaic peoples being *was* these timeless, paradigmatic acts which were significant, secure, and impervious to time's decay. Their religion consisted of replicating these acts through rites that were myth-ordained and myth-prescribed. Through these rites they fused their lives with Being, merging them with the meaningful and the real.

Note how little ethics entered into this first originating phase of religion. The reason is that at this stage ethics did not pose much of a problem, little more than it does for subhuman animals. People were living for the most part in small groups, in tribes or tiny villages wherein everyone knew everyone else and cooperated pretty much as do members of a normal family.

2. Following the terminology of Karl Jaspers, I shall call the second period the Axial Age, for during it human history took a marked turn, a giant swing on its axis, so to speak. This is the period that witnessed the rise of the geniuses the world still honors: the great prophets of Israel, Zarathustra in Persia, Buddha and the Upanishadic seers in India, Lao Tzu and Confucius in China. This burst of religious creativity across the full arc of the civilized world, an extraordinary proliferation of prophetic genius diffused in space but condensed in time and amounting to nothing short of a mass religious mutation—this remarkable phenomenon has often been described but never satisfactorily explained. I submit that it was at root the spirit's response to a marked change in the human condition, a crisis in history's development.

By the first millennium B.C. or shortly before, agricultural improvement had advanced population and settled existence to the point where people were dealing regularly with persons outside their primary group. As a consequence, familial feelings no longer sufficed to keep society intact. Perceptive souls—we call them prophets, seers, rishis, sages, magi—saw this and summoned religion to emerge from its archaic phase to help meet the problem.

Rites and rituals are no longer enough, they said in effect. You must watch how you behave toward others, for human discord can reduce life to shambles. Interpersonal relations are not the sum of religion, but religion stops in its tracks if it tries to skirt them. *Yogas* (spiritual techniques) must be prefaced by *yamas* (moral precepts), *dhyana* (meditation) and *prajna* (wisdom) by *sila* (ethical observances). "If you are offering your gift at the altar, and there remember that your brother has something against you, leave your gift there before the altar and go; first be reconciled to your brother, and then come and offer your gift" (Matthew 5:23–24). For "he who does not love his brother whom he has seen, cannot love God whom he has not seen" (I John 4:20).

Hence the Golden Rules of the great religions which we have reaffirmed this week: Christianity's "Do unto others . . ."; Judaism's "What doth the Lord require of thee but to do justice, love mercy . . ."; Jainism's *ahimsa* and *apari-*

graha; Buddhism's *metta* and *karuna,* its "boundless heart toward all beings"; Hinduism's "highest [yogin] who judges pleasure or pain everywhere by the same standard as he applies to himself" (Gita, VI, 32); Islam's man who "gives his wealth . . . to kinsfolk and to orphans and to the needy and the wayfarer . . . who sets slaves free . . . and payeth the poor due"; Sikhism's "humility to serve"; Confucius' human-hearted *jen.* These counsels to concern for the well-being of others have been the glory of the religions during their axial periods.

3. This brings us to the third great period in human history. I shall call it simply the Modern Age and mark it as having been inaugurated by the rise of modern science in the seventeenth century and the Enlightenment in the eighteenth. The Modern Age differs from its predecessors in seeing social structures as malleable. In previous ages, institutions—family systems, caste and class, feudalism, kingship, chief and emperor—were regarded in much the way we regard the laws of nature; they were ingrained in the nature of things. Now they are recognized as contingent, and by the same token fallible. The corollary is immense. For if society *can* be changed, it often *should* be changed, in which case its members are responsible for seeing to it that it is changed.

Obviously this new perspective enlarges the scope of ethics enormously. Whereas religion's ethical dimension was minimal in the Archaic Period and personal in the Axial Period, today it has become both personal and social, both individual and collective. For to repeat: if social structures can be good or evil and are subject to human volition, people are responsible for their quality.

II

Against the backdrop of these three stages of human history the question of religious relevance becomes more manageable. What makes religion relevant depends on the age in question. Archaic religion was relevant without containing much in the way of ethics at all, for ethics was not then a pressing problem. But if religion had idled ethically in the Axial Period when ethics had become a problem, it would have lost step with relevance and disappeared.

Similarly today, social ethics having emerged as a new human responsibility, if religion defaults on this responsibility it will lose the relevance it has thus far enjoyed. Personal kindness is no longer enough. Institutions affect human well-being no less than do inter-personal relations. This being so, enlightened compassion calls for social responsibility as much as for face-to-face goodwill.

Item: It is now an established fact that if a child does not get a certain minimum of protein before the age of six he or she will be mentally deficient for the rest of life. In Calcutta (where I am writing this) 100,000 inhabitants have no homes but the streets, where gutters serve as bathrooms and sidewalk corners are at once bedrooms for human beings and stables for beasts. Here in this Calcutta where "Above the packed and pestilent town / Death looks down" no amount of personal kindness is going to insure that all children will receive the protein they need if for no other reason than that most of the persons who are in a position to see to it that they do live geographically removed. Direct, face-to-face kindness (the "cup of water given in my name") won't solve the problem, but indirect, organized institutional kindness (UNICEF, or Save the Children Federation, or more equitable trade agreements) might.

Item: It took all of human history up to the middle of this century to develop an economy—that of the United States—capable of growing at the rate of 2½% per annum. Such a growth rate, if sustained, would enable children to be roughly twice as wealthy as their parents. Less than twenty years separate us from 1950, and already two economies (the West German and the Japanese) are pushing 10% per annum growth. If economies sustain this order of growth, children stand to be roughly six times richer than their parents and thirty-six times richer than their grandparents. These figures point up the fact that after capital accumulation reaches take-off momentum it increases exponentially. This places nations that take off early at an enormous advantage; they leave other nations not just behind but increasingly behind. The gap between them and less developed nations widens. The consequence is that if events proceed on present course, the world is going to become in the remainder of our century even more unbalanced in wealth and power than it is already. As the population explosion is centering in the "have not" nations, the "have" nations will represent a decreasing proportion of the world's population while possessing an increasing proportion of the world's wealth and power. Pointing as this does towards a world composed of islands of affluence off a mainland of misery, the situation is neither just nor healthy.

Item: Ten years ago it came clearly to view that for the first time in human history enough metabolic and mechanical energy is available to provide high standards of living for everyone in North America almost immediately and everyone in the world within forty years despite the population explosion. All that stands between us and such universal affluence is invention of the social institutions needed to effect the requisite distribution.

In a way nothing is new here for human well-being has always been affected by its social matrix. The novelty is that, brought to the realization that social institutions are to an appreciable extent humanly contrived, we now acknowledge our partial responsibility for them. We have reached the point in history where we see that to be indifferent to social institutions is to be indifferent to human life.

Not that religion should be converted into social action. Religion must be socially responsible without equating itself with such responsibility. Moreover, it should engage society in a specific way. These qualifications are subtle, but they are important—sufficiently so as to occupy us for the balance of this statement.

III

Let me recast in slightly different terms the three dimensions of religion which historically have appeared successively. Archaic Religion did not focus on humanity, individually or collectively, at all. It looked beyond the human, to divine metaphysical realities from which humanity derived and in which it remained grounded. Religion anchored the current generation in those timeless realities through rituals which (as was noted) linked finite, ephemeral human acts to heroic paradigms that gave them enduring substance and meaning. It was as if its rituals and their attendant myths plugged human doings into timeless templates that charged them with significance and exempted them from time's decay. In subsequent ages, religion articulated this eternal tie explicitly; it spoke (and continues to speak) of immortality, and of anchoring life in the divine presence and the Eternal Now. The move, though, is the same. It counters time's vicissitudes by binding us to the eternal.

Axial Religion added interpersonal concerns to religion's original Archaic agenda, and nurtured conscience, compassion, self-knowledge, and forgiveness. In adding social responsibility to these two preceding agendas, Modern Religion effects a third extension. But it must be an extension, not a replacement—everything turns on this difference. If in the Axial Period religion had relinquished its eternal concerns when it picked up on love of neighbor, it would have cashed in religion for ethics. It did not, of course, do this; statements like "We love, because he first loved us" (I John 4:19) and "It is not for the love of creatures that creatures are dear, but for the love of the Soul in creatures that creatures are dear" (Bhidad-Aranyaka Upanishad, II, 4) make clear that the ethics of Axial Religion was in direct touch with its religious source. Whether the social thrust of Modern Religion is genuinely religious or only seemingly so, being in actuality indistinguishable from secular social action, depends on whether it represents an extension of religion's prior, transcendent-and-interpersonal concerns—love of God and love of neighbor, respectively—or has cut these lifelines.

Tracing our steps backwards through these three concerns, religion would no longer be religion if it attended only to society, for to do so would contradict its conception of the human self. A perfect society (if that notion makes sense) would not produce perfect selves, for the sufficient reason that human worth cannot be bestowed: it must be achieved, because our inner, self-creating, volitional pole is too much a part of our nature to allow us to be manipulated: we are not automata. Given our vulnerability, external circumstances can crush us, which is why organized religions must do what they can to prevent this from happening; but the opposite does not pertain. Circumstances, however well contrived, cannot fulfill us because (to repeat) fulfillment cannot be conferred. By providing food, controlling temperature, and introducing anodynes if need be, comfort can be bestowed, but not nobility, or even happiness; these must be won individually. Being aware of this fact, religion can never rest its case with doing things for other people. Working on oneself—the cleansing of the inward parts—is always part of its agenda. (We have the dictum that it is never possible to do as much for others as one can do for oneself, namely save one's own soul. The Zen version is earthier: everyone must perform one's own toilet.) Neither the agents of social action nor its beneficiaries are exempt from this stricture.

This is the point of Whitehead's definition of religion as what one does with one's own solitariness, and why Kierkegaard gave such attention to human subjectivity. Because this inner, Archimedean point provides the springboard for both of religion's subsequent extensions—into Axial Religion's interpersonal *karuna* (compassion) and *caritas* as defined by St. Paul in First Corinthians 13, and into Modern Religion's further extension into social ethics—we can turn to this springboard directly. Thus far I have described it as focused on time and eternity, but other issues get drawn in; they are elusive, but terribly real. In earlier times we could (in the West) have named the transcendent or eternal focus of religion which we encounter in the depths of our own inwardness "God," but in our century the contours of that word have blurred, beyond which stands the complicating fact that it has no exact equivalent in Afro-Asian faiths. Archaic, eternal religion is obsessed with "why" questions, beginning with why something exists rather than nothing. It deals with the individual's stance toward the world, whether s/he feels at home in it or alienated from it—the ways s/he belongs to it and does not belong to it but is separate from and stands over against it, pointing thereby to an ultimate beyond it. Eternal religion grapples with the failure that in one form or another visits everyone—how we can live with ourselves and feel acceptable when in so many ways we know that we are not. Its root concern is (as I have said) in some way with time: how everything can matter, as we feel in some sense it does, when in the long run it would appear that nothing matters. Running throughout is the question of meaning; how life can be meaningful when so much of it reads like an idiot's tale. Eternal religion knows that there are no discursive answers to these questions. It ranges time and space for insight— *prajna*, vision, a revelation which, bypassing words, will disclose directly why we exist and why the world is the way it is, in much the same way that loving explains why we are male and female.

IV

Even Marxists now concede that "faith for the Christian (and by implications for Buddhists, Hindus, and the rest) can be a stimulus for social commitment," a marked qualification of their original perception of religion as the opiate of the people. It would be pleasant to think that religion's transcendent and interpersonal dimensions protect it against the special dangers to which social programs are heir—fanaticism, projection, means-ends casuistry, and discouragement—but nothing turns on this. With such safeguards or without them, religion must now address the world.

Its social efforts differ from those of secularists primarily in their interpersonal, transcendent roots, but there is another difference: religion's guiding social goal must be general. Images of a new heaven and a new earth, of lions lying down with lambs, of messiahs and *maitreyas* and swords beaten into plowshares are vague, but in this case savingly vague. For sharpened much further they become ideologies. Ideologies have their uses, but sooner or later all are surprised by history. One or another may merit qualified support at a given moment, but to become tied to any would be to lose the freedom and flexibility religion needs if its social voice is to be timelessly contemporary. Probably no social goal more specific than that every human being—child of God in theistic idiom—should have an equal chance at life's opportunities deserves unqualified religious endorsement.

Though I have argued that religion must now include all three of the components enumerated, it would be foolish to contend that everyone should attend to them equally. People are irreducibly different; in religion this makes for priests and prophets, for hermits and householders. It is even appropriate that there be sects that highlight the components differently, as did Confucianism, Taoism, and Buddhism in traditional China. But in a tradition or culture as a whole the three should be reasonably balanced.

V

I have argued two theses: to remain relevant, religion must become socially involved; to remain religious, such involvement must retain ties with religion's earlier concerns. It happens that with respect to these theses, East and West have, today, complementing strengths and weaknesses. When in May, 1968, the *Ceylon Daily News* quoted the eminent Buddhist authority Dr. Walpola Rahula as asserting that development of a sustaining economy for all of the people is as much a religious duty as any other, and that "cultivating a farm properly is better than building many temples," it showed that Asian religions are not unmindful of the need to involve themselves deeply in their adherents' struggle to pull themselves out of the straightjacket of hunger, underemployment, and indebtedness. Throughout Asia swamis, monks, and lay people are changing the image of Hinduism and Buddhism. Religious leaders of many stripes write tracts on problems of modernization, encouraging lay people and fellow leaders alike to participate in economic and social development. In much of Asia we seem to be witnessing something like a Protestant Reformation in its Weberian sense.

If Max Weber were living today, he would have to revise his judgment of the Asian religions; he would find "worldly asceticism" beginning to operate in them too to break barriers to economic, social, and political modernization. But the qualifying phrase "beginning to operate" is important. By virtue of their strong prophetic heritage and even more because industrialization has shown them how much society *can* be changed, Western religions can still help Afro-Asian faiths to see the necessity of social participation. Meanwhile Asian religions can alert those of the West to the danger that threatens *them,* the danger of focusing exclusively on society, neglecting religion's interpersonal, transcendent roots, and becoming in consequence unrelievedly secular. In "Up to Our Steeple in Politics," two ministers chide their fellow Christians for swallowing the prevailing American assumption that "the political order . . . is the *only* source and authority to which we can and ought to repair for relief from what ails us. . . . Politics has become *the* end. We have been gulled into believing that whatever ails us . . . can be cured exclusively by political and social nostrums."

"If there be East and West / It is not wisdom," sang that delightful Tibetan saint Milarepa. In view of what East has to learn from West today about religious *relevance,* and West from East about *religious* relevance, his words acquire new meaning.

HISTORICAL UPDATE

In the four decades since this essay was written, the fate of our planet has emerged as yet another human responsibility, its newest frontier. Consequently, the picture that was sketched above should now be emended to read as follows: Religion began in the individual's direct relationship with the transhistorical and ultimate—God by whatsoever name. From this inviolate starting point and continuing center, it has proceeded to shoulder, successively, concern for interpersonal relations and society's institutions and structures. To live up to its calling, it must now add to these agendas, concern for other species and life's sustaining environment.

BOOK FOUR

The Big Picture

17

Educating the Intellect

On Opening the Eye of the Heart

The topic I wish to reflect on in this essay takes the form of a question. Is there a faculty of knowing that has not evolved from our sensory equipment but instead precedes and empowers the senses while doing much more? My *conclusion* is that there is such an organ. I shall begin by calling it the Eye of the Heart; but then, building on the metaphors I rely on in Section I, I shall shift in Section II to the abstractions of philosophy where I will call the organ the Intellect. There are many reasons why it is important to recognize the Intellect, but I will concentrate on one. The Intellect, or the Eye of the Heart, accomplishes what Mark Taylor tells us no modern epistemology has been able to do. It enables us to get from the knowing subject to its object, from the epistemic subject that *knows* to the object *that* it knows. Modern epistemology's inability to effect this splice accounts for a great deal of the confusion of our time, so the stakes are high; whether we rise to them is another matter. Procedurally, each of the three key terms in my title—Education, Intellect, and the Eye of the Heart—will be allotted a section in my paper, in reverse order.

I. THE EYE OF THE HEART

References to an Invisible Eye that complements our corporeal eyes are widespread in "the wisdom traditions"—my phrase for the major religions in their traditional, sapiential strands; the phrase distinguishes those strands from their institutional, scientific, and sociological involvements. Plato speaks of the Eye of the Soul that "outshines ten thousand [corporeal] eyes," and the Tibetans of opening the Third Eye. In Indian philosophy, Nyaya recognizes *pratyakṣa* as a *pramāṇa* (instrument of knowing) which enables seers to see transcendental realities. Last year a Taoist master from Taiwan sought me out to open my Eye of the Tao, my *shin meng,* or *tsung yang fa mung.* Both Matthew and Luke speak of a Single Eye which lights the whole body like a lamp and without which "how great is the darkness!" (Matt. 6:22–23).

What is this Eye in question, for which I shall use the Sufis' designation, Eye of the Heart? What Heart is referred to? Why does it have an Eye, and why do we need to open it?

It goes without saying that this Heart is not the physical organ that pumps blood; nor is it the seat of our sentiments, the faculty that experiences anguish and joy. Rather, it is the seat of knowledge. There is such a thing as heart knowledge. In the *Upanishads,* as in the Islamic tradition and elsewhere, the seat of knowledge is located in the heart, not the mind. In Chinese, the character for heart *(hsin)* doubles for both mind and heart but is literally heart. In contrast with modernity, which situates knowing in the mind and brain, sacred traditions identify knowing, particularly essential knowing, with the heart. They consider the Heart—the incorporeal heart of which the physical heart is a material prolongation or extension—to be a distinct instrument of knowing that exists as a part of the inclusive anatomy of the human self: physical, psychological, and spiritual. The reason that all wisdom traditions speak of the Heart is that there *is,* I am arguing, such a faculty or organ which constitutes the seat and center of the human state. It is central because it is directly joined to the Center of Reality itself. It is because of the centrality of the heart for the human organism—it sends forth lifegiving blood and receives it back to clean it—that tradition speaks of the Eye of the *Heart,* and not, say, of the liver or the lungs. The corporeal heart animates our physical body in the way the Heart whose Eye we are addressing animates our knowing and our metaphysical selves generally.

Having noted the symbolic appropriateness of the heart, why the eye? Why do traditions speak of the Eye of the Heart and not some other organ? Why not the ear of the heart, or the tongue of the heart? That is because of the scope that vision commands. We can taste and touch only what contacts our bodies. Smell reaches beyond our bodies, and hearing reaches farther still, but we can only see the stars, not smell or hear them. Vision sweeps out the vastest world our senses disclose, and this is why Hindus speak of the Eye of Shiva and the Third Eye, not the ear of Shiva or the third ear.

Having noted the metaphorical appropriateness of "eye" and "heart," I must now say what these are metaphors *for.* What is the traditions' view of the human self that receives these references?

In that view the self is not a simple dualism—a body here and a mind that floats somehow above it. Rather, there are "layers" of body, of which the physical (or gross) body is the cover. (The Hindu scheme is the most explicit about this, with its doctrine of the Five Sheaths and Three Bodies.) All of these bodies have their own centers. We oversimplify disastrously when we think that we are inwardly minds, and outwardly the bodies that physicians deal with. Descartes's simplistic mind/body dualism went a long way toward removing God and spirit from our immediate awareness, and it did so by removing the intermediate spaces in the human self. These intermediate spaces have no meaning to moderns. Ironically, at the very moment that Descartes was erasing intermediate psychic spaces with his dualism, Paracelsus and others in his camp were speaking of astral bodies and the like; Descartes's disjunction couldn't dispel the human intuition that there *are* things besides mind and matter. In our own century, this intuition has spawned research on parapsychology and all kinds of New Age interest in shamanism, channelling, and the paranormal generally. The interest is commendable, but it is lost in the confusion of trying to traverse the labyrinthine soul without a roadmap. The current interest in subtle and astral bodies, along with energies like *ch'i* and *kundalini,* is really an attempt to rediscover in this century regions of the self that the wisdom traditions took note of.

If we pick up with the Hindu formulation because of its explicitness, the rough account is this: animating the gross body, which we can see and touch and weigh, is the subtle body which has its own senses, the *indriyas,* which hear and see and touch and taste metaphysical, invisible realities. All scriptures allude to these occult senses; a nineteenth-century Persian Sufi writes: "Open the Eye of thine Heart so as to see the world of the Spirit" (Hatif Isfahani). In the semitic traditions, God speaks. If we think of physical speech as involving airwaves and vocal cords, this is metaphorical; but in its own domain, on its own ontological plane, it is literal. If there were nothing in us which on the inner and esoteric level corresponds to physical speech and hearing, there would be no possibility of the divine communicating to us. The references to these corresponding senses in the various scriptures imply the existence of inner organs to which our physical sense organs correspond by emanational extension. There is metaphysical seeing—intuitive discernment is my favorite phrase for it—and the Eye of the Heart is the invisible, and presumably immaterial, faculty that effects that seeing.

Why, though, is that Eye depicted as single? Our bodies have two eyes; why shouldn't there be two Eyes of the Heart? In the center of Shiva's forehead, why is there only a single jewel?

The answer is: Our physical eyes are multiple because the physical world they open onto is multiple; in Chinese idiom it is the realm of the ten thousand things. To comprehend the world's plurality, our eyes too must be plural. But that plurality is kept to a minimum—two—because existentially that's the way the world comes to us or "at us." It splits on every hand into yin/yang disjunctions:

subject and object, good and evil, self and other. When Adam and Eve ate the forbidden apple, "the [significantly plural] *eyes* of both were opened" (Gen. 3:7) and the world split, concomitantly, in two—into the knowledge of good and evil. Spirit must heal that rift, and with it all other dualities, not by erasing them but by pulling them together in the way the hand gathers its multiple fingers into the singularity of hand. Because spirit's vocation is, precisely, to transcend dualities, its eye *must* be one. It looks toward the shining point where things transgress their separateness and all lines intersect.

Implied, here, is the answer to why the Eye of the Heart must be opened and not left shut. In the long run we are impelled to open it because the world we ultimately belong to is the world of oneness, and our final felicity, our *ānanda,* the peace that we seek and cannot be happy without, cannot be had unless duality is transcended. Our entire life is the attempt to overcome separation, and the whole tragedy of life springs from our failure to accomplish that task. All human love is a partial overcoming of duality, and all pain of separation is duality seen at close range. Internally, there is no happiness unless we overcome the barrier that separates us from our own selves. Even when I say "I," I am not fully myself, for I am not attuned to the deepest part of myself that is more *than* myself. This may sound abstract, but sooner or later, in one way or another, we must all be brought to this truth because of who we are. That some of us are materialists and atheists makes no difference. Because we are all human, consciously or unconsciously we all seek to overcome the separation between us and the God who is the true object of our desire, whether we envision that God as within us or without. Happy or unhappy as the case may be, the ultimate object of our desire is to be joined to the Reality for which we were created.

The wisdom traditions tell us *how* to open the Eye of the Heart, but I will not go into their instructions which are mainly versions of Hinduism's four yogas. Instead, I shall conclude this section by considering a final question. Why must the Eye of the Heart be opened instead of being open to begin with? Our physical eyes are open from birth. Why isn't the Eye of the Heart?

However we interpret their mythologies, the mainstream answer of the traditions runs something like this:

The fact that we talk about sight suggests that we have not always been blind. The fact that we seek peace though we live in a world full of war means that the experience of peace could not have been totally alien to us. This suggests that the fact that the Eye of the Heart is cited, independently, in so many traditions means that it is a human possibility that it be open. Most, if not all, of the traditions have an explanation for why the eye has closed. It has to do with the flow of time—what the Hindus would call the circling of the cosmic cycles. We are not, today, fully ourselves. We are not what we should be because we live at a particular cosmic moment that doesn't happen to be the Golden Age. The mark of the

Golden Age—the time of Eden, the *krita yuga,* or the Age of the Grand Harmony that Confucius looked back to—was that the Eye of the Heart was then open. People then didn't need revelations or religion. Adam walked directly with God. In an Islamic gloss on that story, the Ninety-nine Beautiful Names, now reserved for Allah, applied originally to Adam as well. He had direct knowledge of things, and was his own prophet. Comparably in the Hindu tradition: in the Vedic Age no special *rishis* were needed, for everyone's Eye was open. But time occasions distancing from the divine source, so gradually the Eye of the Heart closes.

This, roughly, is how the doctrine of the Eye of the Heart shapes up—most directly in Sufism, but with strong analogies in the wisdom traditions generally. I turn now to relate that concept to the second substantive term in my title, the Intellect. Whereas this section has employed the language of religion, fixing on sensible objects—eyes and hearts—to point them toward deeper intangible realities, my next section will ride the momentum thus gained, but will wax philosophical. The intent will be to use abstract language to describe the Eye of the Heart more precisely.

II. THE INTELLECT

In using "Intellect" as the philosophical name for our object, I think of myself as retrieving (on balance) the view of the human mind that preceded the rise of modern science and its pivotal representative, Descartes. In that earlier view, the mind's central faculty was called *nous* in Greek, and *intellectus* in Latin. (Vedanta's *buddhi* and the Buddhist *prajñā* could easily be included.) As I am using broad strokes, I shall not go into the differences between Plato's, Aristotle's, and Plotinus's concepts of *nous,* or how those differences shook down into the *intellectus* of Saint Thomas and the scholastics. When modernity started to think of the mind differently, it lost interest in the Intellect to the point where now it doesn't even warrant an entry in the five-volume *Dictionary of the History of Ideas* (the *history* of ideas!) or its index either. So I shall begin from scratch. Working my way back from the way we now think of the mind, I shall argue that we overlook things that our predecessors had better in view. The ones that concern me coalesce, as I have said, in their notion of Intellect.

We can begin with a mental capacity that baffles current epistemologists completely, one that differs markedly from reason. Reason performs logical operations on information that is in full view and can be described or defined. Through and through, though, we find that our understanding is floated and furthered by operations that are mysterious because all that we seem able to know about them is that we have no idea as to how they work. We have hunches that pay off. Or we find that we know what to do in complicated situations without being able to explain exactly *how* we know. This ability is unconscious, yet it enables us to perform enormously complicated tasks, from reading and writing to farming and composing music. Expertise is coming to be recognized as more intuitive than cognitive psychologists had supposed. These students of behavior and learning are finding that when faced with exceptionally subtle tasks, people who "feel" or intuit their ways through them are more creative than those who consciously try to think their way through the situations. This explains why computer programmers no less than psychologists have had trouble getting the experts to articulate the rules they follow. The experts do not follow rules. Workers in artificial intelligence are coming to see that "human intelligence can never be replaced with machine intelligence because we are not ourselves 'thinking machines.' Each of us has, and uses every day, a power of intuitive intelligence that enables us to understand, to speak, and to cope skillfully with our everyday environment." Somehow it summarizes everything we have ever experienced and done, and enables that summary to shape our present decisions. Programmers cannot instruct their machines to do this because no one has the slightest idea how we ourselves do it.

An example that I have cited before bears repeating because it is so remarkable. Japanese chicken sexers are able to decide with 99 percent accuracy the sex of a chick, even though the female and male genitalia of young chicks are ostensibly indistinguishable. No analytic approach to learning the art could ever approach such accuracy. Aspiring chicken sexers learn only by looking over the shoulders of experienced workers, who cannot explain how they themselves do it.

We find this example startling, but the talent it shocks us into noticing is one that we all possess. Thus far I have stayed with its importance for thinking, but it orders our practical life as well via a virtue we can call prudence. Prudence is a subliminally mobile but focused concentration which again (as in cognition) works for us instinctively, without our knowing how it works or even thinking of it as a distinct operation. Functioning in something of the manner of a hidden gyroscope it monitors our inclinations, directing our "yeses" and our "nos," those two magical words of the will. To do this, it spins no system of ideas. Instead, it synthesizes all we have learned and brings this synthesis to every decision we make. In doing so it provides dozens of answers to dozens of questions, and—because it gives no evidence of caring about their mutual agreement—conveys the impression that each particular answer is absolutely *ad hoc*. This gives it an air of practical poetry, for each particular answer arises spontaneously and ingenuously, while being for the most part appropriate and, for the moment in question, conclusive. Its spontaneity is only seeming, however, for if we reflect on the matter we find that all its *ad hoc* answers arise from a whole that directs them and makes them appropriate; its activities are prodigiously married. The integral truth of our being from which it springs envelops and inspires everything we consciously and even unconsciously do, giving our lives their form and style and seeing to it that each action and decision reflect that style.

I propose that we use the practical and cognitive power I have been pointing to as our entree to the intellect. In this first formulation, we can characterize it as an invisible and mysterious X—invisible because it attaches to no anatomical organ; mysterious because we don't know how it works—that powers and directs our conscious thoughts and actions.

In a way, nothing that I have thus far said is news. For some time Michael Polanyi, evolutionary biologists, and developmental psychologists have been talking about cognitive underpinnings that are indispensable to our knowing but which operate unconsciously. The Intellect, though, differs from "tacit knowing" of this sort in a decisive respect. All the above-mentioned investigators assume that mental operations that we can't explain ride the wave of simpler operations that are rationally explicable. In short, they assume that the more derives from the less. I, for my part, am positing the opposite: that the Intellect is prior to, and the driving power of, all other modes of knowing. To make the difference plain, I shall summarize the evolutionary hypothesis that cognitive psychology works with.

From a "population" of stimulus-response pairs, born of random responses to a given stimulus, the nervous system reinforces pairs that are adaptive. This "selects" them by increasing the probability that they will recur while their maladaptive or merely neutral brethren suffer "extinction" by failing to reproduce. The analogy with Darwinism is very strong, very satisfying, and very familiar. It is equally strong in the so-called dry, as opposed to biological or wet, approach to the study of learning and intelligence, the science of artificial intelligence which works with "thinking machines." Problem-solving computer programs are designed to generate and test. At a given point or points, the program sets up generating and testing units. The generating unit invents candidates for the problem's solution and transmits them to the testing unit, which accepts or rejects them on the basis of stored criteria. This again is like natural selection, as Herbert Simon points out. Artificial intelligence and cognitive psychology work from opposite ends of the scale. Artificial intelligence begins with mechanisms that obviously lack intelligence—magnetic tapes whose segments do or do not conduct electrical currents—and tries to construct intelligence from these, whereas cognitive psychology begins with creatures that obviously have intelligence and tries to work back to neuron firings, nerve reflexes, and selector mechanisms that are as mechanical as computer operations. Forward or backward, though, the object is the same: to derive intelligence from things that do not possess it—or at the very least, things that possess it in lesser degree. For, as Daniel Dennett has written,

> psychology must not of course be question-begging. It must not explain intelligence in terms of intelligence, for instance by assigning responsibility for the existence of intelligence in creatures to the munificence of an intelligent Creator, or by putting clever homunculi at the control panels of the nervous system. If that were the best psychology could do, then psychology could not do the job assigned to it.

What I am seriously suggesting is that, given the way it has set things up, psychology *can't* do the job that it has assigned itself. One phenomenon that won't fit its model—Aldous Huxley called my attention to it during the semester that he was visiting professor at the Massachusetts Institute of Technology—is the talking parrot.

What goes on when a parrot imitates the voice of its owner, or the bark of a dog, or human laughter? Presumably, it has some sort of conscious life. It hears the voice, it hears the bark or the laughter, and presumably, in a way that rudimentarily corresponds to our wish to do something, it wishes to imitate this. But then what happens? When you come to think of it, it is one of the most extraordinary things you can imagine. Something incomparably more intelligent than the parrot itself sets to work and proceeds to activate a series of sound organs that are totally different from those of human beings. People have teeth, a soft palate, and a flat tongue, and the parrot has no teeth, a rough tongue, and a beak. From these, however, it proceeds to organize its absolutely different apparatus to reproduce words and laughter—so exactly that we are very often deceived by it into thinking that what is in fact the parrot talking is the person himself or herself making an utterance. The more we reflect on this, the stranger it is, because obviously in the course of evolutionary history parrots have not been imitating human beings from time immemorial; people arrived after the parrots' adaptive mechanisms were in place. We have here an *ad hoc* piece of intelligent action, carried on by some form of intelligence within the parrot, that cannot be explained by its evolutionary conditioning. This doesn't prove that the Intellect precedes the learning that the developmental model works with, but it leaves the door open to that possibility.

We now have two propositions about the Intellect: (a) it operates subliminally and mysteriously, and (b) it precedes and empowers simpler cognitive components rather than deriving from them. From this base we shall now posit a third feature, (c). It connects us to the world. Working through our sense organs it brings the world to us sensuously, while through the cerebral cortex it enables us to think about the world and reason generally.

This third property is my strongest reason for introducing the Intellect, for anything that holds the hope of removing the wedge that modernity has driven between us and our world deserves attention. I quoted Mark Taylor as saying that no modern epistemology has been able to get from subject to object, and I suspect that this is the root cause of the alienation that so characterizes our age. The failure Taylor points to should not surprise us, for if we begin with Descartes's mind/matter disjunction—which translates into the self/world divide—there's nothing more basic that can unite them. Garbage in, garbage out, as computer programmers say; to hope to arrive at the known after distancing it from the knower categorically is Kafka's cage going in search of a bird. So why accept Descartes's premise to begin with? He had *his* reasons for doing so, but as they were historical ones, having to do with the need to create an epistemology that would give free rein to science, and we live in different times that have their own needs, there is no reason why Descartes's needs should shackle us.

Logically, the epistemological issue reduces to this. Aristotle distinguished between reason (which grasps universals) and sensation (which locks into the world's particulars), both of which faculties are in direct touch with the world. Because the universals in the knowing soul are the same as those in the object known, "actual knowledge is identical with its object" (*De Anima* 430.20). Descartes replaced Aristotle's reason/sensation distinction with the distinction between consciousness, which resides within us, and the material world, which lacks consciousness and is outside our consciousness. This distinction has led to an epistemic impasse (inability to get from the knower to the known) and human alienation (our sense of being adrift in an alien universe). Why, then, should we continue to let it replace the notion of mind that preceded it? My answer, of course, is that we should *not* let it do so, but as my argument turns as much on Cartesian failures as on Aristotelian successes, I will cite those failures and not just assert their existence.

Epistemic Impasse

If we try to connect an animal in the wilds to its environment via what textbooks say about the physiology of perception, we encounter so many inexplicable gaps that rationally we would have to conclude that the animal does not perceive its world at all. This is the psychological outworking of philosophy's inability to bridge Descartes's mind/matter divide. Yet all the while the animal behaves as if it perceives the world; it proceeds toward food and shelter almost unerringly. With J.J. Gibson's *The Ecological Approach to Visual Perception* pointing the way, animal psychologists are coming to see that they have lost sight of this incontrovertible fact. Trying to account for knowledge as inference from noetic bits does not work. We must begin the other way around, Gibson insists: with the recognition that there is a world out there (realism), and that animals are oriented to it.

Human Alienation

I will let Richard Rorty tell the story.

> The Cartesian change from mind-as-reason to mind-as-inner-arena [marked] the triumph of the quest for certainty over the quest for wisdom. [It opened] the way for philosophers either to attain the rigor of the mathematician or the mathematical physicist, or to explain the appearance of rigor in these fields, rather than to help people attain peace of mind. Science, rather than living, became philosophy's subject, and epistemology its center.

It is dissatisfaction with this denouement that drives me back to pre-Cartesian views of the mind which, in their most impressive instances, always centered in the Intellect. None of the different ways that *nous* was nuanced doubt that it locks into world; no Kantian unknowable *noumena* trouble their worlds. Hilary Armstrong characterizes Plotinus's Intellect as "the level of intuitive thought that is identical with its object and does not see it as in some sense external." This is virtually identical with Aristotle's position as earlier quoted.

I ask one final question here: Is the Intellect divine?

Authorities differ somewhat on this question. For Alexander the Aphrodisian and Ibn Sina, Aristotle's Agent Intellect is the Deity communicating itself to individuals through the Affectable Intellect which belongs to individual souls only. For Ibn Rushd, both Agent and Affectable Intellects are separate from individual souls and are alike in all souls, but are less than God. For Thomas Aquinas, the Intellect in both its active and passive aspects belongs to individual souls.

We can leave them to these differences. All of the philosophers mentioned would accept Eckhart's minimal formulation that "there is something in the soul *(aliquid est in anima)* which is uncreated and uncreatable"; which something, of course, is God, God being the only reality that is not created. That God is omniscient and we are not does not refute Eckhart, who does not say our souls are pure Intellect, or Intellect only. Eckhart's wording leaves room for other components of the soul to obscure the Intellect, or crowd it into a corner in the way the Vedantic *kosa* —sheaths that overlay the Ātman—explicitly assert.

I have for the most part steered away from technicalities concerning the Intellect, but a letter from a philosopher at the University of Iowa, James Duerlinger, contains a conclusion reached about Aristotle's view that is interesting enough to quote, even though I cannot pursue it.

> Philosophers have reconstructed Aristotle's active mind into a force that abstracts universals from particulars so that the passive mind can have objects. Far from the truth. The active mind is the divine activity of pure self-knowledge present in our souls, producing in them, as out of soul-stuff, likenesses of itself, these likenesses being our own minds, our organs of thought, which are soul-stuff made capable of thinking themselves—gaining self-knowledge, when they become likenesses of the forms of sensible things. Our minds are images of the divine mind, but which, unlike it (which thinks itself per se) think themselves per accidens. In other words, when we think of the forms of things we imitate the divine self-creation—we achieve the divine life as far as our minds are capable. The divine activity produces the form of our minds, whose matter is the soul-stuff Aristotle calls the affectable/passive mind; and it is the very same activity for the sake of which there is eternal motion in the heavens, as laid out in *Metaphysics*.

III. EDUCATION

"If the sun and moon should doubt, / They'd immediately go out," Blake wrote. Doubting the Intellect, we, comparably, have caused *it* to "go out"; which is to say, drop from our attention. This explains why I have left little room for this closing section on education. There's little point in talking about educating the Intellect if we don't believe that it exists. The first order of business is to challenge the assumption that it doesn't exist.

Having done that, I shall enter a single point on its education; it relates to education for virtue. An important component of traditional epistemology was its concept of *adequatio*. Distinct kinds of objects call for distinct faculties to register them, ones that are adequate for their recognition. The skin can fathom the sun's warmth, but not its luminosity. Sense organs can register the solidity of a book and how the words on its pages appear, but minds are needed to comprehend the words' meanings.

It follows that if there are spiritual objects, spiritual faculties of discernment will be required to take note of them. In human beings, this faculty is the Intellect. It came as something of a shock to me to realize as I began this concluding section of my paper that I had completed everything I had intended to say about the Intellect without as much as mentioning its spiritual capacities. That's shocking, but it's explainable. My strategy was to approach the Intellect by way of epistemology, and current epistemology doesn't recognize spirit. And the reason that it doesn't is clear. Faculties for knowing presuppose realities they might know, and there is no general agreement today that spiritual realities exist, much less what they might be. So accounts of knowing proceed without them.

Not long ago things were different. The colleges in this country were founded to train ministers; and from England we have the anecdote of the student at Balliol College who, on confiding to his don (Benjamin Jowett) that he had lost his faith in God, was ordered to find it before breakfast the next morning. Page Smith's book *Killing the Spirit: Higher Education in America* traces the course of events since then; and another Smith—that redoubtable watchdog, Wilfred Cantwell Smith—picked up the fact that in Harvard University's latest book-length statement of aims for undergraduate education the word "truth" doesn't appear.

These, though, are thoughts for another season; songs—or dirges?—for another day.

18

Do Drugs Have
Religious Import?

For several years following my initiation, entheogens were the center of my reflective and social life. Reflectively, to have become overnight a visionary—one who not merely believes in the existence of a more momentous world than this one but who has actually visited it—was no small matter. How could what felt like an epochal change in my life have been crowded into a few hours and occasioned by a chemical? I knew how my MIT colleagues—Hans-Lukas Teuber, its renowned experimental psychologist, and its equally legendary professor of microbiology, Jerome Lettvin—would answer that question. The mescaline had scrambled the synapses in the nerve connections of my brain, creating irregular associations between its centers for vision, alarm, euphoria, and excitement, et cetera, et cetera—we get the idea. I was not persuaded. Still, if chemistry does not tell the whole story, what is that story? And what part do chemicals, replacing angels as divine intermediaries, play in it?

Questions like these assaulted me with an urgency that reconstructed my social life. Family and friends remained in place, but beyond those I sought out associates who shared my compulsion to talk about and understand our shared secret. This is the stuff of which churches are made, and within the Harvard Project an ad hoc "church" emerged. Its glue was our resistance to epiphenomenal, reductionistic explanations of our revelations, and our certainty—equal to that of Huxley, Hofmann, Wasson, and William James, the giants in whose footsteps we thought of ourselves as walking—that it was impossible to close our accounts with reality without taking these revelations into consideration. What to make of the entheogens was the question, and we lived for the times when, like Socrates and his friends, we could hang out together to talk.

The Harvard Project was hospitable. Open-ended, it wanted to explore the effects of psychoactive chemicals in all promising directions, so our "church" had its blessing and benefactions. Once every month or so we gathered to take our sacramental in a vaguely ritualistic context—incense, candles, favorite poems, passages from sacred texts, and spontaneous inputs in the style of Quaker meetings. In between those "services" we gathered to talk philosophically. We were but one satellite in Leary's project, which served as an umbrella under which those of its subjects who wanted to follow up on their experiences clustered and networked. An organization sprang up, the International Federation for Internal Freedom, which for ten years published a journal, the Psychedelic Review. It attracted some notable contributors, among them Robert Graves, Aldous Huxley, Albert Hofmann, and Gordon Wasson.

Lisa Bieberman and Peter John (who went on to become a Methodist minister) deserve to be mentioned for holding our "church" together; without pay or public recognition, they gave virtually their full time to it. Readers of this book may recognize the names of several other members of our group for the parts they played in the history of the entheogens. Walter Houston Clark, professor of the psychology of religion at Andover-Newton Theological Seminary, became the most ardent crusader for the substances, arguing that they were the only things in sight that could restore the experiential component to the mainstream churches, without which they would not survive. Walter Pahnke's Good Friday Experiment is the subject of chapter 7 in this book; it is difficult to imagine how the history of the entheogens might have been different had he not died in a scuba-diving accident, for he brought to his serious involvement with mysticism the scientific training of a medical doctor and his intention to devote his career to studying the resources of chemicals for religion. Paul Lee, who at the time was Paul Tillich's teaching assistant at Harvard, went on to teach philosophy at the University of California, Santa Cruz, before leaving academia to devote himself full-time to studying herbs.

The essay that follows sets forth the conclusions I reached about the entheogens in the course of the three years that I was involved with the Harvard Project. Titled "Do Drugs Have Religious Import?" it appeared in the October 1, 1964, issue of the Journal of Philosophy. I am told that it has been anthologized more times than any other article in that journal, over twenty times to date. I have made a few minor alterations to clarify points that might otherwise be obscure.

———

I. DRUGS AND RELIGION VIEWED HISTORICALLY

In their trial-and-error life explorations, peoples almost everywhere have stumbled upon connections between vegetables (eaten or brewed) and actions (yogic breathing exercises; fast, whirling-dervish dances; self-flagellations) that induce dramatic alterations in consciousness. From the psychopharmacological standpoint we now understand these states to be the products of changes in brain chemistry. From the sociological perspective we see that they tend to be connected in some way with religion. If we discount the wine used in Christian communion services, the instances closest to us in time and space are the Peyote sacrament of the Native American Church and Mexico's two-thousand-year-old tradition of using sacred mushrooms, the latter rendered in Aztec as "God's Flesh," a striking parallel to "the body of our Lord" in the Christian Eucharist. Further away are the *soma* of the Hindus, the *haoma* and hemp of the Zoroastrians, Dionysus the Greek who "everywhere taught men the culture of the vine and the mysteries of his worship and everywhere was accepted as a god," the *benzoin* of Southeast Asia, Zen's tea whose fifth cup purifies and whose sixth "calls to the realm of the immortals," the *pituri* of the Australian aborigines, and probably the mystic *kykeon* that was drunk at the climactic close of the sixth day of the Eleusinian Mysteries. There is no need to extend the list, as a reasonably complete account is given in Philippe de Felice's comprehensive study of the subject, *Poisons Sacrés, Ivresses Divines.*

More interesting than the fact that consciousness-changing devices have been linked with religion is the possibility that they may actually have initiated many of the religious perspectives which, taking root in history, continued after their entheogenic origins were forgotten. Bergson saw the first movement of Hindus and Greeks toward "dynamic religion" as associated with the "divine rapture" found in intoxicating beverages, and more recently Robert Graves, Gordon Wasson, and Alan Watts have suggested that most religions have arisen from such chemically induced theophanies. Mary Barnard is the most explicit proponent of this thesis. "Which was more likely to happen first," she asks; "the spontaneously generated idea of an afterlife in which the disembodied soul, liberated from the restrictions of time and space, experiences eternal bliss, or the accidental discovery of hallucinogenic plants that give a sense of euphoria, dislocate the center of consciousness, and distort time and space, making them balloon outward in greatly expanded vistas?" Her own answer is that "the latter experience might have had an almost explosive effect on the largely dormant minds of men, causing them to think of things they had never thought of before. This, if you like, is direct revelation." Her use of the subjunctive "might" renders this formulation of her answer equivocal, but she concludes her essay on a note that is categorical: "Looking at the matter coldly, unintoxicated and unentranced, I am willing to prophesy that fifty theobotanists working for fifty years would make the current theories concerning the origins of much mythology and theology as out-of-date as pre-Copernican astronomy."

This is an important hypothesis—one which must surely engage the attention of historians of religion for some time to come. But I am content here to forego prophecy and limit myself to the points where the drugs surface in serious religious study.

II. DRUGS AND RELIGION
VIEWED PHENOMENOLOGICALLY

Phenomenology attempts a careful description of human experience. The question that drugs pose for the phenomenology of religion, therefore, is whether the experiences they induce differ from religious experiences reached without them and, if so, how.

Even the Bible notes that substance-altered psychic states bear *some* resemblance to religious ones. Peter had to appeal to a circumstantial point—the early hour of the day—to defend those who were caught up in the Pentecostal experience against the charge that they were merely drunk: "These men are not drunk, as you suppose, since it is only the third hour of the day" (Acts 2:15); and Paul initiates the comparison when he admonishes the Ephesians not to "get drunk with wine, but to be filled with the spirit" (Ephesians 5:18). Are such comparisons, which have counterparts in virtually every religion, superficial? How far can they be pushed?

Not all the way, students of religion have thus far insisted. With respect to the new drugs, Professor R. C. Zaehner has drawn the line emphatically. "The importance of Huxley's *Doors of Perception*," he writes, "is that in it the author clearly makes the claim that what he experienced under the influence of mescaline is closely comparable to a genuine mystical experience. If he is right, the conclusions are alarming." Zaehner thinks that Huxley is not right, but I believe that it is Zaehner who is mistaken.

There are, of course, innumerable drug experiences that have no religious features; they can be sensual as readily as spiritual, trivial as readily as transforming, capricious as readily as sacramental. If there is one point about which every student of psychoactivating agents agrees, it is that there is no such thing as *the* drug experience per se—no experience that the drugs, as it were, secrete. Every experience is a mix of three ingredients: drug, set (the psychological makeup of the individual), and setting (the social and physical environment in which it is taken). But given the right set and setting, the drugs can induce religious experiences that are indistinguishable from such experiences that occur spontaneously. Nor need the sets and settings be exceptional. The way the statistics are currently running, it looks as if from one-fourth to one-third of the general population will have religious experiences if they take certain drugs under naturalistic conditions, meaning conditions in which the researcher supports the subject but does not interfere with the direction the experience takes. Among subjects who have strong religious proclivities, the proportion of those who will have religious experiences jumps to three-fourths. If such subjects take the drugs in religious settings, the percentage soars to nine out of ten.

How do we know that the experiences these people have really are religious? We can begin with the fact that they say they are. The "one-fourth to one-third of the general population" figure is drawn from two sources. Ten months after they had had their experiences, 24 percent of the 194 subjects in a study by the California psychiatrist Oscar Janiger characterized their experiences as having been religious. Thirty-two percent of the seventy-four subjects in Ditman and Hayman's study reported, looking back on their LSD experience, that it looked as if it had been "very much" or "quite a bit" a religious experience; 42 percent checked as true the statement that they "were left with a greater awareness of God, or a higher power, or ultimate reality." The statement that three-fourths of subjects having religious "sets" will have religious experiences comes from the reports of sixty-nine religious professionals who took the drugs while the Harvard project was in progress.

In the absence of (a) a single definition of religious experience generally acceptable to psychologists of religion, and (b) foolproof ways of ascertaining whether actual experiences exemplify any definition, I am not sure there is a better way of telling whether the experiences of the 333 men and women involved in the above studies were religious than by their reports that they seemed so to them. But if more rigorous methods are preferred, they exist; they have been utilized, and they confirm the conviction of the man in the street that drug experiences can indeed be religious. In his doctoral study at Harvard University, Walter Pahnke worked out a typology of religious experience (in this instance, mystical experience) based on classic reports that Walter Stace included in his *Mysticism and Philosophy*. Pahnke then administered psilocybin to fifteen theology professors and students (half of the total population of thirty) in the setting of a Good Friday service. The drug was given in a "double-blind" experiment, meaning that neither Dr. Pahnke nor his subjects knew which fifteen were getting psilocybin and which fifteen received placebos to constitute a control group. Subsequently the subjects' reports of their experiences were rated independently by three former schoolteachers on the degree (strong, moderate, slight, or none) to which each report evinced the nine traits of mystical experience that Stace enumerates. The results showed that "those subjects who received psilocybin experienced phenomena which were indistinguishable from, if not identical with, the categories defined by our typology of mysticism."

With the thought that the reader might like to test his or her own powers of discernment on the question being considered, I insert here a simple test I gave to members of the Woodrow Wilson Society at Princeton University. I presented them with two accounts of religious experiences, one drug-occasioned, the other not, and asked them to guess which was which.

1

Suddenly I burst into a vast, new, indescribably wonderful universe. Although I am writing this over a year later, the thrill of the surprise and amazement, the awesomeness of the revelation, the engulfment in an overwhelming feeling-wave of gratitude and blessed wonderment, are as fresh, and the memory of the experience is as vivid, as if it had happened five minutes ago. And yet to concoct anything by way of description that would even hint at the magnitude, the sense of ultimate reality . . . this seems such an impossible task. The knowledge which has infused and affected every aspect of my life came instantaneously and with such complete force of certainty that it was impossible, then or since, to doubt its validity.

2

All at once, without warning of any kind, I found myself wrapped in a flame-colored cloud. For an instant I thought of fire . . . the next, I knew that the fire was within myself. Directly afterward there came upon me a sense of exultation, of immense joyousness accompanied or immediately followed by an intellectual illumination impossible to describe. Among other things, I did not merely come to believe, but I saw that the universe is not composed of dead matter, but is, on the contrary, a living Presence; I became conscious in myself of eternal life. . . . I saw that all men are immortal: that the cosmic order is such that without any peradventure all things work together for the good of each and all; that the foundation principle of the world . . . is what we call love, and that the happiness of each and all is in the long run absolutely certain.

On the occasion referred to, twice as many students (46) answered incorrectly as answered correctly (23).

III. DRUGS AND RELIGION
VIEWED PHILOSOPHICALLY

I wish to explore the possibility of validating drug-induced religious experiences on grounds that they come up with the same basic claims about reality that religions always do. To begin with the weakest of all arguments, the argument from authority: William James (whom I class among the religious for his sensibilities) did not discount *his* insights that occurred while his brain chemistry was altered. The paragraph in which he retrospectively evaluates his nitrous oxide experiences has become classic, and I quote it here for its pertinence to the point under consideration.

One conclusion was forced upon my mind at that time, and my impression of its truth has ever since remained unshaken. It is that our normal waking consciousness, rational consciousness as we call it, is but one special type of consciousness, whilst all about it, parted from it by the filmiest of screens, there lie potential forms of consciousness entirely different. We may go through life without suspecting their existence; but apply the requisite stimulus, and at a touch they are there in all their completeness, definite types of mentality which probably somewhere have their field of application and adaptation. No account of the universe in its totality can be final which leaves these other forms of consciousness quite disregarded. How to regard them is the question—for they are so discontinuous with ordinary consciousness. Yet they may determine attitudes though they cannot furnish formulas, and open a region though they fail to give a map. At any rate, they forbid a premature closing of our accounts with reality. Looking back on my own experiences, they all converge toward a kind of insight to which I cannot help ascribing some metaphysical significance. [From *The Varieties of Religious Experience*]

To James's argument I add two arguments that try to provide something by way of reasons. Drug experiences that assume a religious cast tend to have fearful and/or beatific features, and my hypotheses relate to these two features of the experience.

Beginning with the ominous, "fear of the Lord" awe-full feature, I have already registered in the frontispiece of this book Gordon Wasson's account, which (being short) I reenter here. "Ecstasy! In common parlance ecstasy is fun. But ecstasy is not fun. Your very soul is seized and shaken until it tingles. After all, who will choose to feel undiluted awe? The unknowing vulgar abuse the word; we must recapture its full and terrifying sense."

Emotionally the drug experience can be like having forty-foot waves crash over you for several hours while you cling desperately to a life raft which may be swept from under you at any moment. It seems quite possible that such an ordeal, like any experience of a close call, could awaken fundamental sentiments respecting life, death, and destiny, and trigger the "no atheists in foxholes" effect. Similarly, as the subject emerges from the ordeal and realizes that he will not be permanently insane as he had feared, he may experience waves of overwhelming relief and gratitude like those that patients recovering from critical illnesses frequently report. Here is one such report.

It happened on the day when my bed was pushed out of doors to the open gallery of the hospital. I cannot now recall whether the revelation came suddenly or gradually; I only remember finding myself in the very midst of those wonderful moments, beholding life for the first time in all its young intoxication of loveliness, in its unspeakable joy, beauty, and importance. I cannot say exactly what the mysterious change was. I saw no new thing, but I saw all the usual things in a miraculous new light—in what I believe is their true light. I saw for the first time how wildly beautiful and joyous, beyond any words of mine to describe, is the whole of life. Every human being moving across that porch, every sparrow that flew, every branch tossing in the wind, was caught in and was a part of the whole mad ecstasy of loveliness, of joy, of importance, of intoxication of life.

If we do not discount religious intuitions because they are prompted by battle-fields and physical crises; if we regard the latter as "calling us to our senses" more often than they seduce us into delusions, need comparable intuitions be discounted simply because the crises that trigger them are of an inner, psychic variety?

Turning from the fearful to the beatific aspects of the drug experience, some of the latter may be explainable by the hypothesis just stated; that is, they may be occasioned by the relief that attends the sense of escape from high danger. But this hypothesis cannot possibly account for all of the blissful episodes that chemicals occasion for the simple reason that the positive episodes often come first, or to persons who experience no negative episodes whatever. Dr. Sanford Unger of the National Institute of Mental Health reports that among his subjects "50 to 60% will not manifest any real disturbance worthy of discussion, yet around 75% will have at least one episode in which exaltation, rapture, and joy are the key descriptions." How are we to account for the drug's capacity to induce peak experiences, such as the following, which are not preceded by fear?

> A feeling of great peace and contentment seemed to flow through my entire body. All sound ceased and I seemed to be floating in a great, very very still void or hemisphere. It is impossible to describe the overpowering feeling of peace, content-ment, and being a part of goodness itself that I felt. I could feel my body dissolving and actually becoming a part of the goodness and peace that was all around me. Words can't describe this. I feel an awe and wonder that such a feeling could have occurred to me.

Consider the following argument: Like every other form of life, human nature has become distinctive through specialization. Human beings have specialized in developing a cerebral cortex. The analytic powers of this instrument are a stand-ing wonder, but the instrument seems less able to provide people with the sense that they are meaningfully related to their environment: to life, the world, and history in their wholeness. As Albert Camus describes the situation, "If I were a cat among animals, this life would have a meaning, or rather this problem would not arise, for I should belong to this world. I would *be* this world to which I am now opposed by my whole consciousness." Note that it is Camus's consciousness that opposes him to his world. The drugs do not knock this consciousness out, but while they leave it operative they also activate areas of the brain that normally lie below its threshold of awareness. One of the clearest objective signs that the drugs are taking effect is the dilation they produce in the pupils of the eyes, and one of the most predictable subjective signs is the intensification of visual perception. Both of these responses are controlled by portions of the brain that lie deep, further to the rear than the mechanisms that govern consciousness. Meanwhile we know that the human organism is joined to its world in innumerable ways that our senses do not pick up—through gravitational fields, bodily respiration, and the like: the list could be multiplied until the human skin begins to look more like a traffic maze than a boundary. Perhaps the deeper regions of the brain which evolved earlier and are more like those of the lower animals—"If I were a cat I should belong to this world"—can sense this relatedness better than can the cerebral cortex which now demands our attention. If so, when the drugs rearrange the neurohumors that chemically transmit impulses across synapses between neurons, human consciousness and its submerged, intuitive, ecological awareness might for a spell become interlaced. This is, of course, no more than a hypothesis, but how else are we to account for the extraordinary incidence under the drugs of that kind of insight the keynote of which James described as "invariably a reconciliation"? "It is as if," he continues, "the opposites of the world, whose contradictoriness and conflict make all our difficulties and troubles, were melted into one and the same genus, but one of the species, the nobler and better one, is itself the genus, and so soaks up and absorbs its opposites into itself."

IV. DRUGS AND RELIGION VIEWED "RELIGIOUSLY"

Suppose that drugs can induce experiences indistinguishable from religious experiences and that we can respect their reports. Do they shed any light, I now ask, not on life, but on the nature of the religious life?

One thing they may do is throw religious experience itself into perspective by clarifying its relation to the religious life as a whole. Drugs appear to be able to induce religious experiences; it is less evident that they can produce religious lives. It follows that religion is more than a string of experiences. This is hardly news, but it may be a useful reminder, especially to those who incline toward "the religion of religious experience"; which is to say toward lives bent on the acquisition of desired states of experience irrespective of their relation to life's other demands and components.

Despite the dangers of the "faculty psychology" that was in vogue in the first half of this century, it remains useful to regard human beings as having minds, wills, and feelings. One of the lessons of religious history is that to be adequate, a faith must activate all three components of human nature. Overly rationalistic religions grow arid, and moralistic ones grow leaden. Those that emphasize experience have their comparable pitfalls, as evidenced by Taoism's struggle (not always successful) to keep from degenerating into quietism, and the vehemence with which Zen Buddhism insists that once students have attained *satori*, they must be driven out of it and back into the world. The case of Zen is especially pertinent here, for it pivots on an enlightenment experience—*satori,* or *kensho*—which some (but not all) Zen Buddhists say resembles the LSD experience. Alike or different, the point is that Zen recognizes that unless the experience is joined to discipline, it will come to naught.

> Even the Buddha continued to sit. Without *joriki,* the particular power developed through *zazen* [seated meditation], the vision of oneness attained in enlightenment in time becomes clouded and eventually fades into a pleasant memory instead of remaining an omnipresent reality shaping our daily life. To be able to live in accordance with what the mind's eye has revealed through *satori* requires, like the purification of character and the development of personality, a ripening period of *zazen.* [From an early draft of Philip Kapleau's *The Three Pillars of Zen*]

If the religion of religious experience is a snare and a delusion, it follows that no religion that fixes its faith primarily in substances that induce religious experiences can be expected to come to a good end. What promised to be a shortcut will prove to be a short circuit; what began as a religion will end as a religious surrogate. Whether chemical substances can be helpful adjuncts to faith is another question. The Peyote-using Native American Church seems to indicate that they can be; anthropologists give this church a good report, noting among other things that its members resist alcohol better than do nonmembers. The conclusion to which the evidence seems currently to point is that it is indeed possible for chemicals to enhance the religious life, but only when they are set within the context of faith (conviction that what they disclose is true) and discipline (exercise of the will toward fulfilling what the disclosures ask of us).

Nowhere today in Western civilization are both of these conditions met. Faith has declined in churches and synagogues, and the counterculture lacks discipline. This might lead us to forget about the drugs, were it not for the fact that the distinctive religious emotion, and the one that drugs can unquestionably occasion—Otto's *mysterium tremendum, majestas, mysterium fascinans;* in a phrase, the phenomenon of religious awe—seems to be declining sharply. As Paul Tillich said in an address to the Hillel Society at Harvard several years ago:

> The question our century puts before us is: Is it possible to regain the lost dimension, the encounter with the Holy, the dimension that cuts through the world of subjectivity and objectivity and goes down to that which is not world but is the mystery of the Ground of Being?

Tillich may be right; this may be the religious question of our century. For if (as I have argued) religion cannot be equated with religious experiences, neither can it long survive their absence.

19

The Levels of Reality

Nor was it above my mind as oil above the water it floats on, nor as the sky is above earth; it was above because it made me, and I was below because made by it.

AUGUSTINE, *CONFESSIONS*, VII, 10

The triumphs of modern science went to man's head in something of the way rum does, causing him to grow loose in his logic. He came to think that what science discovers somehow casts doubt on things it does not discover; that the success it realizes in its own domain throws into question the reality of domains its devices cannot touch. In short, he came to assume that science implies scientism: the belief that no realities save ones that conform to the matrices science works with—space, time, matter/energy, and in the end number—exist.

It was not always so, but today a sadness comes over us as we think back over the way this *reductio* leveled the world view that preceded it. Traditionally men had honored, even venerated, their ancestors as being essentially wiser than themselves because closer to the source of things. Now forefathers came to be regarded as "children of the race," laboring under children's immaturity. Their *ens perfectissimum* was a mirage, a wish-fulfilling security blanket spun of thin air to compensate for the hardships of real life. Or alternatively, their convictions regarding the human soul were opiates invented by the privileged to quiet, as if by lobotomy, those who without them might press for a fair share of the world's perquisites.

Reviewing the way the new evicted the old—myopia parading as vision, eternity-blindness as enlightenment and the dawn of a brighter day—we find our thoughts turning to the Native Americans. They too watched a landscape dismantled, in their case a physical landscape of almost magical richness. Untapped, unravaged, its grains of soil had been to them beads in the garment of the Great Spirit; its trees were temple pillars, its earth too sacred to be trodden save by soft skin moccasins. Across this unparalleled expanse of virgin nature there poured hordes possessing a capacity so strange that they seemed to the natives they dispossessed to represent a different breed: the capacity to look on everything in creation as material for exploitation, seeing trees only as timber, deer only as meat, mountains as no more than potential quarries. For the victims of this "civilizing mission," as the predators chose to call their conquest, there could only be, in the words of a former U.S. Commissioner of Indian Affairs, a "sadness deeper than imagination can hold—sadness of men completely conscious, watching the universe being destroyed by a numberless and scorning foe." For the Indians "had what the world has lost . . . the ancient, lost reverence and passion for human personality joined with the ancient, lost reverence and passion for the earth and its web of life."

Collier's account emphasizes the quality of sadness rather than anger in the Indians' response. Inasmuch as humanity is in some way one, the response may have included an element of pity for us all. In any case, it appears of a piece with our wistfulness as we think of the destruction of the primordial world view that occurred concurrently and relatedly through scientism's reduction of its qualitative aspects to modalities that are basically quantitative. This ontological strip mining asked man to sacrifice a good part of that which made for him the reality of the world—its beauty, its holiness and crucial expanses of truth—in return for a mathematical scheme whose prime advantage was to help man manipulate matter on its own plane. The discontinuous character of number ordained in advance that such a predominantly quantitative approach would miss the immense tissue of being, its side that consists of pure continuity and relations kept necessarily in balance.

In point of fact, however, continuity and equilibrium exist before discontinuity and crisis; they are more real than these latter and incomparably more precious. But this the modern mind has forgotten. In the face of its lapse, logic can do no more. Short of a historical breakdown which would render routine ineffectual and force us to attend again to things that matter most, we wait for art; for metaphysicians who, imbued with that species of truth that is beauty in its mental mode, are (like Plato) concomitantly poets. By irradiating the human imagination that has atrophied in this *kali yuga*, this age of iron, such men might restore to it the supple, winged condition it requires if it is to come within light-years of Truth. They might return to our inner eye—almost, one might say, to our sense of touch—ontological spaces we have forgotten exist, landscapes crowded with presences the knowing of which can turn men into saints. If the "remembrance of things past" they conjured were vivid enough for us to enter it as confidently as we step out of our front doors, we might, as we have said, rejoin the human race. For to reverse an earlier image, epistemologically their work would be archaeological: a stripping back of deposits of scientistic pseudoinferences that hide the contours, extravagant but defined, of the primordial outlook whose regions appear largely as blanks in the cosmologies modernity has reduced to cosmography.

Archaeology is an appropriate metaphor for the inward probe toward reality, and this we shall come to in the next chapter. For the present, however, we shall table our natural interest in how the levels appear in man and establish their existence in their own right. This calls for reverting to outbound, stratospheric imagery, a mounting of the vertical arm of the three-dimensional cross as it pierces through "cloud-lands"—in the last resort they are all maya—to the apex that alone is fully real, the Infinite.

Disregarding domains that are inferior to our own and therefore lie below the horizontal arm of the cross, common numbering of the worlds is threefold: terrestrial, intermediary, and celestial. Beyond these three lies a fourth domain that is discontinuous with the others. Not itself a world, it is the Infinite which is their uncreated source.

I. THE TERRESTRIAL PLANE

We begin with the terrestrial plane, which alternatively we shall call the gross, the material, the sensible, the corporeal, the phenomenal, or the human plane. Strictly speaking, the last of these appellations is a misnomer, because, as we have mentioned in passing already and will consider in detail in the next chapter, man in the fullness of his being intersects the planes in their entirety. Even so, the designation is convenient, for the plane in question is the one we are most directly in touch with. Its distinctive categories are space, time, energy/matter, and number, the last being a mode to which the first three lend themselves.

Four is a schematization, of course, for the actual number is (as we have said) indefinite. And because the four are in reality classes, we can expect subdivisions to appear in each. These are most apparent on the terrestrial plane, where animal, vegetable, and mineral demarcate themselves obviously; the other planes are difficult enough to see in overview without trying to read the fine print. On the terrestrial plane an upper, border region announces itself in the data that frontier physics encounters. Such data belong to the terrestrial world inasmuch as they continue to participate in some way in space, time, and matter/energy as quantifiable, but the way in which they so participate is, to say the least, peculiar. In this twilight border region, parallel lines converge, things relocate without traversing space, and particles have only probable positions. Phenomena are beginning to phase out of the grossly physical. The terrestrial announces its dependence on the plane above it.

II. THE INTERMEDIATE PLANE

This next plane up is named, neutrally, the intermediate. Alternatively we shall refer to it as the subtle, the animic, or the psychic plane, inasmuch as it is often encountered in phantasms that have no sensible counterparts.

These phantasms can be animate or inanimate: the plane houses both. Those that are animate are the various species of discarnates: ghosts; departed souls that are provisionally in limbo, or traversing the intermediate *bardos* (planes), as the Tibetans would say; the "controls" that spiritualists and mediums claim to be in touch with insofar as their claims are valid; and our own subtle bodies *(suksma-sarira)* insofar as they are disengaged, as in sleep, from their gross, exterior envelopes. These subtle bodies are often called "etheric" or "astral," and their adventures—central to shamanism—described as astral projections, but we must remember that spatial imagery never fits precisely on planes above our own. The highest planes contain no literal space whatever. The intermediate plane is spatial in a way, but the way differs markedly from that of terrestrial space: the peculiarities that we just noted in post-Newtonian physics derive from the fact that its novelties are first steps in the direction of space of the intermediary order. All this must be kept in mind when we hear talk of astral projection and the dream journeys of shamans. As with everything on the higher planes, such notions become absurd if we force them into terrestrial armor, a costuming that in this case generates pictures of psychic pellets slipping through dermal pores to rocket this way or that to who knows what fantastic wonderlands. The truth at issue will emerge if we balance such astronautical images with opposing ones in which the subtle body remains securely within its corporeal sheath while time and space wash through it, and its indriyic net—*indriyas*: subtle correlates of our physical sense organs (Sanskrit)—selects the information it seeks. Or let the explanatory model be ESP, the psychic counterpart of gravitation's action at a distance. This eliminates spatial imagery altogether.

Passing to the impersonal furniture of the psychic plane, we encounter most importantly the archetypes. Their actual abode is on the next plane up, but lower planes derive from the higher, so the archetypes appear on the subtle plane as reflections of their originals—each world in creation is no more than a tissue of shadows entirely dependent on the archetypes in the world above, phenomena being (as we might say) divine qualities eroded in an illusory manner by nothingness. Thus the archetypes turn up on the terrestrial plane as well, in the "forms" that shape objects out of a matter that would otherwise be inchoate. On the subtle plane which we are currently considering, however, we encounter them more directly, though not yet unalloyed.

When on the next plane we do find them in their unalloyed state, they turn out to be Plato's Forms or Ideas, but here on the intermediate plane they stand closer to the archetypes Jung explored. The images he found recurring in the dreams of his patients coincided to such a degree with the world's mythologies (of which his patients were largely innocent) that he concluded that the symbols themselves must reside in man's collective unconscious. But not passively—not as colors on a painter's palette, to be dipped into for the artist's needs. They have an energy of their own, sufficient to have caused Jung to regard them as the psychic counterparts of biological instincts. Physically man's life is vectored by his biological drives; psychically it is molded by the surging pressure of the archetypes. In the end Jung risked a further correlation. The archetypes seemed close enough to the patterns he saw emerging in the theories and experiments of twentieth-century physics for him to conclude that archetypes are *psychoid*. By this he meant that they shape matter (nature) as well as mind (psyche). They transcend the split between these two and are neutral toward it, favoring neither one side nor the other.

This account has a double virtue. First, it establishes the fact that the intermediate plane governs the terrestrial plane in its entirety, its corporeal as well as its psychic aspects; to underscore the completeness of its suzerainty, Sufis call it the Domain of Royalty *(malakut)*. The Indian notion of *siddhis*—yogic powers, certain of which can influence external bodies directly, in psychokinesis as we would say—moves in the same direction, as does the concept of magic as the action of subtle force on corporeal matter.

The second respect in which Jung's notion of archetypes is appropriate here is in the justice it does to their formative powers; they "create" or project forth the terrestrial plane, which is no more than their exterior covering. Several times in this study we have inveighed against reductionism, but let us be clear. Its error does not lie in its attempt to understand one type of reality in terms of another. Virtually all explanation proceeds in this fashion, and explanation is needed, for true reality is never the most obvious; one might almost say that one of the ways truth betrays the fact that it is such is in the care it takes to remain elusive, if one may put the matter paradoxically. The mistake of reductionism—spirit reduced to metamorphosed matter (Darwinism), truth reduced to ideology (Marxism), psyche reduced to sex (Freud: there is no way "to sweeten the sour apple")—lies in its attempt to explain the greater in terms of the less, with the not surprising consequence that the greater is thereby lessened. It is this, at root, that sets us against the modern outlook and turns us back toward tradition where the drift is always the reverse: to explain the lesser by means of the more, a mode of explanation that tends to augment rather than deplete, for in both cases explanation produces a kind of rub-off. The terrestrial plane proceeds from and is explained by the intermediate, the intermediate by the celestial, and the celestial by the Infinite. Thus everything derives, ultimately, from the Infinite. And since "derives" cannot in this last case involve separation—the Infinite is like a celestial void: nothing escapes from it—everything abides in the Infinite's luster.

We tend to think of mind as an epiphenomenon, as a gloss on matter with spirit a patina on that gloss. The truth is the reverse. Matter is the rarity; it obtrudes from the psychic with perhaps the frequency of a few stalactites from the roof of an enormous cavern. Or it is like our earth and its planets—tiny bits of matter floating in an ocean of space. Our lives are plunged in the animic world like crystals floating in a liquid, though appearances make us suppose that the animic is within our bodies or behind the physical shell of things. This supposition causes us to underrate the mental. Apart from the fact that it closes the door on the domain to which magic pertains, it again makes the higher depend on the lower and keeps us from seeing the faculties that make man distinctively human in their full extent.

This holds not only when these faculties are in working order, but when they are not. Insanity is now regarded as "mental illness": we place its victims in hospitals and pity them in the way we do those who have lost their bodily health. (The victims themselves often dispute this assessment, of course, but they are the ones who are mad, so their judgment is discounted.) In point of fact, however, insanity is seldom simply a lack. We recognize this, despite the changes we have effected in vocabulary, in the fear that insanity, unlike disease, continues to inspire within us, the inkling of strange seas beating against the shores of our familiar island. A man may have "lost his reason" only to have had it replaced, for better or worse, by something else. Rarely is he simply reduced like an amputee, and when we treat him as such he feels deeply if obscurely insulted even if we are insensitive to our impertinence.

Mindful of the psychic plane and the way the human is lodged within it, traditional societies tend to regard the insane with a species of awe and respect, seeing them as caught in psychic vortices that work at cross-purposes to ours while possessing something of the autonomy and coherence that ours exhibit. Our madhouses, too, may contain souls that are ravaged by principalities and powers on the psychic plane; in a word, possessed. The phenomenal response to a recent film, *The Exorcist,* shows that our unconscious minds remain open to this notion, but current psychiatric theory is so opposed to it that it will be useful to have an example to show that there are cases that almost require it. The following eyewitness account by Peter Goullart is condensed from his book *The Monastery of Jade Mountain:*

> The energumen, a rather emaciated man of about twenty-five, lay on an iron bedstead on a rush mat. He was very pale and there was a wild, roving look in his fevered eyes. The Taoist priest, holding an elongated ivory tablet held ceremonially in both hands in front of his chest, approached the bed slowly. There was a visible transformation on the energumen's face. His eyes were filled with malice as he watched the priest's measured advance with a sly cunning and hatred. Suddenly he gave a bestial whoop and jumped up in his bed, the four attendants rushing to hold him.
>
> "No! No! You cannot drive us out. We are two against one. Our power is greater than yours." The sentences poured out of the energumen's distorted mouth in a strange, shrill voice, which sounded mechanical, inhuman—as if pronounced by

a parrot. The priest looked at the victim intensely, gathering all his inner strength; beads of perspiration appeared on his thin face.

"Come out! Come out! I command you to come out!" He was repeating in a strong metallic voice with great force. "I am using the power of the One compared to whom you are nothing. In His name I command you to come out." Inmobile, he continued to focus his powers on the energumen's face. The man was struggling in the bed with incredible strength against the four men who held him. Animal growls and howls issued from time to time from his mouth which became square, his teeth gleaming like the fangs of a dog. I had the impression that a pack of wild animals was fighting inside his body. Terrible threats poured out of the contorted mouth, now fringed in white foam, and interspersed with such incredible obscenities that women had to plug their ears with their fingers.

Again the abbott cried his command to the unseen adversaries to leave the prostrate man. There was a burst of horrible laughter from the victim's throat and suddenly with a mighty heave of his supernaturally strengthened arms he threw off the men who held him and jumped at the priest's throat like a mad bloodhound. But he was over-powered again. This time they bound him with ropes and fastened the ends to the bedposts. The abbott, still immobile, continued his conjurations in a metallic voice, his eyes never leaving the body. With unutterable horror, we saw that it began to swell visibly. On and on the dreadful process continued until he became a grotesque balloon of a man.

"Leave him! Leave him!" cried the monk concentrating still harder. Convulsion shook the monstrous swollen body. It seemed that all the apertures of the body were opened by the unseen powers hiding in it and streams of malodorous excreta and effluvia flowed on to the ground in incredible profusion. For an hour this continued and then the energumen, resuming his normal size, seemed to come to rest, with his eyes watching the unmoved priest who was still reading.

The priest stopped reading; with sweat pouring down his face, he backed down to the altar, laid down the tablet and took up the ritual sword. Threateningly and commandingly he stood again over the energumen.

"The struggle is useless!" he cried. "Leave him! Leave him in the name of the Supreme Power who never meant you to steal this man's body!" Another scene of horror evolved itself before our dazed eyes. The man on the bed became rigid and his muscles seemed to contract, turning him into a figure of stone. Slowly, very slowly, the iron bedstead, as if impelled by an enormous weight, caved in, its middle touching the ground. The attendants seized the inert man by his feet and arms. The weight was such that none of them could lift him up and they asked for assistance from the onlookers. Seven men could hardly lift him for he was heavy as a cast-iron statue. Suddenly he became light again and they put him on a wooden bed which had been brought in. A long time passed with the abbott reading and commanding interminably. At last he sprinkled the inert man with holy water and advanced to him again with a sword. His concentration was so deep that he did not seem to see anybody. He was utterly exhausted and swayed slightly. Two novices came up to support him.

"I have won!" he cried triumphantly in a strange voice. "Get out! Get out!" The energumen stirred and fell into dreadful convulsions. His eyes rolled up and only the whites were visible. His breathing was stertorous and he clawed his body until he was covered with blood. Foam was issuing from his mouth and a loud gurgling sound.

"Damn you! Damn you!" came a wild scream from the foaming lips. "We are going but you shall pay for it with your life." There was a terrific struggle on the bed, the poor man twisting and rolling like a mortally-wounded snake and his colour changing all the time. Suddenly he fell flat on his back and was still. His eyes opened. His gaze was normal and he saw his parents who now came forward.

"My parents!" he cried weakly. "Where am I?" He was very feeble and they carried him out in a specially ordered sedan chair. The abbott himself was in a terrible state of prostration and was half-carried and half-dragged away by his novices.

The word *possession* usually, as here, connotes demonic possession, and this underscores the fact that the psychic plane houses evil as well as good. For the popular mind, which (as we have seen) ranks the worlds on the scale of euphoria, this fact necessitates splitting the psychic plane in two: lodging its beatific components in heavens above the earth and its hellish ones in realms below—the effect can be achieved by rounding the intermediate plane into a circle that envelops the terrestrial plane. But for the reflective mind whose ordering principle is power—and more basically, being—the moral and affective differences that loom so large in popular thought are secondary. Evil is worse than good, but its power can rival it at points, which means that at these points the two are ontically on a par. And if the power in question exceeds the terrestrial, this par lies above the terrestrial plane. The primordial, Zarathustrian war between the opposites proceeds on the intermediate plane; we inherit its spill and backwash. Sufis recognize the ambiguous character of the psychic plane by calling it God's Footstool—the place where Rigor and Mercy, his two feet, reside—whereas the celestial plane is his Throne: that plane is beatific throughout, for on his throne God sits complete. According to the Tibetan Book of the Dead, the intermediate *bardos* (planes) that a soul must traverse before it reenters a human body run the full gamut from terror to bliss. The opposites they house are the same as those we experience here, but there they are experienced more intensely. We visit those *bardos* nightly, the Indians say, when, subtle bodies disjoined from gross, we dream.

A final point about the intermediate plane brings up again the place of space and time within it. We have already noted that this plane does not elude these categories entirely; for this reason it can be classed with the terrestrial plane, the two together constituting the manifest world or nature in the inclusive meaning of these terms. It can even be the object of empirical research as in parapsychology and depth psychology, though the teeth on the rim of its wheel, so to speak, are rather flexible and barely mesh with the cogs of consensual objectivity which even these sciences, if they are to be such, must honor as the final indices of the real. But though space and time pertain in some ways to the psychic realm, the ways themselves are significantly different from those that hold on the gross, corporeal plane. To accommodate the psychic counterparts of the spatio-temporal peculiarities that manifest themselves in frontier physics, Jung coined the word "synchronicity." We need not juggle the full theory behind that word; our interest is in a single point. If Jung was accurate in reporting that meaningful "coincidences"—as in Arthur Koestler's *The Roots of Coincidence*—increased for his patients as they became aware of the archetypal symbols and situations that were working in their lives, this fact supports our present thrust. In addition to creating the terrestrial world, the archetypes order it in ways that partially exceed its linear laws of causation.

III. THE CELESTIAL PLANE

The intermediate plane is not a miscellany. It is not even enough to say that it is an integrated and ordered whole. One must add that it is a conscious whole, for as one mounts the levels of being, awareness intensifies and integration increases. The subtle state coalesces in its totality in the "universal or total soul," as Plotinus called it, though in the terminology we are using it is the universal or total mind. As with organs and the organisms of which they are members, individual minds can be distinguished from the world mind, but they are not separate from it.

The world mind is the supreme expression of the divine in the manifest world, but it is far from God's totality. The question of what more his nature contains carries us to the plane above the intermediate, the celestial.

When a man effects a project—wages a campaign, let us say—he is truly present within it. A part of his nature surfaces in the campaign, clearer than if we had been left to infer how he might have performed in the face of its demands. Even so, the undertaking treats us to but a facet of his being. We assume that underlying *what* the person does is the person who does those things. In the case in question, he involves himself in the campaign, but by no stretch of the imagination can he be equated with this involvement.

Comparably with God. To the end that nothing that is possible be left undone—if it were, the Infinite would not be such—God actualizes (creates) being in the mode of mutiplicity and individuation. In addition he enters and abides in his creation—the terrestrial and intermediate planes combined—as the mind that organizes and empowers it. All the while he transcends his creation and exceeds his involvement with it. According to Hindu cosmology, during the nights of Brahma in which he sleeps, the terrestrial and intermediate planes vanish completely; the "big bang" reverses—matter vanishes into spreading black holes?—leaving nothing for the (no longer existing) astronomers to detect. The lower realms, now reabsorbed into the celestial, are shown to have been but episodes in the divine expanse.

Mystics, endowed with the "eye of the heart," can intuit this celestial expanse; others must rely on reports or inferences. Regarding the last of these, we have noted more than once that unaided logic can infer nothing regarding higher realms from ones that have been severed from them completely—realms viewed only in terms of what excludes them from ones that are higher: the externality of their components, their fragmentariness, their incorrigible limitations. But if a lower plane is viewed through the eyes of what might be called "ontic sensibility," it is noticed that the plane is illumined. Seeking the source of its illumination, sight turns upward and logic perceives the contours of the planes from which the illumination issues.

Such "ontological logic" points invariably toward greater being and less division. Thus the celestial plane dwarfs the ones below it in the plenitude of its existence and at the same time is less fragmented. Multiplicity reduces in its case to the basic *kinds* of existents, the archetypes; we encountered them in a derivative mode on the intermediate plane, but come now upon the originals which, combining and recombining, give form and structure to the worlds below.

To us these "universals," as they are sometimes called, seem abstract, for in the phenomenal world we never encounter beauty, say, by itself but only as a property of concrete things that are beautiful. However, to regard objects as concrete and their properties abstract is like calling water spray concrete and wetness abstract. Objects are ephemeral, qualities endure; the qualities we encounter in tangible objects are fragile attenuations of the intense, undiluted, and stable condition the archetypes enjoy in their own right, on their own plane. In addition to archetypes of single qualities, there are archetypes that are combinations of these. A species is an instance. Roses come from Roseness, which is incomparably more real than the flowers that line the garden walk.

The celestial plane can be viewed impersonally, in which case the archetypes are, as we noted earlier by way of anticipation, the Platonic forms; viewed collectively, as comprising and implying one another, they constitute the Idea of the Good. It is more natural, however, to use personal imagery, for of things we directly know, persons are the best, and as we ascend the ladder of reality, value keeps step with being. Even Plato uses personal terms when in the *Sophist* he has the Eleatic stranger attribute to the "friends of the forms" the view that the forms are alive. Plotinus in typical fashion converts Plato's allusion into settled fact: the forms are unequivocally alive, which makes the Intelligence that comprehends them even more so. In conventional terminology the celestial plane is the abode of God Transcendent: God before he creates the world and the fullness of God that exceeds his creation after he has accomplished it. It goes without saying that God's nature is integrated, but this does not keep it from being composed of attributes. It is meaningful to speak of his love, his will, his judgment, his mercy, and the like.

We are obviously here in the realm of theism in its classic Western sense. The celestial sphere is the sphere of the personal God. God of Abraham, Isaac, and Jacob rather than of the philosophers, he creates the world by deliberate intent, presides over history providentially, and knows and loves his creatures—not a sparrow falls but he registers that fact (Matt. 10:29); "not so much as the weight of an ant in heaven and earth escapes from Him" (Koran, XXXIV: 3).

About theism in this eminently personal mode three points must be made:

1. The view is natural. Satirists, eyes peeled for man's pretensions, use this as a count against it: "If cattle . . . were able to draw . . . they would make the bodies of the gods such as they had themselves," said Xenophanes; the gods of triangles, said Montesquieu, would have three sides. But there is no reason to disparage what is natural; as a rule it tokens what is fit and appropriate. To be put off by the anthropomorphic character of God in scripture amounts in last resort to being disaffected with ourselves, for the reality we call God necessarily assumes toward us a human demeanor to the end that we may enter as fully as possible into what is ultimately impenetrable. "Thought flows into man," said Shankara, "as molten metal is poured into the founder's mold." The very intensity of the God-idea makes it occupy man wholly, more or less as water fills a vessel to the brim. It assumes the shape of that which contains and limits it, and becomes anthropomorphic.

But is God personal only in the way he appears to us, or is he personal in himself, in his own right and nature? This introduces the second point.

2. Theism is true. It is not the final truth; God's personal mode is not his final mode; it is not the final reality. Even so, it is vastly more real than are the creatures who encounter him in this mode, so the fact that the mode is not final presents no problem. Only persons who sense *themselves* to be not finally real—*anatta*, no-self—will sense the same of the God of theism. And for them it does not matter that in the last analysis God is not the kind of God who loves them, for at this level there is no "them" to be loved. Insofar as one takes oneself seriously, as all of us do most of the time and most of us do all of the time, the God of theism is to be taken seriously too. Not only do we love; we are loved. Not only do we hope; we are hoped for. Not only do we find or miss meaning; we are meant.

Nevertheless:

3. Theism is not the final truth. Its vision of God is modeled after capacities that are distinctively human, and noble as these capacities are—the capacity to make discriminating judgments, the capacity to exercise responsible decision and choice, the ability to carry out long-range purposes—they require for their exercise contexts that stand over and against their subject and thereby limit him. But the final reality is unlimited, for it is infinite; to put the point in an aphorism,

nothing *finite* can be *final*. Being persons ourselves, we tend to see in God the part or aspect of his nature that is kin to us. But part is never whole: man *has* reflexes (knee jerks, eye blinks); he is not *himself* a reflex, not in his wholeness. Or to move closer to the dignity of the topic at hand, man possesses reason while at the same time exceeding his possession: reason is his tool, not his definition. Several paragraphs above we noted that God is anthropomorphic. Now we add that there is a sense in which he is not; to wit, the sense in which he transcends all descriptions, anthropomorphic ones included—mystics often use the word "Godhead" for this transpersonal mode. Religious sensibility demands this cor-relate as much as does logic, for much as we yearn for a God who resembles us, such a God could never satisfy us completely: we know ourselves too well. It is a truism that a God we could comprehend would not command our worship. If he could be squeezed into the miserably inadequate vessel of our minds we would not avert our eyes—no shudder would run through us; there would be no *horror religiosus,* no religious awe. It is not enough to say that God's attributes exceed ours inexhaustibly; the attributes themselves must be transcended, for in the last analysis they derive, all but infinity, from limitation, which finally is what religion works to transcend. The difference in degree must phase into a difference in kind.

IV. THE INFINITE

"The difference between most people and myself," wrote Jung toward the close of his life, "is that for me the 'dividing walls' are transparent." Remove the walls entirely, including any that might serve as boundaries or perimeters, and we have God in his ultimate nature: the Infinite.

As with God in his personal mode, so too with his Infinite. Several points must be registered, in this case four.

1. Only negative terms characterize it literally. This begins with the word "Infinite" itself, which asserts only that its object is not finite, and holds equally for other characterizations such as unconditioned, ineffable, and immutable. In Hinduism the Infinite is *nir-guna* (without qualities); in Buddhism it is *nir-vana* (nondrawing, as a fire whose fuel is exhausted has ceased to draw) and *sunyata* (emptiness, a void); in Taoism it is the Tao that cannot be spoken; in Judaism it is *'en-sof,* the not-finite. The Infinite cannot be defined positively because defini-tions compare: either they liken what they define to something or they distin-guish it from something. If they distinguish, we are back with negation: the object defined is not what it is contrasted with. And if they liken? But the Infinite is all-inclusive, so there is nothing other than it to which it *can* be likened.

2. Positive terms apply to the Infinite only analogically. When Vedantists say that Brahman is *Sat, Chit,* and *Ananda* (Being, Awareness, and Bliss) they mean

that the terms are more accurate than their opposites. The Infinite is more like a lion that exists than like a unicorn that does not, more like creatures that experience than like objects that do not, more like ourselves when we are fulfilled than when we are wanting. But that is all the assertions claim. We cannot presume that Being in its infinity bears more than a trace of resemblance to the being we encounter in rocks or mountains or waterfalls. And because the connotation of "being" derives preponderantly from the modes in which we encounter it directly, it would be misleading to claim that the word characterizes the Infinite literally. Only if the claim is converted into its negation—the assertion that the Infinite hasn't zero-being (doesn't not-exist)—is it literally true; short of this the word functions analogically. The same holds for "awareness," "bliss," and all other posited attributes.

3. The degree to which positive terms seem apposite will vary. The reason is: it depends on the experience (or the imaginative capacity) of the person who is using them. When Spinoza said that God's knowledge resembles our knowledge to the extent that the Dog Star resembles a dog, it was because in his discernment the Infinite exceeded the finite in about that ratio. Others whose "ceilings" are lower will not find the disparity as great. The governing law reads: the more developed the sense of the Infinite, the more distant from the finite it appears and the less literal positive designations will seem.

4. The most effective way to underscore the negative side of analogy—how much attributes when predicated of the Infinite differ from the modes in which we usually encounter them—is through paradox. The device can also be seen as one by which the mystics who (to borrow one of their own profound words) have "suffered" the weight of the Infinite try to raise the sensibility ceilings of the uninitiated with respect to the Infinite's otherness. The opposing forces that paradox generates cause it to function as a verbal lever. The mystic may begin, for example, by establishing as fulcrum the fact that God is light. This holds both metaphorically (light everywhere symbolizes knowledge) and literally inasmuch as God-incursion is often accompanied by light that is physically sensed: Christ in his transfiguration, Saul on the Damascus road, saints in the Eastern Orthodox tradition. But in saying "light" the mystic will be misunderstood, for neither the literal nor the symbolic light he intends is the light the world knows—on the literal side, for example, it has the power of an arc lamp with no sense of glare or strain. Immediately, therefore, he must press against the word's usual connotations. So: "God is not light"; if "light" denotes its conventional referents, God is darkness. The countervailing forces raise the far end of the lever toward light of a different order. If the alchemy works, our minds are expanded and our souls as well.

These four points speak to language and the Infinite. What within their stipulations need be added before this chapter may close?

Of the (necessarily negative) predicates that apply to the Infinite literally, the most important two are "unbounded" and "undifferentiated"—we are back with the fact that walls, internal *or* peripheral, dividing *or* enclosing, have no place at being's summit. The Infinite is unbounded because as we have had more than one occasion to remark, a boundary would limit it and contradict its infinity. It is undifferentiated, because differentiation implies distinction and thereby in some respect separation, separation in turn implies distance, and in the realm of the spirit distance symbolizes ignorance epistemologically and privation affectively. A Something that excludes nothing save distinctions we cannot begin to image any more than we can image light that is simultaneously wave and particle, electrons that jump orbit without traversing the intervening distance, or a particle that passes through alternative slits simultaneously without dividing. But if physics does not stop with the image-able, need metaphysics?

Physics can relinquish imagery because it still has mathematics' terra firma to walk on. Metaphysics lacks this support. It reaches a point where, numbers long ago having been abandoned, thought itself faces a drop-off. There are some who mistake this point for the end of the world; whatever can be neither imaged nor coherently conceived, they argue, does not exist. But truth does not need us and is in no way dependent upon our powers of conceptualization. There are regions of being—the unimaginable perfection of totality is at the moment the case in point—that are quite unrelated to the contours of the human mind. The mind is comfortable with facts and fictions. It is not made for grasping ultimates.

Other persons concede that the fact that we cannot conceive of something is no proof that it does not exist, but contend that if it does exist it is for all practical purposes irrelevant. But the fact that ultimates exceed the reach of our bread-and-butter faculties and can never be captured by minds that insist upon absolute rights of possession does not mean that these ultimates have no contact with the world we inhabit or with the human self in its totality. It is only because we invest all our interests in the specifiable, which to be such must perforce be partial and ephemeral, that no concern remains for that which is total and eternal and therefore unspecifiable. Even so, because it is total it cannot be escaped. The belief, normal to mankind, that meaning inheres in everything that exists and everything that happens derives at depth from the fact that the Ultimate, or Infinite as we are calling it, is omnipresent.

Being everywhere, it is, of course, in man; in the natural world it is in man preeminently.

20

The Levels of Selfhood

He is the Self within and without; yea, within and without.
MAITRAYANA UPANISHAD, V. 2

In truth I say to you that within this fathom-high body . . . lies the world and the rising of the world and the ceasing of the world.
THE BUDDHA

For the kingdom of Heaven, nay rather, the King of Heaven . . . is within us.
GREGORY PALAMAS

As without, so within—the isomorphism of man and the cosmos is a basic premise of the traditional outlook. If man does indeed mirror the cosmos, a quick review of the traditional cosmology will alert us to its regions that call for human counterparts. Visualized, that cosmology shows the earth, symbolic of the terrestrial sphere, enveloped by the intermediate sphere, which in turn is enclosed by the celestial, the three concentric spheres together being superimposed on a background that is Infinite.

Considered in itself each sphere appears as a complete and homogeneous whole, while from the perspective of the area that encloses and permeates it, it is but a content. Thus the terrestrial world knows not the intermediate world, nor the latter the celestial, though each world is known and dominated by the one that exceeds and enfolds it.

Positioned, as we are, at the center of these realms, when we look out we look up, when we look in we look down. In the latter case empowering is sensed to erupt from below and proceed from within: vital organs are encased in skeletal armor, seeds slumber in husks, kernels are guarded by shells less animate. Now we are ready to delineate the echelons of selfhood that derive from and reflect the ontological planes the preceding chapter established.

I. BODY

We begin with man's surface aspect, his body. One hundred fifty pounds, more or less, of protoplasm that we can see, touch, and maneuver, it is the most evident part of our makeup, so need not detain us long. Pages could be given to its wonders. We could describe the cells that are its building blocks, each equipped with hundreds or thousands of allosteric enzyme molecules a million billion times finer than the most delicate cybernetic relays man can devise. Or we could note the brain that is the body's apex; with its 10 billion neurons any one of which can be related to as many as 25,000 others for a number of possible associations that exceeds the number of atoms in the universe, it is the most highly organized three pounds of matter we know. There is no need to dwell on details. We leap over them to consider the sentience that infuses the human frame.

II. MIND

Mechanists consider mind to be a part of the body, but this is a mistake. The brain is a part of the body, but mind and brain are not identical. The brain breathes mind like the lungs breathe air.

It is not possible to prove these assertions, for as we just said, each plane when viewed from within presents itself as a complete and self-sufficient whole. But though this rules out the possibility of demonstrating the existence of ontological "mores" of whatever sort, intimations of such mores are likely to obtrude, for the lesser is in fact not self-contained. Whether a given individual picks up on these intimations—"hath ears to hear"—depends on his sensitivity.

Intimations of the fact that the mind, though obviously implicated with the brain is not reducible to it are of three sorts.

Wilder Penfield, dean of living neurophysiologists if anyone deserves such a title, thinks that by applying electrodes to the memory and motor regions of the cerebral cortex of patients undergoing brain surgery the surgeon can make them remember past events and move their bodily members, but there is no brain-spot which, if electrically stimulated, will induce patients to believe or to decide. Stressing that years of studying the mechanisms of the human brain have forced him to retain rather than abandon the distinction between mind and these mechanisms, Penfield concludes that:

> Mind must be viewed as a basic *element* in itself. . . . The mind seems to act independently of the brain in the same sense that a programmer acts independently of his computer. . . . It will always be quite impossible to explain the mind on the basis of neuronal action within the brain. . . . Mind comes into action and goes out of action with the highest brain-mechanism. But the mind has energy [and] the form of that energy is different from that of neuronal potentials that travel the axone pathways.

Still in the area of neurophysiology is the recent discovery that the two hemi-spheres of the human brain serve different functions. Its left hemisphere works predominantly with the analytic, logical thinking of language and mathematics. Meanwhile the right hemisphere proceeds holistically. Instead of following trails of linear reason and "single causation" as does the left hemisphere, it takes in fields in a gulp; it grasps intuitively, in patterned gestalts. It thinks, but because it bypasses language, it thinks tacitly. This mode of mentation equips it for artistic endeavor, pattern recognition—our ability to identify faces at a glance—and the orientation of our bodies in space: walking, swimming, or riding a bicycle. Since these right hemisphere functions involve space, whereas talk takes time, we can say that the right hemisphere functions predominantly spatially and the left temporally. If the right hemisphere is in closer touch with the subtle plane than is the left, then "Time is an invention of man, but space—space belongs to the gods" (the painter Max Beckmann).

Since only the human brain is thus divided, no other species even prefiguring it, the division is obviously related to man's attendant monopoly, language. But why must linguistic competence be compartmentalized? Why does it not pervade the cerebral cortex as a whole? Because, it would seem, our entire being cannot be accommodated to it. This being the case, a part of the brain must be kept language-free. Only so can capacities that are incommensurate with language yet indispensable to life remain intact.

If it is impossible for man to manage the whole of his terrestrial life by means of language, it goes without saying that transverbal faculties must enter even more if he is to traffic with supraterrestrial planes, which differ in kind from the plane that language is primarily designed to cope with and mirror. Without empowerment by the psychic order, man cannot live: we see empirical evidence of this in the laboratory discovery that experimental subjects who are allowed to sleep but not to dream go mad; metaphysically it follows from the double fact that (a) the lesser is ordered and empowered by the greater, and (b) the psychic plane is greater than the corporeal. The psychic cannot, however, be fitted into corporeal categories which are also, in the main, the categories of language. Speaking in the manner of a Platonic myth, we might say that the mind, contemplating its descent into matter, foresaw that it would have to school itself in its ways. It did so by pouring its direct and luminous intellection into molds—concepts, words, language—that splintered it, for "rational" and "ratiocination" presuppose what the words suggest: a process in which we *ration* or divide up reality into separate things to facilitate discussion. The categories of matter and the language that in part reflects, in part creates, these categories. But if mind was to save the world—redeem it from total opacity and lifelessness—part of its nature had to remain outside those categories, for reason, being *founded* in distinctions, can at best only grope toward wholeness; indirectly through inference, and sequentially through time. The parallel with the two natures of Christ is exact: The mind assumes the conditions of the fall with its left (distinctively human) hemisphere while keeping its right hemisphere transcendent. That both hemispheres are requisite for man's full functioning is but one more evidence of his amphibious nature. He lives in the world while not being of it.

At the beginning of this section we said that there are three lines of argument that point toward the conclusion that mind exceeds the terrestrial plane. Neurophysiology we have noted; of the other two, one is theoretical and the other empirical.

The theoretical argument asks if matter can ever account for sentience, or mind in the widest sense of the word. This is a time-worn issue, of course, one of the thorniest in the entire history of philosophy. What we can say briefly is that no convincing materialistic explanation of mind has been forthcoming. Matter is located in space; one can specify precisely where a given tree, let us say, resides. But if one asks where his perception of the tree is located he can expect difficulties. The difficulties increase if he asks how tall his perception of the tree is; not how tall is the tree he sees, but how tall is his seeing of it. Conscious experience is refractory to measurement.

That in some way I see because I have eyes and move my arms and legs because I want to seems as incontrovertible as anything can be; both our observation of life and the fact that within limits we can take it in hand and squeeze it like an orange presuppose body-mind interaction. But as to the character of the interaction—it is no more explicable today than it was in the time of Aristotle, but in reality it is less explicable, for Aristotle's nature included its subtle half whereas the current conception, which prunes nature to almost its quantifiable components, is less accommodating.

The matter comes to this: From the side of insentient matter the gulf that separates it from sentience is infinite; no bridge can reach the other bank. A ton of feathers presents no problem, but of items that weigh nothing whatever, no number will produce even an ounce. The doctrine of "emergent evolution" contributes nothing here. Proceeding from the fact that gases that cannot be poured may condense into liquids that can be poured, it argues that new qualities do arise. In riding such analogies it overlooks the fact that a clear continuity joins liquid to gas—the two are alternative arrangements of molecules in motion—whereas no common substratum linking sentience to insentience has been proposed. A substratum linking insentience to sentience does exist; depending on the level of reality on which the question is raised, it is form, existence, being, or the Infinite. But nothing answering to physical categories links the terrestrial plane to those above.

Such are the theoretical considerations that suggest that mind exceeds matter. A final line of argument is empirical. Instead of arguing that mind is a distinctive kind of entity, it argues that it functions in distinctive ways. It plays by different rules, conforms to laws that differ in kind from those that matter exemplifies.

So much for the existence of mind as a stratum of self that is neither reducible to the brain nor finally dependent on it. Turning to our experience of this stratum, we note that it takes two forms: waking and dreaming.

The "feel" of mind as we encounter it awake is so familiar that we overlook the mystery it parades in broad daylight. For on the one hand it truly reaches the physical world and no philosophical artifice can convince us of the contrary; meanwhile it consists of nothing but a tissue of images conditioned by what our senses can pick up, our interests induce them to pick up, and our past experience feeds in by ways of interpretation that elicit expectations. Everything that constitutes for us the world—its brute stubbornness, its continuity, its logical coherence—is a flow of phantasms, a gossamer of Berkeleian impressions. It is futile to try to know the world outside this magic lantern show, since it comes to us only through its "slides." All the while the world insists—and we cannot but agree—that we are not looking at a screen at all. The screen is a window through which we see the world itself, an autonomous order.

No theory of perception removes this miracle, the fact that an entity in one region of space flashes forth to assume—in truth *become*—the form (though not the matter) of entities removed: the sparkle in a mountain stream, the red on the throat of a ring-necked pheasant. Or causes those qualities to come to it—with mind we are on the intermediate plane where "wheres" cannot be pinpointed on the terrestrial map. When we move from perception to memory, imagination, and abstract thought the mysteries compound. If physiological psychology ever gives the impression of explaining these phenomena we should not be misled: it removes their mysteries in the way daylight banishes stars. Given sufficient pertinacity, reason's flailings can worry the mystery out of anything. In fact, of course, it is our sensibilities that die: "'Tis ye, 'tis your estranged faces, That miss the many-splendoured thing." Alternatively, "It is not the eyes which grow blind. It is the hearts within the breasts that grow blind" (Koran, XXII, 46).

Daily, when we sleep, mind changes its register. In deep or dreamless sleep its content—assuming, with India, that it then continues to have a content—is out of sight; presumably it is too undifferentiated to be recalled. Dreams, on the other hand, *can* be remembered, but we must not overlook the evaporation that occurs in the process. As we pass into wakefulness a sort of decantation takes place, of which we can, however, take note inasmuch as it is by degrees that a dream's force subsides and its otherworldliness eases into linguistic molds.

In dream the subtle body retires from the gross. The communication lines to its physical senses are disconnected, and it returns to its natural medium. For the duration of its "home leave" its pedestrian rendezvous with matter is suspended and it swims untrammeled in the psychic sphere. Because that sphere is its native habitat—the environment that is continuous with the stuff of which the mind is composed—the homecoming refreshes and restores. "He giveth his beloved—sleep."

Not that the dream world is more pleasant. Terrors lie in wait each time we turn out the light, nightmares being on average as common as dreams of peace. Nor do we see more clearly while asleep; if anything maya is compounded. We know less where we are and for this reason can take ourselves less in hand, a point the religions make by rating earthly life precious because of the opportunity it affords us to alter our condition toward final ends. Not pleasurableness but vividness and power are the respects in which dreams outrank our waking consciousness.

Dreams are invariably and by nature vivid because they know no habituation: each encounter with a rose or goblin is as if we were meeting it for the first time. As to power, the case is ambiguous. In one sense dreams have little power, for as we just noted, being disjoined from will, they do not in themselves affect our futures as much as our deliberate doings can. We cannot say that they have no power, for men have been known to emerge from dreams with perspectives that changed the course of their entire lives, as in Dostoevsky's story "The Dream of a Ridiculous Man." On the whole, however, the force dreams possess is passive rather than active; their emotional intensity is out of proportion to the difference they make. Beyond their freedom from habituation that has been remarked, their intensity derives from the fact that they put us in touch with forces that are more deep-lying and causative than the ones we notice in daily life. The dream lecture in the course of which I discover that I am prepared in neither content nor attire may be fictional with respect to real life—read: the waking world. Certainly I breathe easier when I awake and realize that it was, as I say to myself, only a dream. The fact remains that the anxiety the dream confronts me with is more real—calls more tunes, throws more switches in my moods and behavior—than the satisfaction I may feel later in the day in the course of an actual lecture for which I have prepared and donned trousers; in this sense we are indeed "such stuff as dreams are made on." Dream research has come up with exceptionally concrete evidence to document the fact that in dreams we are close to the center of life's vitalities. Eighty percent of the time men dream they have erections.

III. SOUL

The conditions that govern this earthly cockpit in which we are stationed are local and relative. To daydream is to gaze out its windows at cloud kingdoms or stars so bright they seem at fingertip; at such times we forget for a spell our cabined condition and risk air's rhapsody of the deep. Sleep springs us from our carrier and brings the weightlessness of dream; death severs the lifeline to our transport, and for a time we stride the clouds like titans. "For a time," because there is a dimension of our selves that exceeds even the stratosphere, an essence no universe, subtle or gross, can contain. The ancients called it soul *(psyche, anima, sarira atman, nephesh,* or *nafs),* and though on the cosmological map it lies beyond the reach of the strongest telescope, we can join it in a twinkling once we learn its register. For it is closer to our essence by far than is the mind with which we usually identify.

The soul is the final locus of our individuality. Situated as it were behind the senses, it sees through the eyes without being seen, hears with the ears without itself being heard. Similarly it lies deeper than mind. If we equate mind with the stream of consciousness, the soul is the source of this stream; it is also its witness while never itself appearing within the stream as a datum to be observed. It underlies, in fact, not only the flux of mind, but all the changes through which an individual passes; it thereby provides the sense in which these changes can be considered to be *his.* No collection of the traits I possess—my age, my appearance, what have you—constitutes the essential "me," for the traits change while I remain in some sense myself. To switch to the vocabulary of George Herbert Mead, the fragments of self that present themselves for identification constitute the "me" while the "I" that supports them as a clotheshorse supports the garments we drape over it remains concealed. To try to get the "I" into the field of vision is like trying to see my eyes by stepping back a pace; with every backward move I make, it retreats correlatively. But though the "me" is the only part of myself I can objectify, I sense it to be the object of a subject that is its source and superior.

This superior is the soul. We sense it indelibly in the incommunicable sense of what it feels like to be oneself instead of anyone else who has ever lived, but beyond this we know it only indirectly, by its effects. The way it supplies us with life is completely invisible, as is the way it directs the trajectory of our ontogenetic development: from the moment of conception it decrees that the raw materials the body assimilates in food and drink and air will be transformed according to incredible foreordinations to produce from among illimitable possibilities precisely—a human being. These workings of the soul are not only hidden from the subject they create; for the most part they elude even the laboratory scrutinies of science—microbiology gives only a barest glimpse of the drama involved. Where we do sense our souls is first, to repeat, in our discernment of our individuality—the fact that from conception to death we are the same person, which person is distinct from all others—and second, in our wants. For if we ask what we sense ourselves to be, there is no better initial answer than that we are creatures that want.

To center on a single point: the soul's essential dynamism. In the faint glimpses of itself that the soul affords us, it appears less as a thing than as a movement, a bridge more than a destination. Restlessness is built into it as a metaphysical principle. And though its reachings often seem random, they have a direction.

What is this direction?

Ever since man appeared on this planet he seems to have been searching for an object that he could love, serve, and adore wholeheartedly; an object which, being of the highest and most permanent beauty and perfection, would never permit his love for it to dwindle, deteriorate, or suffer frustration. The search has led to difficulties. It has brought him face to face with calamity and taken from him a toll of heavy sacrifice including the sacrifice of life itself. Yet he persists. The relentless urge of his nature compels him to continue at all costs. The entire history of the race—political, moral, legal, socio-cultural, intellectual, economic, and religious, from earliest times to the present day—is the record of man's search for some beckoning object.

And again we ask, what is this object?

The metaphysical answer is more basic. The soul is programmed to perpetuate its existence and then to augment it. Its tropism is toward being and its increase.

This is obvious in the case of drives like hunger and sex, but it holds for other outreaches as well, indeed for every outreach. We seek wealth and power because they strengthen our support system, fame and power because they increase our social stature. Friendship at once shores up our lives by the positive regard it elicits from others and enlarges our lives by stretching them, so to speak, to include the lives of others within them: we rejoice with those who rejoice and weep with those who mourn. Knowledge extends our understanding—"The world spreads out on either side / No wider than the mind is wide"—and beauty foretells the inner harmony of things. In the latter case, it is a quickening of spirit that signals augmented being rather than an enlargement in size, which is being's usual metaphorical quantifier.

Not that we see that being is invariably what we want. What the lover senses himself as wanting is his beloved. In this he is not mistaken, of course; the point concerns only *why* he loves her. That question the lover himself does not ask: immersed completely in the universe of love, its object is self-evidently its final cause. But if our object is to understand, the question "why" obtrudes. The beloved attracts because she configurates the precise aperture through which being can pour through to her lover in largest portions. Or change the image. Among innumerable pieces of quartz that lie strewn about the floor of a quarry it may chance that one alone bends the sun's rays at the exact angle that sends them toward my eyes. Doing so makes the quartz gleam. Yet it is the sun's light I see; were cloud to intervene, the quartz would turn to slag. So it goes: every emptiness we feel is "being" eclipsed, all restlessness a flailing for the being that we need, all joy the evidence of being found.

Kings lick the earth whereof the fair are made,
For God hath mingled in the dusty earth
A draught of Beauty from His choicest cup.
'Tis *that,* fond lover—not these lips of clay—
Thou art kissing with a hundred ecstasies,
Think, then, what must it be when undefiled!
(Jalal al-Din Rumi)

Even the addict who prowls the streets for his angry "fix" and the assassin who stalks his fated prey are reaching out for being. The alleys that they walk are blind ones; judged in terms of the larger being they preclude or the damage they work on the being of others they stand condemned. But if it were possible to consider the cocaine's "rush" by itself, apart from its consequences, it would be judged good; the same holds for the satisfaction that sweeps over the assassin as he effects his revenge. *Esse qua esse bonum est.* Being as being is good; more being is better.

It was Aristotle who saw every movement in the universe as ultimately caused by the irresistible attraction of being's superlative instance, the Unmoved Mover. *That* is the magnet; that, the far-off divine event toward which creation moves. St. Thomas detailed his insight: the dynamic pulse and throb of creation is the love of all things for the Infinite; in Dante's echo, it is "l'amor che muove il sole e l'altre stelle," the Love that moves the sun and the other stars. From the lowest level of reality, where even matter reaches out for form, to the highest heavens where angels gravitate around the Throne, a single breath and motion sweeps through existence, the search of each existent for the Good.

Our interest here is the way man, specifically his soul, instances this tendency. So sweetly are things disposed that it appears to the soul not so much that it is led as that it goes as it were of itself. Desiring self-fulfillment, it actively, of its own free will, goes where this fulfillment is to be found. And because the soul is finite, it appears to the soul as if its fulfillment were to be found in finite things: wealth, fame, power, a loved one, whatever. And again we say: in its way this is not inaccurate. But a telltale clue betrays the fact that such immediate objects of desire are but proximate ends that front for one that stands behind them and with respect to which they are but installments. This clue is the fact that we invest these manifestly finite objects with infinite worth. As infinite attractiveness is obviously not an objective property of our desired objects, a paradox ensues: we want infinitely, to the point of sacrificing our lives at times, things that are finite. Our usual way of explaining this paradox is to say that our evaluations are bestowed. The lover projects his estimate on the beloved—lays it on her, she may sometimes feel. The phenomenon admits of another interpretation. It is not so much that he projects infinity—infinite worth—upon her as that he glimpses infinity—the Infinite—through her. She has, for the duration that his passion lasts, become for him a symbol as (for Dante) was Beatrice: she in whom Heaven's glory walked the earth bodily. Symbols can be more or less effective and more or less durable, but within these limits they are the apertures we mentioned. However foolish the swain's love, while it lasts something, at least, of the Shekinah (Presence) hovers. God is near. The lover is in heaven.

For the most part the soul flits from symbol to symbol. Being flashes for a moment, now here, now there, only to withdraw. The object that admitted its light almost blindingly closes over, and we wonder, as we say, what we saw in *her*. In the long run the closures are providential, for they keep us from getting caught on ontological rungs that are incapable of satisfying us as much as ones that are higher. At the time, however, the closures are painful. When no replacement appears, our inward indigence turns everything to wasteland; at this juncture macrocosm mirrors microcosm. Searching for a love that is unerodable, Plato depicted in the *Symposium* the possibility of passing from the love of beautiful objects to the love of that within these that makes them beautiful: from the love of a particular woman to the love of the femininity they have in common, to suggest an example that was not his. From this one might proceed, he argued, until one arrived at the love of the Good itself, whereupon, it being the Form that composes all lesser forms, one could in some respect love everything and so never be without an object for his affections.

For most temperaments this route is too abstract. Its alternative is to love not the Good but God. The object of this preference, as we pointed out in the preceding chapter, is not a fiction. On pain of anthropomorphism we must be on guard not to ascribe to God properties that make us distinctively human: our *kind* of knowledge, our *mode* of love. And we must not overlook that exceptional type of spiritual personality who, having sloughed off his own image and achieved within himself a kind of total nudity, can know God otherwise than through a human prototype; this type we shall treat in the next section. But between anthropomorphism on the one riverbank and transpersonalism on the other flow the waters of the living God. It is not just, as we have noted, that the lion knows a leonine deity. We must go further and say that what we see through the tinted glass of our finite human discernments is nonetheless there, and if an in-ways-humanized image serves as bridge to a region beyond the limitations under which all images must labor, then *al-hamdu lillah*—praise be to Allah, as the Muslims would say.

It is not easy to gauge the spiritual temperature of an age nor to discern the mode its spirituality assumes, but the prevalence of phrases like "the death of God," or better, "the eclipse of God," suggests that men seem to be "saying thou to the universe" less than they did in the past, and hearing less in the way of personalized responses from it. It may be that the mechanization of our industrial environment—steel sheets and girders, concrete piers and asphalt roads, belching blast furnaces, heavy coal smoke, and dead neon signs—this enveloping insentience has led us unconsciously to assume that all environments are inanimate, whereas in fact, of course, above the smog the stars still shine and the angels sing. If deep is answering to deep less today it is not because the depths have changed, certainly not on their objective side. If our world has changed, this only reflects the change in the idea we now have of it. God has not retreated; it is we who have turned away.

So far have we strayed that we need a firsthand account to remind us what it was like to live in the conviction that from beginning to end existence thrills to the life of the living God. To emphasize the fact that personalized experiences of God were not restricted to saints and seers, we present as illustration here an account by an anonymous layman:

> I remember the night, and almost the very spot on the hilltop, where my soul opened out, as it were, into the Infinite, and there was a rushing together of the two worlds, the inner and the outer. It was deep calling unto deep—the deep that my own struggle had opened up within being answered by the unfathomable deep without, reaching beyond the stars. I stood alone with Him who had made me, and all the beauty of the world, and love, and sorrow, and even temptation. I did not seek Him, but felt the perfect unison of my spirit with His. The ordinary sense of things around me faded. For the moment nothing but an ineffable joy and exultation remained. It is impossible fully to describe the experience. It was like the effect of some great orchestra when all the separate notes have melted into one swelling harmony that leaves the listener conscious of nothing save that his soul is being wafted upwards, and almost bursting with its own emotion. The perfect stillness of the night was thrilled by a more solemn silence. The darkness held a presence that was all the more felt because it was not seen. I could not any more have doubted that *He* was there than that I was. Indeed, I felt myself to be, if possible, the less real of the two. (Quoted in William James's *Varieties of Religious Experience*)

Happiness, it is said, has no history. History recounts wars and plagues and famines. All the while on the underside of its mantle of disaster a different kind of drama has never ceased from being woven. A private, interior drama consisting of scenes like the one just described, it reaches the pages of history only when it makes an exceptional impact, as did St. Paul's experience on the Damascus road or Luther's sudden comprehension of the full import of "I believe in the forgiveness of sins." Yet precisely because it is an interior drama it touches the wellsprings of joy and resiliency. Those who are tapped for its cast can lie down on nettles, lie down with vipers, and scarcely notice where they are. The world is not relinquished, but it assumes its proper place. It

> is not all;
> Is harsh with envy, greed, assault,—or blooms

With friendship, courage, truth, is beautiful;
Yet is at best but an inn on a thoroughfare:
Provincial, one might call the mind contented there.
(Edna St. Vincent Millay, *Conversation at Midnight*)

The phenomenology of the soul's romance with its Creator admits of three distinguishable modes. In the first the accent falls on the love the soul feels for God. The troubadours come to mind here, as do the seekers of the grail and the seventh- to ninth-century Alvars of South India, *alvar* meaning literally "diver" (into the ocean of divine consciousness). These ecstatic devotees of Vishnu pressed into devotional service the entire complement of human emotions, from the tenderness of a doting mother to the terror of an abandoned child, but it was in the half-crazed, near-hysterical longing of a lover for his absent love that their fervor reached its peak:

When will the time come when I shall see Him without intermission and place my crowned head at His feet? When will the time come when my tears of ecstasy shall flow on seeing the wonderful Lord? When will the time come when my mind gazing at His moon-like face will melt into Him? (*Kulasekhara Alvar*)

A favorite allegory in Sufi tales concerns the shaikh who abdicates his eminence in the world and to the incomprehension and disgust of those who had envied and respected him now lives only to gain the company of some simple wench who has won his heart. His beard mats up and his clothes become rags, for his thoughts are so completely on her that none remain for his own person. Even death is no deterrent, for whereas her continued absence is intolerable, in her presence he could die in peace.

In the second mode, the accent falls on God's love for man.

Posit a lover whose existence has centered for months in an anguished and unrequited yearning like that of the shaikh just depicted. Though his passion is spurned he nevertheless longs for nothing so much as to be in his beloved's presence: in her absence he consoles himself with recollections of the times he was with her and anticipations of ones when he will see her again. If after months of such seemingly hopeless longing the swain were to find that the princess was beginning to take an interest in him, could we imagine his state? Not only does he want, he is wanted; not only does he love, he is loved. And should it transpire that from a modest beginning the princess's regard for him were to rise to an intensity that rivaled his own—the intensity of his desperation when it seemed that his love was hopeless and of his rapture when it began to look as if it were not—would we then be able to follow his emotions to their Himalayan heights? It is on record that such are the emotions that visit the soul when it discovers that it is literally loved by the God who made and rules the universe. The following is the account of Mrs. Jonathan Edwards:

> Last night was the sweetest night I ever had in my life. I never before, for so long a time together, enjoyed so much of the light and rest and sweetness of heaven in my soul. . . . Part of the night I lay awake, sometimes asleep, and sometimes between sleeping and waking. But all night I continued in a constant, clear, and lively sense of the heavenly sweetness of Christ's excellent love, of his nearness to me, and of my dearness to him; with an inexpressibly sweet calmness of soul in an entire rest in him. I seemed to myself to perceive a glow of divine love come down from the heart of Christ in heaven into my heart in a constant stream, like a stream or pencil of sweet light.

In our analogy we spoke of the princess's love as rivaling the swain's, but in the present case God's love exceeds the soul's, for the soul is finite, with the consequence that what is total for it is no match for the love that flows from a source that is illimitable. It must have been this sense—the sense that the Lord of all Being loved them with a strength that exceeded their own, loved to the point of sacrificing his very Son for them—that empowered the early Christians to launch what numerically was to become the foremost religion in the world.

Our account of the soul, the theme Plato esteemed to be "of large and more than mortal discourse" (*Phaedrus,* 246a), is complete. Having identified its essential tendency as "that veritable love, that sharp desire" (Plotinus) and its final object as Being, if one thinks "abstractly," or God in his personal mode if one does not, the way is clear to move to the final rung on the scale of reality and the deepest element in man. But lest it be inferred from this projected move that we do not take the soul's God seriously, that we regard him as no more than an edifying fiction or symbol, we close this section with words that count the more because written by the man who more than any other has secured for us the personal God without loading him with finality—the two things must be said together. Speaking of the levels within the self and the ascending importance of those which, lying deeper, are more substantial, Frithjof Schuon writes:

> According to some people, it is enough to convince oneself, as it were by auto-suggestion, that one is neither the body nor the mind. This truth is not realizable, however, until body and mind have conformed on their plane to what may be called the "Divine Will"; one cannot attain *Atma* without God or in opposition to God. The "personal Divinity" only allows those who adore Him to understand that He is not the absolute Reality.

We can see why this is so. To identify (merge) with what is pitted against us (feared and resented) is out of the question; only love can draw us, first toward, and then into, another. Only when the demandingness of separative existence (the *tanha*-craving of body and mind) has fallen away, leaving us identified with the region of self that loves its matrix and knows its love to be reciprocated—only selves that are living at this barely separate level can think of taking the final step of relinquishing their individuality entirely, if "thinking" has any application in a state that is on the verge of simply dissolving into the Godhead. As long as the sense of separateness continues, which is to say in some degree until death, the self must love and worship the Other its life confronts, for to repeat, this is the only attitude (affective stance) that can counter the alienation of separateness and cause it to diminish. To the degree that a soul worships, it does not demand to be "I," and so is not opposed in principle to the thought, should it arise, that "I am not my finite self; I am the Atman." It is in this way that an adoring soul is the only possible bridge to Spirit.

IV. SPIRIT

If soul is the element in man that relates to God, Spirit is the element that is identical with Him—not with his personal mode, for on the celestial plane God and soul remain distinct, but with God's mode that is infinite. Spirit is the Atman that *is* Brahman, the aspect of man that *is* the Buddha-nature, the element in man which, exceeding the soul's full panoply, is that "something in the soul that is uncreated and uncreatable" (Eckhart). It is the true man in Lin Chi the Ch'an master's assertion that "beyond the mass of reddish flesh is the true man who has no title"; and the basis for the most famous of Sufi claims: Mansur al-Hallaj's assertion, "*ana'l-Haqq*, I am the Absolute Truth, or the True Reality."

We speak of identity, and this is right, for on this final stratum the subject-object dichotomy is transcended. Still, man's finitude remains, which means that the identity must not be read simplistically. Spirit is Infinite, but man is finite because he is not Spirit only. His specifically human overlay—body, mind, and soul—veils the Spirit within him. As the Jains say, a lamp's flame may be bright, but let its chimney be coated with dust or soot and the lamplight will be dim. Spirit's presence in man does not render him omnipotent or omniscient, nor relieve him of limitations that dog even the greatest saints: "Why callest me good? there is none good but one, that is, God" (Matt. 19:17). But though it does not render man omnipotent, Spirit does, as we might put the matter, remove his impotence. It does so by providing him with a vantage point from which he can see that his station requires the limitations his humanity imposes. By itself that realization would produce only resignation, but the something in man that enables him to see that he must be limited also does the limiting, if we may use this perhaps curious way of registering the fact that the Infinite cannot tolerate a second of its kind: some things are obvious. Spirit decrees that body, being corporeal, must naturally be limited. Man accepts that decree for his physical component; for his mind and soul as well, in their respective ways. Meanwhile his Spirit remains free, it being the sovereign that imposes the decree rather than the prisoner who submits to it.

The shifting of the ballast of man's self-recognition from servant to Sovereign proceeds by stages. Following a Sufi formulation, we may distinguish between the Lore of Certainty, the Eye of Certainty, and the Truth of Certainty, the first being likened to hearing about fire, the second to seeing fire, and the third to being burned by fire. Spirit is the bedrock of our lifestream, but the waters that course over it are for the most part too roiled to allow the bed to be seen. Where the banks widen and the current slows, however, sediment settles and we glimpse our support. Always in this life some water intervenes to veil, but at the moment the point is the opposite one. Not only is the bed there throughout; it is truly the bed that we see even when we see it obscurely. Man is Spirit while not Spirit unalloyed.

Back now to Lin Chi's "true man who has no title" residing beyond the mass of reddish flesh. He has no title—is not man or woman, young or old, rich or poor—because as we spelled out at some length in "The Levels of Reality," the Infinite which Spirit overlaps defies positive characterization. Since "Spirit" and "Infinite" are, like "Atman" and "Brahman," but two words for a single reality, we summarize what was said about it under the caption "The Infinite." Though it is possible to intuit it directly, we can think of it only by invoking a double negative. Peripherally Spirit is without boundaries; internally it is without barriers. It knows neither walls that encompass nor walls that divide.

Between thought (which proceeds indirectly through concepts) and intuition (which directly identifies) lies a middle ground. We scarcely know what to call it. Symbolism? Art in its sacred sector? It uses the stones of earth to raise on its flatlands spires that point toward heaven. This middle mode of concourse plays while logic works. It is unquestionably alert, while being in some respects passive to the point of dissociation, for to shift gears an engine must disengage and pass through neutral. Playing with the second of the above stipulations about spirit—its indifference to internal divisions—we note first that it is possible for nondifferentiation to climb to the point where the world's divisions vanish completely. Ramakrishna reports his experience of this condition as follows:

> Suddenly the blessed Mother revealed Herself. The buildings with their different parts, the temple, and everything else vanished from my sight, leaving no trace whatsoever, and in their stead I saw a limitless, infinite effulgent Ocean of Consciousness. As far as the eye could see, the shining billows were madly rushing at me from all sides with a terrific noise, to swallow me up! What was happening in the outside world I did not know; but within me there was a steady flow of undiluted bliss.

But though corporeal distinctions can be thus erased, the instances in which they are erased constitute an exceptional class. Normally distinctions remain but are softened. Or they remain precise while changing from barriers to bridges.

> "I," table, flower, fragrance, the chirping of birds, are all undeniably present, but being in reality nonexistent they do not present themselves as solid, self-subsistent entities. They are transparent and permeable. Reflecting each other, interpenetrating each other, and dissolving themselves into each other, they form an integral whole which is nothing other than the direct appearance of the primary level of Reality. In this sense, sensible perception, wherein distinctions loom so large, is reduced almost to nullity. It loses its functional basis, it does not work properly, in the presence of the trans-subjective and trans-objective awareness of the interfusion of all things where "gnat," instead of presenting itself as an independent external entity, means rather its identification with Being and an other things so that they end up by being fused into one. (Adapted from the writings of Toshihiko Izutsu)

In and through the body and *ahamkara* (ego sense) of every human being Lin Chi's man with no title is untiringly alive. He is not the personal God; he is the all-embracing Infinite. He is the actor who has internalized the play so completely that he identifies more with it than with his role in it: he will make the audience despise him if the play requires that he do so. We can generalize this image. Every figure presupposes a ground against which it is seen or thought. But since in the final analysis the individual could not exist without its ground or be conceived without presupposing it, the two are—in last analysis, we repeat—inseparable. In a way that is absolutely crucial, a thing's ground is an aspect of the thing itself. Seen with the "eye of the heart," the organ of spiritual vision, this body of flesh and blood which in corporeal respects is frail as foam, fleeting as dew, is at the same time, in this very moment and on this very spot, the infinite and eternal Life instancing itself in this particular respect. Normally, as we have noted, the perception does not involve the total dissolution of finitude in the ocean of Godhead. Rather it is the experience of finitude *as* infinity, or temporality *as* eternity, the opposites blended in ineffable yet palpable whole. It is as if an iceberg were suddenly to realize that it is H_2O.

The fact that the notion of the Infinite appeals to us is itself evidence of Spirit's reality, for metaphysical arguments would never convince were there not within us a trace of that which they set out to communicate—if the certainty they seek to awaken were not already sleeping in the substance of our souls. At the same time we resist the notion, for it requires that we shift our identification from the parts of our being that press palpably upon us. The writing of this chapter happened to span a Christmas in which there was a two-year-old in the house, and it became evident again how strong the *ahamkara,* or ego sense, is ingrained within us. One had remembered from one's own children the insatiability of the ego's wants: the Christmases when what counted was not what the presents were but their quantity, with the inevitable tears when the number proved finite. It took a grandchild, however, to revive the memory of an earlier stage when the life task was to firm up the sense of selfhood itself. At this state not even numbers mattered as much as who the numbers were for. Before each present was opened, it was imperative that it be paraded and acknowledgment secured from each person assembled that "This is *my* present. This present is *mine!*" The sands of the Sahara, and a grain pops up to announce: I exist!

Once personal identity is established the issue shifts to what that identity is to be attached to. An eighth birthday and the boy was happy until he went to bed and the light was out. Then, in the aloneness of the dark, time paid him its first visit, whispering that he would never be seven again. And the prospect was intolerable. Since seven was what the boy sensed himself to be, the day that had just ended being insufficient to offset his identification with the plans and projects of the days and weeks that had preceded it, time's notice fell as death warrant. The death of himself-as-seven was the death of *him,* the only "him" that at the time was in view. He jumped from his bed and ran to his parents sobbing, "Take the presents back; I don't want them. I just want to be seven."

We smile at the boy's naïveté, but we know what he meant. For with the exception of those supernatural moments when reality breaks through the carapace of time like lightning and reveals the landscape in which we *are* infinite, every human has his age seven, his less than total self, with which he myopically identifies. The referent is elastic. An addict while his tissues scream knows himself as little more than a demanding body. At the other end of the spectrum are the times when one's cup runs over to the point where it would be easy to lay down one's life if the need arose. But almost invariably there is some point where selfhood is sensed to end and the not-self begin. This not-self, too, can be variously viewed: it can appear as a predominantly hostile world of alien objects and circumstances that kick and buffet, or as everlasting arms from whose embrace it is impossible to fall. One must come to the point where they are seen as the latter before one can take the final step in self-abandonment and identify with one's surround, which is why the preceding section asserted that the door that leads from soul to spirit is the door of love: love of Being-as-a-whole or of the God who is its Lord. For Spirit to permeate the self's entirety, the components of the self must be aligned: body in temperance, mind in understanding (Gautama's Right Views), and soul in love. But the immediate point is that even when the environment is seen to be benign, as long as it presents itself as distinct and other there will be imponderables which must be written off to God's inscrutable ways. The only alternative is to remove the dichotomy itself.

The removal is effected by perceiving the "other" as one's destiny. As we despair of equaling a formulation of this point that has come our way, we quote from Gai Eaton's "Man as Viceroy" at some length.

> There is no radical distinction to be made between what a man is given in the way of mind, emotional make-up and body on the one hand and, on the other, what he is given in the way of outward circumstances and environment. Together they form a significant whole and all are aspects of a particular individual life.
>
> The being between birth and death scrawls—in matter and in events—a pattern which, taken as a whole, expresses his unique identity. This man, So-and-So, is not a sealed personality moving through an alien environment. He is the sum total of all that he does and all that happens to him and all that comes within his range, spread out (from our point of view) in time and space, but a single, timeless fact in the mind of God. What we are and where we are cannot ultimately be divided. And to accept our destiny is to accept ourselves, recognizing that what happens to us is as much a part of our nature—in the widest sense—as the most intimate contours of our own selfhood. It is sometimes said that the fatal bullet has its victim's name upon it and fits no other flesh.
>
> In the last resort, a man looks at the love or anger or fear within himself and says, So this is me. Looks at his withered hand or wounded foot and says, So this is me. Looks at the woman he has married or the garden he has planted and says, So this is me. Looks finally upon his enemy and upon his death and says, So this is me. But in saying this he bears witness to the fact that he is also incomparably more than an itemised list of the elements that make up his individuality and its inseparable field of action.
>
> And in acknowledging so much that is a part of ourselves (since our boundaries extend to the furthest horizons we can see from our particular vantage point) we make an act of recognition which actualises what was inherent in us from the start—almost as though we existed only to discover what was always there—recognising our name-tag on everything that comes our way. But the part of us that is our destiny, streaming in upon us in the form of "outside" events through the course of time, can be recognised as belonging to our own particular pattern only when it has happened. The religious man can say, "Thy will be done!" as a statement of his intention to accept this will when it has been done and is apparent to him, but it is not our nature to be able to foresee the future except under the most unusual circumstances. In general, acceptance of destiny is acceptance of what has happened, not of what might happen (but might be prevented).

Assuming that the acceptance in question is in the mode of affirmation and not solely resignation, acceptance of one's destiny as part of one's selfhood is an aspect of that love of being or God that opens us to the Infinite. But enough: the point has been made or it will not be made here. We close with a Sufi tale, "The Tale of the Sands," that epitomizes what this section has tried to say.

A stream, from its source in far-off mountains, passing through every kind and description of countryside, at last reached the sands of the desert. Just as it had crossed every other barrier, the stream tried to cross this one, but it found that as fast as it ran into the sand, its waters disappeared.

It was convinced, however, that its destiny was to cross this desert, and yet there was no way. Now a hidden voice, coming from the desert itself, whispered: 'The Wind crosses the desert, and so can the stream.'

The stream objected that it was dashing itself against the sand, and only getting absorbed: that the wind could fly, and this was why it could cross a desert.

'By hurtling in your own accustomed way you cannot get across. You will either disappear or become a marsh. You must allow the wind to carry you over, to your destination.'

But how could this happen? 'By allowing yourself to be absorbed in the wind.'

This idea was not acceptable to the stream. After all, it had never been absorbed before. It did not want to lose its individuality. And, once having lost it, how was one to know that it could ever be regained?

'The wind,' said the sand, 'performs this function. It takes up water, carries it over the desert, and then lets it fall again. Falling as rain, the water again becomes a river.'

'How can I know that this is true?'

'It is so, and if you do not believe it, you cannot become more than a quagmire, and even that could take many, many years; and it certainly is not the same as a stream.'

'But can I not remain the same stream that I am today?'

'You cannot in either case remain so,' the whisper said. 'Your essential part is carried away and forms a stream again. You are called what you are even today because you do not know which part of you is the essential one.'

When he heard this, certain echoes began to arise in the thoughts of the stream. Dimly, he remembered a state in which he—or some part of him, was it?—had been held in the arms of a wind. He also remembered—or did he?—that this was the real thing, not necessarily the obvious thing, to do.

And the stream raised his vapour into the welcoming arms of the wind, which gently and easily bore it upwards and along, letting it fall softly as soon as they reached the roof of a mountain, many, many miles away. And because he had had his doubts, the stream was able to remember and record more strongly in his mind the details of the experience. He reflected, 'Yes, now I have learned my true identity.'

The stream was learning. But the sands whispered: 'We know, because we see it happen day after day: and because we, the sands, extend from the riverside all the way to the mountain.'

And that is why it is said that the way in which the Stream of Life is to continue on its journey is written in the Sands.

21

Western Philosophy as a Great Religion

In a striking paper titled "*Philosophia* as One of the Religious Traditions of Mankind," Wilfred Cantwell Smith argues that the Greek legacy in Western civilization deserves to be ranked as one of the world's great religions. We couldn't recognize this earlier, he says, because our notion of religion was too tightly tied to Judaism and Christianity. A century of work in comparative religion has now loosened this parochial mooring; it has enabled us to bring the entire human heritage into view, lining up its components in our mind's eye, arraying them side by side, and according reasonable justice to each. This, in turn, has given us a better understanding of what a religious tradition looks like—what it is that makes it such. Among other advantages, this new understanding doubles back to "proffer a substantial reinterpretation of Western data," including the realization that

> it is legitimate and helpful to consider . . . the Greek tradition in Western civilization, rationalist-idealist-humanist, within the generic context of various [other] religious traditions of mankind. It is neither absurd, nor trite, to reinterpret it as one of our planet's major religious traditions: different, of course, from each of the others yet comparable, and understood most truly when so contrasted and compared.

Like so many of Professor Smith's insights, I find this one exciting, although I propose to develop it differently from the way he projected in his paper. First let me say why I think a fresh look at our Western philosophical heritage is in order.

I

Worldviews derive from epistemologies, which in turn derive from motivations. That the driving motivation of modern science is to control is, I take it, too obvious to need documenting. The epistemology that has fashioned our modern outlook derives from this same animus: we wove its net with the hope that the kind of knowledge it would lift from the sea of being would be the kind that would augment our effectiveness in dealing with life as a whole, *effectiveness* being defined here in its problem-solving sense. I shall limit myself to a single witness for each of the two remaining links in my propaedeutic chain: Ernest Gellner for epistemology, and Hannah Arendt for its consequent ontology or worldview.

I choose Gellner for epistemology because, being a sociologist as well as a philosopher, his perceptions carry more than private weight. I am not saying, of course, that he is infallible or even necessarily right—only that, as a philosopher-sociologist who trains his sociological equipment on philosophy as a discipline, his findings lay claim to more than private standing. Gellner focuses on the way Western philosophers have come to see things rather than on the way he himself sees them.

What is this way? Gellner admits that at first glance there seems to be no "way" in the singular; what greets us is, to use the title of the opening section of his *Legitimation of Belief,* "The Pluralist Chorus." But beneath this surface variety—even cacophony—a trend can be discerned. Most generally, it is the trend toward acceptance of epistemology as contemporary philosophy's focal task; more specifically, it is an "emerging consensus" that, to be recognized as legitimate, beliefs must now pass two tests, or "insistences" as he calls them. "There is the empiricist insistence that faiths ... must stand ready to be judged by ... something reasonably close to the ordinary notion of 'experience'.... Secondly, there is the 'mechanistic' insistence on impersonal ... explanations."

Gellner proceeds to ground these two insistences in the prometheanism I have charged with calling the tune for modern Western epistemology:

> We have of course no guarantee that the world must be such as to be amenable to such explanations; we can only show that *we* are constrained to think so. It was Kant's merit to see that this compulsion is in us, not in things. it was Weber's to see that it is historically a specific kind of mind, not human mind as such, which is subject to this compulsion. What it amounts to is in the end simple: if there is to be effective knowledge or explanation *at all,* it must have this form, for any other kind of 'explanation' ... is *ipso facto* powerless.

"We have become habituated to and dependent on effective knowledge, and hence have bound ourselves to this kind of genuine explanation," Gellner continues. The view of the world it produces is inevitable—I am speaking now for myself, to make the transition from Gellner to Arendt, from epistemology to ontology. Empiricism and mechanism being ill-suited to deal with transcendence and the unseen, the epistemology of prometheanism necessarily delivers a naturalistic world. "What has come to an end," Hannah Arendt wrote toward the close of her life, "is the . . . distinction between the sensual and the supersensual, together with the notion, at least as old as Parmenides, that whatever is not given to the senses . . . is more real, more truthful, more meaningful than what appears; that it is not just beyond sense perception but *above* the world of the senses."

That says it: our (promethean) motivation has elicited our (mechanistic-empiricist) epistemology, which in turn has brought forward a naturalistic metaphysics. Now the price of focusing attention on one thing is, of course, inattention to other things: when a botanist peers down his or her microscope at a leaf cell, the leaf as a whole disappears. This simple analogy alone should cause us to have second thoughts about our prevailing naturalism, so obviously is it a product of a partial epistemology. But one of the tolls that has been exacted from us on the road we have traveled is interest in truth for its own sake. Preoccupied with "effective knowledge" (Gellner's term), we have grown forgetful of Being; the self-centeredness that prompts prometheanism in the first place carries right through to the end. If motivations forge epistemologies that forge ontologies, these ontologies in turn forge anthropologies, meaning, by this last word, lives as conditioned by the worlds in which they live.

What is the feel of the life that naturalism has generated? As early as two centuries ago, Gellner points out, Kant saw "the inescapable price of this Faustian purchase of real *[sic]* knowledge. [In delivering] cognitive effectiveness [it] exacts its inherent moral, 'dehumanizing' price. . . . The price of real knowledge is that our identities, freedom, norms, are no longer underwritten by our vision and comprehension of things. On the contrary we are doomed to suffer from a tension between cognition and identity." A hundred years later, Hannah Arendt continues, Nietzsche deepened Kant's analysis. Picking up on the point we have already cited from her, that the distinction between the sensual and the supersensual has been brought to an end, she proceeds as follows:

> Meanwhile, in increasingly strident voices, the defenders of metaphysics have warned us of the danger of nihilism inherent in this development; and although they themselves seldom invoke it, they have an important argument in their favor: it is indeed true that once the suprasensual realm is discarded, its opposite, the world of appearances as understood for so many centuries, is also annihilated. The sensual, as still understood by the positivists, cannot survive the death of the supersensual. No one knew this better than Nietzsche who, with his poetic and metaphoric description of the assassination of God in *Zarathustra,* has caused so much confusion in these matters. In a significant passage in *The Twilight of Idols,* he clarifies what the word *God* meant in *Zarathustra.* It was merely a symbol for the suprasensual realm as understood by metaphysics; he now uses instead of *God* the word *true world* and says:

"We have abolished the true world. What has remained? The apparent one perhaps? Oh no! With the true world we have also abolished the apparent one."

Kant for the eighteenth century, Nietzsche for the nineteenth—for the twentieth I shall choose a sociologist at my own university, Manfred Stanley:

> It is by now a Sunday-supplement commonplace that the social, economic and technological modernization of the world is accompanied by a spiritual malaise that has come to be called *alienation*. At its most fundamental level, the diagnosis of alienation is based on the view that modernization forces upon us a world that, although baptized as real by science, is denuded of all humanly recognizable qualities; beauty and ugliness, love and hate, passion and fulfillment, salvation and damnation. It is not, of course, being claimed that such matters are not part of the existential realities of human life. It is rather that the scientific world view makes it illegitimate to speak of them as being "objectively" part of the world, forcing us instead to define such evaluation and such emotional experiences as "merely subjective" projections of people's inner lives.

The world, once an "enchanted garden," to use Max Weber's memorable phrase, has now become disenchanted, deprived of purpose and direction, bereft—in these senses—of life itself. All that which is allegedly basic to the specifically human status in nature comes to be forced back upon the precincts of the "subjective" which, in turn, is pushed by the modern scientific view ever more into the province of dreams and illusions.

Are we ready, now, to take another look at our philosophical past?

II

Professor Smith keeps the Greek philosophical heritage intact, seeing that heritage-as-a-whole as an alternative to the Western family of religions (Judaism, Christianity, and Islam) and the religions of non-Western civilizations. Using a diagram he does not himself introduce, we might visualize his demarcation of the major historical religious alternatives as shown in table 1.

I, on the other hand, want to take as my encompassing unit our Western religious tradition as a whole, in which the Greek component figures as one-fourth, the other three-fourths being Judaism, Christianity, and Islam. Moreover, only a fourth of Western philosophy enters the Western religious tradition: its modern half becomes too fastened to modern science to be religiously important, while half of its original, traditional half was likewise more occupied with worldly than with religious concerns.

Explanations are at once required.

1. In placing Greek *gnosis* at the pinnacle of Western religion I do not mean that it is superior to Judaism, Christianity, and Islam. I mean only that when

Table 1

Judaism	Christianity	Islam	Philosophia: The Greek Heritage	Hinduism	Buddhism	The Chinese Religious Complex

these Semitically originated communities came to conceptualize their deepest insights, a grammar for the purpose awaited them. It was, moreover, a grammar so advanced, so carefully tuned to the highest registers of the human spirit, that Christians, Muslims, and Jews alike embraced it. In Chomskian idiom, they found its grammar to be "generic"—we need think only of the equal enthusiasm with which Philo and Maimonides, Dionysius and Thomas Aquinas, Avicenna and ibn 'Arabi assimilated it. The zenith of the Western religious tradition is Greek in the sense that Greece provided its grammar and vocabulary, but the discernments this equipment was used to articulate were present in the Semitic religions from their start.

2. Analytic philosophers often point out that the novelties that have entered philosophy in our century do not token a break with its past: Aristotle, Anselm, Thomas Aquinas, and Duns Scotus, they contend, were analytic philosophers. Fair enough. But analytic philosophy's preponderantly critical attitude toward religion makes me want to enter the same claim for religious philosophy. It too is solidly grounded in our philosophical past, continuing the Great Tradition.

3. Philosophers who are comparativists will see almost at once what I am up to, for it is in Vedantic idiom that my project can be stated most succinctly. This is not surprising, for the project would never have occurred to me had I not encountered India; it is from her that my controlling paradigm is lifted (table 2).

I want to consider the Greek inheritance in philosophy as our Western version of *Jñāna* yoga. It is common knowledge that India delineates four paths to God, of which *jñāna*, the path of knowledge, is one. Its chief alternative is *bhakti yoga,* the path of love or devotion, for the two remaining paths—those of work and meditation, *karma yoga* and *rāja yoga* respectively—tend to be assimilated by the first two. India accommodates these two great spiritual options in a single tradition, called the *sanātana dharma* or *varṇāśrama,* depending on whether one is thinking of its theoretical or its practical side. But in the West these alternatives have not been partners in a single tradition. They look more like distinct separate traditions that for two thousand years have been trying to work out a modus vivendi.

Athens and Jerusalem, philosophy and religion, the Hebraic and Hellenic components of Western civilization: does the Indian experience have anything to say to us as we continue to work toward a harmonious marriage of these parents

TABLE 2

		The Greek Philosophical Inheritance		The Western Religious Tradition
	Ionian		Italianate (Magna Graecia)	
Traditional	Thales		Pythagoras	
	Anaximander		Parmenides	
	Anaximines		Heraclitus	Greek *gnosis*
	Anaxagoras		Socrates	
	Leucippus		Plato	
	Democritus		Plotinus	
		Philosophy begins to be shaped by modern science		
Modern	(welcomes this move)		(tries to continue the tradition)	Judaism Christianity Islam
	Empiricism		Rationalism	
	Galileo		Renaissance nature	
	Bacon		philosophy	
	Hume		Spinoza	
	Positivism		Romanticism	
	Anglo-American analytic philosophy		Continental philosophy (existentialism & phenomenology)	

that have begotten us? To Indian eyes, Judaism, Christianity, and Islam appear basically as bhaktic or devotional paths which, because they don't provide much room for *jñāna* or *gnosis,* leave the latter housed with the history of philosophy. *Jñāna* visits the Western religions proper, who grant it temporary visas, we might say; but except for the duration of the medieval synthesis it isn't given citizenship. We need only think of Spinoza, Eckhart, and al-Hallaj to be reminded of how restive Judaism, Christianity, and Islam can become when full-fledged gnostics appear in their midsts. Śaṅkara and Nāgārjuna had to contend with the Brahmins and Bhikkus of their traditions too, but in the end they were fully ensconced. Insofar as this essay has a programmatic thrust, it is to propose that the Western religious tradition open its gates comparably to the jnanic strand in its civilization, the strand that originated in Greek philosophy.

III

What is *jñāna* or *gnosis* (spelled with a small "g" to distinguish it from Gnosticism as a specific doctrine) as a religious category?

In *Farewell Happy Fields,* the first volume in her trilogy of memoirs, Kathleen Raine describes in some detail her father's Wesleyan Methodism in Ilford, England. On the verge of manhood he had undergone conversion to "a living faith," which remained thereafter unshaken and enabled him to live a life of many sorrows with deep confidence. He looked for no earthly happiness, for it was clear to him that in this world a human is "a stranger and sojourner." All he asked of his brief time on earth was to perform the tasks life placed before him, for task was precisely what life was—a task to be performed, sure of the reward of the faithful servant in the world to come. Ambition had no place in such a life; it was unimaginable to him, for he did not regard his life as his own but rather his Master's. What his Master willed for his life was that he spend it assisting in the titanic struggle of good against evil. This good was situated in social improvement and service rather than in nature, truth, and beauty. These latter he valued only for their "message," for moral purpose was everything—the question of salvation made it so. This relentless moralism forced a certain narrowness on his life. Still, the fineness of his moral sense infused his conduct with a beauty of its own.

A summarizing paragraph cannot do justice to Dr. Raine's account of this religious universe of her father, but that doesn't matter because it is not that universe itself that concerns us here. I have introduced it only as a foil to bring out what is of moment, namely, his wife's reaction to it. Fortunately Dr. Raine's own account is succinct enough to let her give it directly.

> My mother's evasion, after her marriage, of the religion of John Wesley was not different from her earlier evasion of John Knox; a withdrawal of attention, a failure of interest availed her more than argument and useless opposition. She had, besides, a habit of fainting in church; I never knew her to faint elsewhere, certainly not at the theatre, on the longest walk, or in the hottest greenhouse in Kew. My father I think never knew whether my mother had been "saved" or not; for she always agreed with everything he said. But at over eighty it was the *Upanishads* and the works of A. E. and G. R. S. Mead and even Israel Regardie that my mother would take down from my shelves, or travels in Tibet, or works on spiritualism; never have I seen her read any work of Christian devotion. The supernatural world was for her, as were her vivid nightly dreams, rather an escape from the moral world than, as for my father, a region of it. She confessed to me (she was in her mid-eighties then) that she was not "religious" and had always found the emotionalism of Methodism vulgar; "but I am very interested in the cosmos." Some time before this she had had a slight stroke and thought she was dying. What was it like? I asked her; and my mother's eyes flashed like those of a hawk whose hood is lifted and she said, "I was very interested."

She said she was not religious, but do we believe her? Her disinterest in the kind of religion she saw around her comes through to us (in her daughter's account) categorically, but the account shows something positive at work as well—that to which she was drawn as "religion's" alternative. She was interested, we are told, in the cosmos and in her near-encounter with death. *More* than interested, actually; in these she was "very interested"—the phrase is repeated for both topics. And the question for us becomes: Do we not sense in these interests themselves something religious? Her own protestations to the contrary count for nothing here, of course, since it's precisely the meaning of the word *religion* that is at stake. In part her *religiousness* (in our enlarged definition of the word), discloses itself in the objects that interested her, for death and the cosmos are religious themes in ways that ice cream and horse racing are not. But it is in the *way* those objects drew her that the character of her religious impulse, its jnanic character, is disclosed. In contrasting her mother's interest to her father's, Dr. Raine highlights its form. Her mother's interest was disinterested in a way her father's was not; it was the "disinterested interest" that is the hallmark of jnanic religion. A wife's confession that she was "not 'religious' . . . but" has brought us to the distinctive feature of jnanic religion or gnosis. It is religion in the presiding mode of pure interest—pure, disinterested interest, to repeat the paradoxical formulation. Hypnotized by the strangeness of a new and unfamiliar beauty, the person is fascinated, engrossed, awestruck, transfixed. The jnanic vision is so totally its own reward that the question "What's in it for me?" doesn't even intrude. In pure cases there is no "me" in the picture at all.

I am not contending that self-transcending vision is the only important thing in religion or even in jnanic religion. Questions of action (what's to be done) and the meaning of one's own individual life inevitably enter and must be dealt with—justice interested the West's paradigmatic *jñāna* yogin, Socrates, only slightly less than did wisdom. I am, though, claiming that important as these other components are, to the *jñāna* yogin they are secondary to the religious object as it transcends finally not only oneself but humanity and the entire created universe. If we cannot recognize a position that fixes on the strange, transhuman beauty of being as it passes in awe-inspiring recessions from the natural world into the infinite; or, if acknowledging that such a position exists we nevertheless refuse to grant it full religious status, I should end my essay here. For if Western philosophy is religious, it is so in the mode I have tried to describe; and if that mode is not authentically religious, Western philosophy is not a great religion.

IV

The preceding section tried to identify the heart of the jnanic position. In this final section I shall argue the religiousness of this position as it appears in the

West, primarily in the gnostic strand of Greek-originated philosophy. I have already observed that the bhaktic, devotional character of Judaism, Christianity, and Islam has obscured the fully religious character of this jnanic stance. My strategy toward removing that prejudice will be to enumerate seven properties we tend spontaneously to recognize as religious and show the extent to which our philosophical tradition has housed them. There is space here only to touch on these seven themes which elsewhere I hope to expand, but perhaps their simple enumeration can help us to see why Peter Brown could note toward the beginning of his biography of Augustine of Hippo that "for centuries now, the *idea* of philosophy had been surrounded with a religious aura."

1. *Philosophy's communal nature*. When Whitehead defined religion as what we do with our solitariness, he was voicing at most a half-truth. More obvious is its deep involvement with our social nature; as people associate around the things they prize, their lives get woven together: synagogues, churches, and the Islamic *ummah* (community) take shape. So it was with the schools of ancient Greek philosophy. The Epicureans, Stoics, Academics, Peripatetics, and Neo-Pythagoreans were not philosophical schools in the abstract sense in which we speak of schools of thought today—positivist, idealist, pragmatic, and the like. They were also cultic communities, half ritual and half philosophy—more like colleges in the medieval, monastic sense than in the sense of even our residential colleges today. Like the *ashrams* of India and American communes today, they often sprang up around central founding figures such as Plato, Aristotle, Zeno the Stoic, Epicurus, or, later, Plotinus—individuals who were not just thinkers or professors but who were regarded as inspired. Correlatively, their students were not students in the contemporary academic sense but more like disciples. They congregated around their masters because they wanted actually to live by their doctrines. The Pythagorean communities are the extreme case here, of course. Their students were more like candidates for the priesthood than candidates for a degree at a modern university.

2. *Its cultic features*. These follow in part from the communal features just noted. Mary Douglas contends that communities become such through the conscious or unconscious rituals that knit lives together more powerfully than does conversation. But my interest here is not in the rituals the Greek philosophers devised or adopted for their own communities. Such rituals existed; we know, to cite a single case, that "Plato's Academy was a religious association with its own divine worship, in which the cultus was of such importance that we find it explicitly laid down that one of its members should be appointed to prepare the sacrifice." But the more important point, I think, is that the philosophers typically participated in the normal rituals of their communities. I see no reason to view this cynically, as if they did so for reasons of prudence or expediency. On the contrary. I take it as evidence that they saw themselves adding their insights

to the religion of their people rather than using these insights to oppose that religion. (Their critique of the crass anthropomorphism and immorality of the Homeric pantheon doesn't counter that statement, for that way of imaging the divine was on its last legs for the populace as a whole.) This is not to say that the relations between priests and the philosophers were always harmonious. Being of different spiritual temperaments they at best felt somewhat awkward with one another, while at worst hostility could flame. Socrates is the classic case, having been condemned in part on the charge of teaching atheism. But the other side of that coin is his denial of the charge. I venture the generalization that whereas exoterics (*bhaktis*) often felt threatened by esoterics (*jñānins*), not fully comprehending what the latter were up to, esoterics (the philosophers) generally saw their spirituality as continuous with that of the people, though of course they did claim to see more deeply into its meaning. The *Republic* opens with Socrates reporting, "I went down yesterday to the Picraeus with Glaucon . . . that I might offer up my prayers to the goddess [Bendis]," and his last words as recorded in the *Phaedo* were, "Clinton, we owe a cock to Ascelepios [the god of healing]; pay it without fail."

3. *Its ultimacy.* In a well-known lecture, John Burnett argues that the core of Socrates' teaching is to be found at *Apology* 29D4 and 30A7 ff., where stress is laid on the care of the soul and how to make it as good as possible:

> Men of Athens, I honour and love you; but I shall obey God rather than you, and while I have life and strength I shall never cease from the practice and teaching of philosophy. . . . I believe that no greater good has ever happened in the state than my service to the God. For I do nothing but go about persuading you all . . . not to take thought for your persons or your properties, but first and chiefly to care about the greatest improvement of the soul.

Quite apart from the word *God* that appears twice in this brief statement, it is impossible to miss its author's conviction of the urgency of his mission. If religion is ultimate concern, we sense it in statements like these by Socrates or we sense it nowhere. The schools of philosophy I referred to several paragraphs back arose during a time of skepticism; the ancestral order had dissolved and men and women were looking for an alternative way to get their bearings. To say that skepticism—rootlessness, rudderlessness—didn't satisfy them is too weak; they found it intolerable and reached for truth as for a lifeline. "To Pythagoras, philosophy was not an engine of curiosity; but a way of life and death." *Our* popular imaginations may picture Epicurus as a man who had good times in beautiful gardens, but his disciples called him *soter,* "savior," for he did one of the greatest things for them that a teacher can do. He freed them from anxiety.

4. *Its involvement of the total self.* Let me lead into this point through an

example that may seem trivial but which points to something important. In his treatise "On Cleanliness" Epictetus writes:

> By the gods, when the young man feels the first stirrings of philosophy I would rather he came to me with his hair sleek than dishevelled and dirty: for that shows a sort of reflection of the beautiful, and a longing for the comely, and where he imagines these to be, there he spends his effort. (*Discourses* 4.11)

To generalize from the case in question, Epictetus is saying that a candidate's capacity for philosophy does not turn on I.Q. alone. It roots down into regions of the person which, while they will definitely affect the mind's performance—will it be able to grow wise?—are not themselves strictly cognitive.

Few professors today could comfortably open their philosophy courses by saying, "If you hope to acquire not just knowledge but wisdom you must change your lives. You must try to tell the truth. You must cease to live in your skin-encapsulated egos with their petty wishes and try instead to identify yourself with the all-embracing Self. Seek God, pray." If on rare occasion a Western philosopher should now say something like this, it would probably be in a course on ethics or aesthetics, not metaphysics or epistemology. Yet this is the way wisdom philosophers (*jñāna* yogins) used regularly to speak. Socrates argued that if you want to keep your ability to philosophize intact it is better to suffer wrong than to do wrong. Plato taught that by using poetry and music the young should be schooled to approve what is to be approved and condemn what is to be condemned to the end that "when reason comes, he will greet her as a friend with whom his education has made him long familiar" (*Republic* 402A). Aristotle echoed that general point when he said that the young are not ready for ethical reflection, being able to understand no more than the grammar of words. In short, factual knowledge is one thing, wisdom and *gnosis* another. In the broadest sense of the word, the latter require virtue. For to borrow an image from Frithjof Schuon, light does not go through an opaque stone and barely illuminates a black wall. The knower must become like crystal or snow.

5. *Its theophanies.* Standard classifications link revelation to religion and reason to philosophy, but again the question is whether these accepted divisions cut where the joints are. For the jnanic philosophy we are dealing with does not proceed through reason alone. We have just seen that the reason it does employ ties in with deeper-lying components of the self, but the point now is that this reason is also fed by transcendent sources. In the *Meno* Plato tells us that wisdom comes to us somehow "by divine dispensation, and Parmenides clearly presents his theory "as a revelation, accorded to him by the Goddess who governs all things in person." I pass over specifics like these to note three general areas where we catch sight of revelation infusing Greek philosophy.

a. The first of these places is in the mythic base out of which philosophy
   arose. In *The Presocratics*, Werner Jaeger points out that these thinkers
   capped the preceding mythic period quite as much as they launched a new
   beginning—Greek philosophy. And the myths they thus rounded off were
   held to be of nonhuman origin. It was not in merely human eulogy that
   Homer was called "the divine poet," for the mythic wisdom of the Greeks,
   like that of the Vedas, was held to be uncreated—eternal. Unlike the
   hypotheses of science, which come and go, it could never become obsolete,
   for it was believed to be not cumulative but a priori. As metaphysicians and
   poets alike testified, it was derived not from experiment but from inspiration. Plato said it came by *anamneses*, "recollection." It is not human but
   divine, belonging not to the ego but to the Self which is common to all.
   Today we might not speak of myths in quite these terms, but if we know
   our subject at all we recognize that myths are wholly different from fables
   deliberately fashioned by individuals to amuse or preserve a lesson learned.
   Myths are never intentionally made nor produced by individual authors.
   The least we can say is that they arise from the cumulative experience of
   countless generations and embody instinct and deep communal feeling.

b. If myth is collective revelation, revelations are also given to individuals. In
   the *Timaeus* 80B, Plato says that to our God-given vision and hearing the
   muses add harmony to those who can use it "intellectually . . . to assist the
   soul's interior revolution, to restore it to order and concord with itself."
   Etymologically, *revelation* derives from *re-velum*, 'the drawing back of
   a veil that conceals,' and Plato's Allegory of the Cave is as powerful an
   account of such disclosure as has ever been written. It is the account of
   the philosopher who is shown something others do not see and who is
   changed—and finds the universe changed—by the revelation.

c. Perhaps the most important kind of revelation is that which manifests itself
   in human form—an incarnation. Christ is the chief instance of this mode,
   of course, but he has his counterpart in Greek philosophy in the figure of
   Socrates. Socrates stands to Plato as Christ stands to St. Paul; we have the
   one through the other. It was Socrates who showed Plato the way. Plato's
   name barely occurs in his dialogues; for decades he effaced himself to leave
   the stage to his master. Compared with his fateful encounter with Socrates,
   everything else Plato encountered was episodic. His entire corpus is the
   effort to recapture the vision of Socrates and hold it up for others. How
   is it possible that there could have been a man of this stature? The question reaches its climax in Alcibiades' euology in the *Symposium*. Bernard
   Loomer once remarked that the euology makes the *Symposium* the New
   Testament of Greek philosophy, and establishes (almost by itself) the Platonic tradition in Western philosophy as one of the world's great religions.

6. *Its intuitive intellect.* In referring above to *jñāna*'s involvement with the total self, I noted that it links reason to human sensibilities that are not cognitive in the strict sense of that word. It follows that in isolation from these deeper sources, reason is a distinctly limited instrument. In Indian philosophy *manas* is augmented by *buddhi,* which Zimmer translates as "intuitive awareness." In Western philosophy reason is supplemented by intellection.

If we watch carefully we can all sense kinds of knowledge that flow from a source in us that is different from reason. We might call this supplementing faculty *insight,* or *intuition* if we don't read that word in its Bergsonian sense. We can even call it *imagination* if we are clear that in doing so we use the word in a way almost opposite to the way Spinoza used it, siding instead with the romantic poets who elevated imagination into a capacity for apprehending realities that can be reached in no other way. For Shelley imagination was "that imperial faculty," and Blake saw the person of imagination as the person of vision, opposed by the person of reason who sees with the corporeal eye only. We are obviously involved here with the doctrine of the intuitive imagination as the distinct organ of perception in the human soul, the "eye of the soul" as Plato called it. In the full-blown medieval doctrine of *intellectus,* the object that this eye perceives is the transcendent.

What lies behind these various locutions—Hegel's distinction between *Verstand* and *Vernunft* and Spinoza's between science and intuition could be added to them—is the fact that in metaphysical matters insight is decisive. This insight cannot be produced by assembling brute data or initiating chains of formal logic, or any combination of these. For the reigning epistemologies of our time this is a scandal, for it opens the prospect of studies that require a certain level of insight as their prerequisite as well as the possibility of issues that cannot be arbitrated by additional evidence. The most each side can do is appeal to its opponent to deepen his or her powers of insight and nurture the intuitive intellect.

7. *Its ontology.* I have saved till last the ontology of the jnanic tradition in Western philosophy because I consider it decisive. Twice in these pages I have alluded to Tillich's definition of religion as "ultimate concern," but it is obvious that that phrase can be read either psychologically or ontologically. Read psychologically, religion is whatever happens to concern a person most, be it sex, ambition, or whatever. Ontologically approached, on the other hand, religion is involvement with what in fact *is* ultimate, ontologically ultimate. For the Western philosophy I have been examining, this ontological ultimate is radically transcendent, which does not keep it from being fully immanent too for those who have eyes to see. Denotatively, it is Anaximander's "boundless" or "infinite," Plato's "Idea of the Good," Plotinus's "One," and Spinoza's "Deus sive natura." It is the initial link in the Great Chain of Being that proceeds from it.

Having examined this chain at some length in my *Forgotten Truth: The Primordial Tradition*, I shall not detail it further here. I shall remark only that though reason cannot climb its links to any great height, to penetrate beyond reason into what the intuitive intellect alone can discern is the strongest drive of the gnostic's nature.

BOOK FIVE

Return to the Personal

22

Encountering God

I must confess that the prospect of sharing what it's like to have a day-to-day, moment-to-moment personal relationship with God made me apprehensive. Why? Was it presumption that I have a moment-to-moment relationship with God—one that I am consciously aware of? Or was my reluctance one of good taste, the issue of whether it's appropriate to parade intimacies in public? Underlying these doubts was the question of whether I know what my relationship to God is. The arrangement feels more like a mystery that is open to my conscious awareness and direct inspection.

In the end, though, the premise that we can learn from one another on this matter prevailed.

When, on the National Broadcasting Company's *Wisdom* series I asked Daisetz Suzuki if he was born with a religious impulse, he answered, "Not born, but it awakened."

"When did it awaken in you?" I wanted to know.

"Well, I do not know exactly. But the starting point was marked, perhaps, when I was sixteen or seventeen. I wanted to get my religious yearnings somehow settled."

I could have answered the same: the deepest yearnings of which I am consciously aware have always been religious. I consider the religious impulse to be a part of the human makeup; the search for cosmic understanding is as much a part of the religious impulse as the search for cosmic belonging. In my case, though, early conditioning doubtless contributed to the strength of the drive.

My relationship with God through my mid-twenties was cast in a Protestant, pietistic mold wherein God was approached through a personal, love-and-service relationship with Christ. I continue to honor that mode and to work on it in part. But, in addition, the Hindu doctrine of the four yogas—the notion that people are of different spiritual temperaments and therefore will approach God in different ways: *jñānis* through knowledge, *bhaktis* through love, *karmic* types through service, and *rajic* types through meditation—freed me to see that there were other channels through which spiritual energies may flow. My personal relationship with Christ, though real, was not very intense, whereas *thoughts* of God could hold me spellbound for an entire night.

Such *jñānic* knowledge is apt to be misunderstood by those who have not experienced it—by those whose yogic strengths lie elsewhere. It has nothing to do with quantity of information or logical dexterity. It is rather that thoughts, for the *jñānic,* possess a body of sorts, a three-dimensional substantiality that makes thoughts real in ways they are not for other people. Plato's ideas, for example— the Good, the True, and the Beautiful—for *the jñānic* (or Gnostics, as they might be called in the West if that word is distinguished from gnosticism) are not the empty abstractions that others take them for. They are almost palpably real. And their reality excites; they all but dance and sing. This distinguishes the *theoria* that discusses them from theories as these typically function in science. The Greek word *theoria* derived from theater, which makes *jñānic* knowledge closer to vision than to thought as we usually use the word. It is seeing, albeit with the eye of the soul. And the vision attracts. Aristotle compounded Goodness, Truth, and Beauty into this Unmoved Mover, which moves the entire universe by force of attraction. But my point is that ideas attract *jñānis,* who are drawn to ideas because they love them—and we are drawn to and become like that which we love. Socrates said that to know the good is to do it. St. Paul disagreed, but he was a different temperamental type—so knowing was not the same for the two men.

This all relates to God, for though I have not used the word, I have been speaking of nothing else. God is the Good, the True, the Beautiful—and Power and Mystery, we should add—fused so completely that the five are not five but one. In my best moments I am drawn to that God as moth to flame, and at such times I do not know whether my happiness is the rarest or the commonest thing on earth, for all earthly things seem to reflect it. But I cannot hold onto it. When those grace-filled moments arrive, it does not seem strange to be so happy, but in retrospect I wonder how such gold of Eden could have been mine.

It is easy to make too much of direct mystical disclosures. Desert stretches provide opportunities for growth that are as important as mountaintop experiences, and theologians assure us that souls can be established in an abiding relationship with God without being sensibly aware of God's presence. The goal is not altered states but altered traits. Aldous Huxley's observation that the task of life is to overcome the fundamental human disability of egoism comes in here, for every step we take in overcoming that is in God's direction.

23

Reflections upon Turning Ninety

May 31, 2009. Ninety years old. As my birthday nears, people are congratulating me as though I'd done something—run a marathon blindfolded, say. That may not be an entirely inaccurate description of reaching ninety, but never before have I been congratulated for doing nothing, or nothing more than continuing to breathe in and out. Behind the congratulations, though, I sometimes detect fears and a need for reassurance that it will be all right. The fears are real. And it will be all right.

A year ago, however, I did do something. I moved from my home on Colusa Avenue, full of air and light and with my study overlooking Berkeley's golden hills, and moved into one room in an assisted-living facility. I left Kendra, my intimate companion of sixty-five years, to cohabit with people in wheelchairs or depressed or with Alzheimer's. "I had already been in assisted living for half a decade," I joke and point to Kendra. "She was the assister." (My increasing physical needs were taking their toll on her health; hence the move.) The first night after the move was a dark night of the soul. Religion relies on that successful plot device, the happy ending. I still believed in one, but after my first night in the assisted-living residence I thought, the happy ending will now have to wait until I am dead.

And then after three days here, it became acceptable, perfectly fine. The move seemed no more than turning the page of a book. On the previous page I had been on Colusa Avenue and on this page I am here, but the story itself has not changed. And ninety, I discover, is a good age for making new friends. The maintenance man, Mr. Lin, has just left my room, and how coincidental: he grew up in China near where I grew up! We have wonderful conversations, in Chinese.

Today Mr. Lin told me how during the Cultural Revolution (when Mao boasted he had eradicated hunger) there was no leaf on any tree; people plucked and ate them, to stave off starvation. "Mr. Lin," I asked, "did you eat the leaves, too?" "Ah, Huston, I am alive, am I not? Yes, I ate the leaves."

People go to nursing homes, I've heard it said, to die. I came to this assisted-living residence, it seems, to cheer people up. I still begin each day with exercise for my body, reading religious classics for my mind, and prayer for my spirit. I have modified the physical exercises, since I can no longer stand on my head (although if my osteoporosis bends me over much more I won't be far from it). Now to the threefold body-mind-spirit morning regimen, I have added a fourth practice. Mentally I take a census of the other residents here, and as each appears in my imagination, I ask how I might improve his or her day.

The other residents are dear, but often their conditions are not. In the dining room the conversation can be minimal. I will use any topic to get the ball rolling: "Mr. Lin told me today that in Chinese astrology this is the year of the rat." The others at the table ask what that means, and soon everyone is free-associating about rats, and we're on our way. We're always on our way, if only we knew it. A former surgeon here has trouble hearing, and I offered to introduce him to a famous hearing expert I know. "No, no, Huston," he answered, "thanks, but I'm fine." I do not understand that attitude. Oliver Sacks says that deafness cuts you off from society even more than blindness. I had a risky cochlear-implant operation to improve my hearing: I want to hear what everyone says, even the chatterbox. It has meaning, and it may help me figure things out.

One week in our Sunday "Spiritual Moments" meeting, Brother James got us going using a deck of cards with a word written on each one, and when he extracted one, we were each to say our associations with that particular word. When the word was *beauty*, I immediately thought: *Kendra!* This week Brother James was absent, so I took his place: in pantomime I drew from an imaginary deck an imaginary card and said the word *gratitude*. Gratitude—what I learned from the *roshi* at the Kyoto monastery half a lifetime ago. I could obsess about my ailments and be an old man in misery. Instead I forget them and wonder how I came to be so fortunate and what I am even doing in an assisted-living facility. Gratitude? If I fail to mention something in a letter but remember before I put it in the mailbox, I feel grateful. The day sings its song of small grace notes. In the bathroom or the elevator I whisper under my breath, "God, you are so good to me"—thirty-five or forty times a day I say it. It seems I finally have a mantra.

"God, you are so good to me." After a lifetime of studying and teaching and writing, of investigating, deliberating, and philosophizing, of heaping qualification upon qualification, how simple it can finally become.

People ask me questions like "Do you still practice Hinduism?" Or "What role does Buddhism play in your life today?" Dare I answer? I have forgotten more about the various religions than I knew in the first place. All that is left of my study of them is . . . me.

My father had black-and-white ideas, a right and a wrong way for every situation. When Kendra and I were first married, I watched her spread jam on her toast, and I repeated my father's stricture: "The first piece of toast, no jam. On the second piece jam is permissible." "But I am eating only one piece," Kendra replied. "Oh," I thought, perplexed, "well . . . in that case I guess it's all right." Six and a half decades of living with Kendra has gotten me over arbitrary notions and helped bring me into the open air of simply being.

Religion teaches us that our lives here on earth are to be used for transformation. Buddhism in particular describes three mental toxins by which we poison ourselves—greed, hatred, and delusion—but it is possible to transform those poisons into three blessings. Kendra would readily admit that her "poison" is hatred, but hatred, when purified, turns into discernment, and Kendra has become the most discerning person I know. (When I was a judge for the Danforth fellowships, I'd turn the applications over to her; she had some magical sixth sense for who the right applicants were.) Care to guess my poison? Me, who wanted to be a big man on campus at Central College, who hungered always for more experience, who enjoyed what small bits of acclaim came his way? Yet Buddhism says that greed, purified, becomes great faith. As I enter my tenth decade on earth, my faith does seem to be enlarging, not in opposition to experience, but coming out of it.

"At age thirty"—this is the sage Confucius speaking—"I could stand on my own feet. At age forty I suffered no more doubts. At fifty I understood the mandate of heaven. But only at age sixty could I do what I wanted without going against the path." Possibly I needed to go through ninety years of life to understand how life itself is the path.

And one day the path shall end. I am thinking now of my beautiful daughter Karen and her premature death. After her death an interviewer asked me—I still hear his question—"Can you believe in God's perfection now?" No, when Karen lay dying, I could no longer see any justice or perfection. Or perhaps I did feel it, through my tears, in the heroic way our daughter met her end. On her last day, after the sarcoma cancer (I described it earlier) had spread into all her organs, causing excruciating pain, she told me, "I have no complaints" and "I am at peace." Her last words were about the sea, which symbolized life to her: how she could even smell it, it was so near. Her death, so unbittered and brave, increases, if not my sense of perfection, my awe. Only Karen or someone upon whom the worst has fallen has the right to absolve life of our possible grievances against it. The father learned nobility of spirit from the daughter.

Socrates called philosophy the practice of dying. I have puzzled over that statement, unsure of what Socrates meant. In the *Phaedo* he said death will be either a restful sleep or a meeting of noble souls in a better world, and hence why fear? With Karen's example before me, I believe death holds no terror for me. Perhaps I have practiced philosophy in the way Socrates intended after all.

How would I like to die? My friend Martin Lings, author of *Return to the Spirit*, wrote his last book when older than I am now. An avid gardener, Martin went into his garden and picked a bloom of uncommon beauty and put it in a vase. And with no more fuss he slumped over, *adieu*. People tell you, however, that you cannot choose how or when you will die. In fact I have known two people who did choose. The abbot of a monastery in Kyoto, upon retirement, retreated into a tiny hut, where one day he summoned the monks and announced he planned to die that coming Friday. "You cannot!" they exclaimed. "Friday begins O Bon!" O Bon is that busy time when the monastery's patrons and parishioners visit; his death would get in the way. Obliging, my friend postponed his dying to the next month. I cannot hope to emulate him, but nonetheless I take a lesson from his example. The lesson: our common fears and assumptions about death may be just that—assumptions—that have little to do with the reality.

People ask me, the professor of religion, "What happens when we die?" Every time, I think of the student who approached the Zen master.

> *Student:* What happens when we die?
> *Zen Master:* I don't know.
> *Student:* But you're a Zen master!
> *Zen Master:* True. Quite true. But I am not a dead Zen master.

I am not a dead religion professor—yet. However, most of us do have unexamined or unconscious assumptions about what happens after we shed this mortal coil. Although none of our surmises can be proved, there may be a reason or resonance why we each imagine what we do. So pull up a chair, have a seat, and I'll tell you (my idea of) what happens when we die.

Charles Tart, in the psychology department at the University of California at Davis, has devoted his career to studying clairvoyance, telepathy, psychokinesis, and out-of-body experiences. I asked him if he thought his consciousness would survive his bodily death. "Yes, definitely," Charles answered, only he did not know whether *he* (or it) would still recognize it as *his* consciousness. Charles's answer raises a question. If we survive beyond this single life span, do we (a) survive as individuals or (b) dissolve into something greater ("the Godhead")? Sri Ramakrishna opted or hoped for the first possibility: "I want to taste sugar. I don't want to be sugar." In *Why Religion Matters* I expressed my intuition: we are each allowed to choose for ourselves the possibility we want.

I give myself poetic license to imagine it. After I shed my body, I will remain conscious of old habits and habitations; I will still be concerned with Kendra,

Gael, Kim, and the whole *dramatis personae* of my life on earth. However, a day will come when no one alive will have heard of Huston Smith, much less have known him. What will be the point of my hanging around then? I will turn my back on this dear world and direct my attention to something more interesting: the beatific vision. So long as I remain involved with my individuality, I'll be aware that it is Huston Smith enjoying this vision. For me, though—mystic that I am at heart—after oscillating back and forth between enjoying the sunset and enjoying Huston-Smith-enjoying-the-sunset, I expect that the uncompromised sunset will become ever more absorbing. The branch of narrowed awareness upon which I rested will sever and fall away. The cord is cut, the bird is set free.

Soon it will be time to say good-bye. Let me end where I began, by saying good-bye first to you, my mother and father. My mother spent her last years in a retirement home in Springfield, Missouri, where she remained admirable as always. Although nearly blind, she would count the doors and, locating the right ones, go into the rooms of those who were bedridden, and comfort and cheer them up. I was in my prime then, flying around the country, lecturing here, there, and everywhere. Whenever the talk was remotely near Springfield, I would visit her, but the visits were brief; I was invariably in a hurry. When I would leave the very next day, my mother would hide her disappointment or try to. What would I not give now—I would give anything—if I could enter her room once more and say, "Mother, guess what? This time I will be staying a long time."

My father was already dead by then. In our family we never said, "I love you." His circumlocution to me was, "Huston, we are so proud of you." After a visit, as I'd be leaving, he would point a finger to his cheek, and I would kiss him there. Now I wish I had said it, and said it with all my heart: "Father, I love you, and always have, and always will."

And good-bye to you, dear reader. Writing was to me more than an academic obligation; it was my passion and my refuge. Although we never met in person, you were like a friend, the thought of whom spurred me to my best efforts.

A playwright, I can only suppose, fusses over the last line, the one that will bring the curtain down. My last line—how typical of me—is not one but three closing lines as I postpone the curtain, unable to choose which is best.

First close: I echo the British author Elizabeth Pakenham (mother of novelist Antonia Fraser), whose last words were "It has all been very interesting."

Second close: My second last line is actually an observation. The older I get, the more the boundary between me and not-me thins and becomes transparent. I look back upon the paths I have traveled and think, This is me. I look across the table at Kendra, my wife of sixty-five years, and think, This is me. I feel my hip replacement and think, This is me. The childish *oneself versus other* becomes the mature *oneself and other* becomes, finally, *oneself as other.*

Third close: I can choose my favorite closing, after all. It is borrowed from the martyr Saint John Chrysostom, who while being drawn and quartered was said to have exclaimed, "Praise, praise for everything. Thanks, thanks for it all." I savor the words in my mind, roll them on my tongue, and repeat them as my own: *Thanks for everything! Praise for it all!*

Conclusion

The Sacred Unconscious

More than once I have foresworn prophecy. There are times, though, when to act as if something *has* happened helps it to happen, and this next statement adopts this approach. Taking the human self as its object, it describes that self "from the further shore," as Buddhists would say.

There is need to see it in that light, for the view from this shore does not do us justice; as Saul Bellow points out in the Nobel Lecture, "we do not think well of ourselves." The complete edition of the works of Sigmund Freud contains over four hundred entries for neurosis and none for health. What account of ourselves is given by psychologists, sociologists, historians, journalists, and writers?

In *The Next Million Years,* a book published around the time of Darwin's centennial, his grandson, Charles Galton Darwin, considered the prospects for genetic engineering. Writing as a geneticist, he concluded that the difficulties were formidable but solvable. What was not solvable, he thought, was the goal of such engineering—agreement as to the kind of person we would like to produce. Nietzsche and Van Gogh were geniuses but went mad—would we want their genes in our gene pool? It's a good question. It tries to define the highest good for man.

Writing as a philosopher and historian of religions, let me venture my perception of this "human best" as follows. If Marx unmasked our social unconscious and Freud our personal unconscious, both piercing through superstructures, or rather substructures, that hide true causes and motives, the supreme human opportunity is to strike deeper still and become aware of the "sacred unconscious" that forms the bottom line of our selfhood.

I shall not go into reasons for assuming that this final unconscious exists; I have discussed some of them in my *Forgotten Truth* where I use the word "spirit" for what I am here calling the sacred unconscious. Nor will I map here our human consciousness to show the relation of this deepest level to ones that are more proximate; that I attempted in my essay "The Levels of Selfhood." Instead I shall try to surmise what our lives would be like if our deepest unconscious were directly available to us. What would a supremely realized human being, here conceived as one that is consciously aware of his or her sacred unconscious, be like? How would such a person look to others and feel to him/herself?

It is easier to say what s-he would not be like than to picture him or her positively, as the "tragic flaw" theory of art reminds us. No writer would dream of trying to create a perfect hero; he would sense instinctively that such a figure would seem completely fictitious—a cardboard cutout. But let the author endow an otherwise strong character with a tragic weakness—Hamlet's indecision is the standard example—and our imaginations will correct that weakness on their own; convincingly, moreover, for we graft the missing virtue onto a character whose imperfection makes him believable. The same principles apply when we try (as here) to describe human wholeness not concretely as the artist does, but abstractly: we are on firmest ground when we state the case negatively. To cite an historical instance, the Buddha's characterization of enlightenment as the absence of hatred, greed, and ignorance draws its force from being solidly anchored in real life: its key terms refer to traits we live with all the time. But if we try to restate his formula in positive terms and say that to be enlightened is to be filled with love, wisdom, and an impartial acceptance of everything, our description becomes abstract. Obviously we have some acquaintance with these virtues, but acquaintance is not what is at stake. The goal is to be suffused with these virtues; to be filled by them completely. That we have only the faintest notion of what these positive terms mean when they are raised to their maximum, goes without saying.

DEFINITION OF A *JIVAMUKTI*

So now we have two wise caveats before us: Darwin's, that we don't know what the *summum bonum* is; and Buddha's, that we do best to approach it negatively. I propose to throw these warnings to the wind and attempt a positive depiction of a *jivamukti,* as the Indians would refer to a fully realized person: a *jiva* (soul) that is *mukti* (liberated, enlightened) in this very life. The project must fail, of course, but that doesn't keep it from being interesting. Perhaps, in keeping with the tragic flaw theory I just alluded to, its very failure may induce the reader to round out in his own imaging the picture which words can never adequately portray.

An enlightened being, I am proposing, is one who is in touch with his deepest unconscious, an unconscious which (for reasons I shall be introducing) deserves to be considered sacred. Our century has acquainted us with regions of our minds that are hidden from us and the powerful ways they control our perceptions. My thesis is that underlying these proximate layers of our unconscious minds is a final substrate that opens mysteriously onto the world as it actually is. To have access to this final substrate is to be objective in the best sense of the word and to possess the virtues and benefits that go with this objectivity.

Normally we are not in touch with this objective component of ourselves—which paradoxically is also our deepest subjective component—because intermediate layers of our unconscious screen it from us while at the same time screening the bulk of the world from us. Our interests, drives, and concerns, their roots largely hidden from our gaze, cause us to see what we want to see and need to see; most of the rest of reality simply passes us by. The Tibetans make this point by saying that when a pickpocket meets a saint, what he sees are his pockets. Moreover, the things we do see we see through lenses that are "prescription ground," so to speak; our interests and conditionings distort the way they appear to us. When poor children are asked to draw a penny they draw it larger than do children for whom pennies are commonplace; it looms larger in their minds' eye. In many such ways, what we take to be objective facts are largely psychological constructs, as the Latin *factum*, "that which is made," reminds us.

This much is now psychological truism. We enter more interesting terrain when we note that at a deeper level the thoughts and feelings that control what we see are themselves shaped by what the Buddha called *the three poisons:* desire (lust, greed, grasping), aversion (fear, hatred, anger), and ignorance. And the greatest of these is ignorance. For it is ignorance—most pointedly ignorance concerning our true identity, who we really are—that causes us to divide the world into what we like and dislike. Thinking that we are separate selves, we seek what augments these selves and shun what threatens them. What we call our "self" is the amalgam of desires and aversions that we have wrapped tightly, like the elastic of a golf ball, around the core of separate identity that is its center.

This tight, constricted, golf-ball self is inevitably in for hard knocks, but what concerns us here is that on average it doesn't feel very good. Anxiety hovers 'round its edges. It can feel victimized and grow embittered. It is easily disappointed and can become unstrung. To others it often seems no prettier than it feels to itself: petty, self-centered, drab, and bored.

I am deliberately putting down this golf-ball self—hurling it to the ground, as it were, to see how high our total self can bounce; how far toward heaven it can rise. To rise, it must break out of the hard rubber strings that are normally stretched so tightly around it, encasing it in what Alan Watts called "the skin-encapsulated ego." If we change our image from rubber to glass and picture the three poisons as a lens that refracts light waves in keeping with our private, importunate demands, then release from such egocentric distortions will come through progressively decreasing our lenses' curve—reducing their bulge. The logical terminus of this would then be clear glass. Through this glass we would be able to see things objectively, as they are in themselves in their own right.

This clear glass, which for purposes of vision is equivalent to no glass at all, is our sacred unconscious. It is helpful to think of it as an absence because, like window glass, it functions best when it calls no attention to itself. But it is precisely its absence that makes the world available to us: "the less there is of self, the more there is of Self," as Eckhart put the matter. From clear glass we have moved to no glass—the removal of everything that might separate subject from object, self from world. Zennists use the image of the Great Round Mirror. When the three poisons are removed from it, it reflects the world just as it is.

To claim that human consciousness can move permanently into this condition may be going too far, but advances along the asymptotic curve that slopes in its direction are clearly perceptible. When our aversion lens is powerful, bulging toward the limits of a semicircle, we like very little that comes our way. The same holds, of course, for our desire lens which is only the convex side of our aversion's concave: the more these bend our evaluations toward our own self-interests, the less we are able to appreciate things in their own right. Blake's formulation of the alternative to this self-centered outlook has become classic. "If the doors of perception were cleansed everything would appear to man as it is, infinite."

The fully realized human being is one whose doors of perception have been cleansed. And these doors, which up to this point I have referred to as windows, I am here envisioning as successive layers of our unconscious minds. Those that are near the surface vary from person to person for they are deposited by our idiosyncratic childhood experiences. At some level, though, we encounter the three poisons (once again, desire, aversion, and ignorance) that are common to mankind and perhaps in some degree essential for our human functioning. But the deepest layer, we have seen, is really a no-layer, for being a glass door ajar, or a mirror that discloses things other than itself, it isn't there. Even if it were there, in what sense could we call it ours? For when we look toward it we see simply—world.

This opening out onto the world's infinity is one good reason for calling this deepest stratum of the human unconscious sacred, for surely holiness has something to do with the whole. But the concreteness of Blake's formulation is instructive. He doesn't tell us that a cleansed perception discloses the Infinite per se. It finds it in the things at hand, in keeping with those Buddhist stories which tell us that the most sacred scriptures are its unwritten pages—an old pine tree gnarled by wind and weather or a skein of geese flying across the autumn sky.

DESCRIPTION OF A *JIVAMUKTI*

Thus far I have defined a *jivamukti;* it remains to describe him or her. What does life feel like to such a person, and how does s-he appear to others.

Basically s-he lives in the unvarying presence of the numinous. This does not mean that s-he is excited or "hyped"; his/her condition has nothing to do with adrenalin flow, or with manic states that call for depressive ones to balance the emotional account. It's more like what Kipling had in mind when he said of one of his characters, "He believed that all things were one big miracle, and when a man knows that much he knows something to go upon." The opposite of the sense of the sacred is not serenity or sobriety. It is drabness; taken-for-grantedness. Lack of interest. The humdrum and prosaic.

All other attributes of a *jivamukti* must be relativized against this one absolute: his/her honed sense of the astounding mystery of everything. All else we say of him must have a yes/no quality. Is s-he always happy? Well, yes and no. On one level s-he emphatically is not; if s-he were s-he couldn't "weep with those who mourn"—s-he would be an unfeeling monster, a callous brute. If anything, a realized soul is *more* in touch with the grief and sorrow that is part and parcel of the human condition, knowing that it, too, needs to be accepted and lived as all life needs to be lived. To reject the shadow side of life, to pass it by with averted eyes refusing our share of common sorrow while expecting our share of common joy would cause the unlived, rejected shadows to deepen in us as fear of death. A story that is told of the recent Zen Master Shaku Soen points up the dialectical stance of the realized soul toward the happiness we are noting. When he was able to do so, he liked to take an evening stroll through a nearby village. One evening he heard wailing in a house he was passing and, on entering quietly, found that the householder had died and his family and neighbors were crying. Immediately he sat down and began crying too. An elderly gentleman, shaken by this display of emotion in a famous master, remarked, "I would have thought that you at least were beyond such things." "But it is this which puts me beyond it," the Master replied through his sobs.

The Master's tears we can understand; the sense in which he was "beyond" them is more difficult to fathom, like the peace that passeth understanding. The peace that comes when a man is hungry and finds food, is sick and recovers, or is lonely and finds a friend—peace of this sort is readily intelligible. But the peace that passeth understanding comes when the pain of life is not relieved. It shimmers on the crest of a wave of pain; it is the spear of frustration transformed into a shaft of light. The Master's sobs were real, yet paradoxically they did not erode the yes-experience of the East's "it is as it should be" and the West's "Thy will be done."

In our efforts to conceive the human best, everything turns on an affirmation that steers between cynicism on the one hand and sent mentality on the other. A realized self isn't incessantly, and thereby oppressively, cheerful—oppressively, not only because we suspect some pretense in his unvarying smile, but because it underscores our moodiness by contrast. Not every room a *jivamukti* enters floods with sunlight; he can flash indignation and upset moneychangers' tables. Not invariance but appropriateness is his hallmark, an appropriateness that has the whole repertoire of emotions at its command. The Catholic Church is right in linking radiance with sanctity, but the paradoxical, "in spite of" character of this radiance must again be stressed. Along with being a gift to be received, life is a task to be performed. The adept performs it: whatever his hand finds to do, he does with all his might. Even if it proves his lot to walk stretches of life as a desert waste, he *walks* them rather than pining for alternatives. Happiness enters as by-product. What matters focally, as the Zen Master Dogen never tired of noting, is resolved.

If a *jivamukti* isn't forever radiating sweetness and light, neither does he constantly emit blasts of energy. He can be forceful when need be; we find it restoring rather than draining to be in his presence, and he has reserves to draw on, as when Socrates stood all night in trance and outpaced the militia with bare feet on ice. In general, though, we sense him/her as relaxed and composed rather than charged—the model of the dynamic and magnetic personality tends to have a lot of ego in it; it demands attention. Remember, everything save the adept's access to inner vistas, the realms of gold I am calling the sacred unconscious, must be relativized. If leadership is called for the adept steps forward, otherwise he is just as happy to follow. He isn't debarred from being a guru, but equally he does not need to be one—he doesn't need disciples to prop up his ego. Focus or periphery, limelight or shadow, it doesn't really matter. Both have their opportunities, both their limitations.

All these relativities I have mentioned—happiness, energy, prominence, impact—pertain to the *jivamukti*'s finite self which he progressively pushes aside as he makes his way toward his final, sacred unconscious. As his goal is an impersonal, impartial one, his identification with it involves a dying to his finite selfhood. This finite self is engaged in a vanishing act, as Coomaraswamy suggested when he wrote, "Blessed is the man on whose tomb can be written, *Hic jacet nemo*—"Here lies no one."

But having insisted above that there is only one absolute or constant in the journey toward this self-naughting; namely, the sense of the sacred, that luminous mystery in which all things are bathed, I must now admit that there is another: the realization of how far we all are from the goal that beckons, how many ranges of hills remain to be crossed, "Why callest thou me good? . . ." As human beings we are made to surpass ourselves and are truly ourselves only when transcending ourselves. Only the slightest of barriers separates us from our sacred unconscious; it is infinitely close to us. But we are infinitely far from it, so for us the barrier looms as a mountain that we must remove with our own hands. We scrape away at the earth, but in vain; the mountain remains. Still we go on digging at the mountain, in the name of God or whatever. For the most part we only hear of the final truth; very rarely do we actually see it. The mountain isn't there. It never was there.

Afterword

The Man Who Took Religion Seriously
Huston Smith in Context

Dana Sawyer

When Huston Smith was growing up in Dzang Zok, China, he couldn't possibly have imagined he would become the leading figure in the academic study of religion for the twentieth century. But that's what happened.

Prior to Huston Smith, the modern mind viewed religion as a waste of time or worse. Freud had said that religion is a delusion we create to comfort ourselves in an uncertain world. We, based on an "infantile model," project a cosmic father or mother onto an indifferent universe to have someone to plead to when things go bad. Karl Marx, to cite another modernist who disparaged religion, argued "religion is the opiate of the masses," distracting us from the necessary revolutions that would bring social equality and justice by feeding us pretty lies to placate us in our misery. In short, by the 1950s when Huston wrote his breakthrough book, *The Religions of Man*, the job of most professors of religion was to explain religion away, as something quaint and outdated, something we'd be better off without. It was the fifties after all, and high time we outgrew our nonscientific ways of making sense of the world. Scholars of religion were generally accepted by their colleagues only if they weren't religious (a condition Huston found analogous to hiring music teachers only if they're deaf), but Huston demanded the freedom to love what he studied and taught.

Huston acknowledged that the story of religion hasn't always been rose colored, but he argued, using an analogy borrowed from a Hindu holy man, that

Dana Sawyer, professor of religion and philosophy at the Maine College of Art and author of a critically acclaimed life of Aldous Huxley, is now completing a biography of Huston Smith.

religion is like a cow: it sometimes kicks, but it also gives milk. Religions have brought wars and persecutions, but they have also inspired much of the world's greatest art and music, and they have given people purpose and meaning for countless ages. In short, Huston was worried in the fifties that academia was too eager to discard something that still gave benefits; furthermore, he pointed out that the deadliest ideologies of the modern world were not religious. The policies of Hitler, Stalin, and Mao claimed more than seventeen million lives, and their ideologies were all secular, not religious. For Huston, this made clear that acceptance of secularism is not implicitly a safeguard against atrocity. He pointed out that fanatical devotion to any perspective is the real problem, not religion per se, and so he won a point with his colleagues—and, of course, with those who valued religion.

A FRESH APPROACH

To ensure that he described the world's religions accurately, Huston came up with a research method all his own. "First, I read their sacred scriptures—including the profound and trusted commentaries on those scriptures," he once explained to me. "Second, I sought out the most authentic and profound living representatives of those views and asked them questions. And third, I would jump into the religions myself—as a participant observer, doing the rituals and practices they prescribed to get an insider's view." Huston traveled around the world to observe rites and rituals firsthand, and he apprenticed himself to various adepts. While in Japan he studied Zen with D. T. Suzuki; in India, he studied Hinduism with swamis of the Ramakrishna order; and in Iran he studied Islam with Seyyed Hossein Nasr, who once told me a story about Huston's eagerness to learn. The two men were crossing a busy street together in Tehran. "We had just come out of a meeting with a group of Sufi mystics, and there we were with cars zipping by us on either side. I was holding Huston's hand, to guide him through traffic, and I turned to see how he was doing. He wasn't even paying attention! He was so deeply in thought about the Sufis that he didn't care about the cars!"

Huston's search for accurate descriptions led him, in 1957, to spend ten weeks at Myoshin-ji, the Temple of the Marvelous Mind, in Kyoto, Japan, to see what it was like to live as a Zen monk. He found that the food was bland and the lifestyle austere, but out of sheer determination he got an insider's view. Once, while talking with him about the experience, I asked what his room was like: he laughed, sat forward in his seat, and said, "You're on the wrong track entirely!" He and the monks were meditating for ten or twelve hours a day in a *sodo,* a long room with a raised platform on either side. "And when night came, and we were finished meditating, we would simply reach up and pull down a sort of comforter. One half of it was used as a mattress and the other half was a cover. So the private room you're wondering about—and that I might have wanted—turned out to be a space about three feet wide."

Furthermore, Huston's difficulties at Myoshin-ji weren't limited to physical discomfort. He was a philosopher whose mind, like that of all philosophers, sometimes roiled with ideas, but even if these ideas seemed profound to him, his Zen master found them only a distraction. Early in the retreat Huston sometimes wrote in a little pad that he kept tucked under his covers on the shelf over his head, but when this was noticed he was called out of the meditation hall and told to stop. As Huston related the story to me: "The head monk said, 'This is a holy place. We do not write in the *zendo*.' So I asked, 'What if you have to write a note home or something?' And he answered: 'Well try not to *have to*, but if you absolutely must, write it in the *banjo*,' which was the squat toilet we all used." Huston smiled at me wryly and sat back in his chair. "So much for the prestige of being an author."

When *The Religions of Man* came out, it was clear that Huston's research method had paid off. His descriptions not only rang true for believers all over the world, but they gave people a sense of pride in their religions. "I was in Delhi, in high school, when I first read that book," Deepak Chopra told me in an interview, in 2009. "What struck me at first was the lucidity of the writing and the depth of understanding. Then I was struck by the fact that it was totally non-opinionated. It was an inquisitive, curious, in-depth look at the religions without any cultural or religious bias. It conveyed the value of the religions—and I appreciated how accurately he had described Hinduism, the religion of my country." Similar reports came from people of all faiths—and they still do.

UNEXPECTED DISCOVERIES

Often while he was gallivanting around the world, Huston encountered ceremonies and practices he had never heard of before—and sometimes nobody had heard of them. The most significant of these surprises came in 1964, in Dalhousie, India. Huston was visiting a Tibetan Buddhist monastery, just days before his first meeting with the Dalai Lama—who was twenty-nine years old at the time—and he witnessed a four-day ceremony that included much chanting. The chants melted into a meaningless drone after a few hours, and Huston was nearly asleep when suddenly he heard what sounded like "an angelic choir." Realizing he was hearing something unique (the ability of specially trained lamas to simultaneously sing one note with their vocal chords while accentuating two additional harmonics with their throats and sinus cavities), he located a tape recorder in a nearby school and made a recording. A few months later, after returning to MIT, where he was then teaching, he became the first person ever to explain (in Western musical terms) the mechanics of Tibetan harmonic chanting. His account was later published in the *American Anthropologist* (April 1967), and this discovery gave him yet another reason to believe he was on the right track, studying cultures on their own turf and with an open mind.

THE PERENNIAL PHILOSOPHER

More than a decade before he published *The Religions of Man*, in spring 1945, Huston was finishing his doctoral dissertation in Berkeley, California. While doing research in the library one night, he accidentally came upon the work of Gerald Heard, and this triggered an insight that gave direction to all Huston's later work. In a nutshell, Huston became convinced, after reading Heard's *Pain, Sex, and Time*, that mystical experiences provide an avenue to truth and meaning overlooked in the modern world.

That same year, Aldous Huxley, a friend of Gerald Heard's, published *The Perennial Philosophy*, an anthology of mysticism that Huston was soon carrying around with him "like a sort of Bible." In that book, Huxley laid out a theory of religion based on the premise that beyond the disagreements between religions regarding beliefs and practices, there is a shared "highest common factor" endemic to them all. This highest factor is derived from a spirituality implicit in man's very being, based on an experience of an underlying, unmanifest foundation of all reality that Huxley referred to as the "Divine Ground of Being." Mystics of all religions, Huxley argued, have experienced this Divine Ground throughout history, and having this experience is the ultimate purpose of our existence. We seek this spiritual enlightenment championed by the mystics whether we are aware of it or not. Gerald Heard had first introduced Huston to this idea, but it was Huxley's specific privileging of mysticism as the root of religion, supported by testimonies from the saints of all traditions, that really captured Huston's imagination and conviction. "And this is why I started carrying Huxley's book everywhere I went."

Huston became so enthused with perennialism and its explanation of religion that in 1947, just before leaving Colorado, where he had a temporary teaching position, for St. Louis and Washington University, he hitchhiked to California to meet Heard and Huxley. He found Gerald tucked up in a monastery that he had started in the Laguna Hills, and Huxley also seemed to be hidden away, living with his wife at a small ranch in the desert about fifty miles north of Los Angeles. Both men were engaged in simple, almost ascetic lives, and this impressed Huston greatly, as they really seemed to be walking their talk and seeking spiritual insight. Bill Moyers once said of Huston, "What he has learned, he has applied to life," and Huston saw this same lived approach in the lives of his mentors.

When Huston got off the bus for that first meeting with Huxley, Huxley, tall and lean at six-foot-four, greeted the young scholar with a warm handshake and suggested they take a walk in the desert. Huston, who was eager to please, promptly agreed.

"He loved the desert," Huston would later write, in a 1988 article for the *L.A. Times.* "He told me, for its symbolic power. Its emptiness emptied his mind. 'The boundlessness of its sands [I paraphrase] spreads a mantle of sameness—hence unity—over the world's multiplicity in something of the way snow does. The Nothingness to which the Desert Fathers were drawn is not a blank negation. It is a no-thing-ness in which everything is so interfused that divisions are transcended. Pure light contains all the frequencies of the rainbow but undemarcated. The Void is the vacuum-plenum complex [the Oneness of Reality in both its forms, as the transcendent 'nothing' as well as the *everything* of the physical universe], grasped by its vacuum pole.'"

Huxley's description that day of the Divine Ground, and the importance of experiencing it, galvanized Huston's acceptance of the perennial philosophy, and he would go on to become its primary defender in academic circles throughout the 1960s, 1970s, and 1980s. These efforts culminated in two of Huston's most important books, *Forgotten Truth* (1976) and *Beyond the Post-Modern Mind* (1989). In these works he addressed the critics of perennialism, answering their attacks with sound reasoning and strong advocacy for the value of mystical insight. Ken Wilber, a contemporary perennialist, whose career Huston helped launch, has called *Forgotten Truth* the best introduction to perennialism ever written, and I see no reason to disagree with his judgment. The book offers a brilliant, short overview, including Huston's specific explanation of the relationship between perennialism and religion.

Of course, few people today recognize the term *perennial philosophy,* and there are scholars who argue that the theory has now faded in importance and credibility, but the fact is that perennialism has become so entrenched in the contemporary mind that we can't see the forest for the trees. For instance, in the self-help area, Ken Wilber's "integral spirituality" and Deepak Chopra's "quantum spirituality" are really just iterations of Huxley's viewpoint. In transpersonal psychology, from Maslow and Stanislav Grof forward, the guiding principle of "self-actualization" (the fulfillment of a secular, and therefore scientifically more acceptable, description of enlightenment) is, again, highly suggestive of, and mostly derived from, perennialism. Furthermore, when Andrew Weil, the famous doctor and author, discusses health and wellness, he often echoes Huxley. For example, Weil (as well as Dean Ornish, Deepak Chopra, and others) endorses "The Journey to Wild Divine," a computer game based on biofeedback that induces serenity while one "quests" for a spiritual, transreligious "awakening." What does this suggest, if not perennialism? Even researchers in the field of psychedelic studies present theories that fit perfectly with Huxley's viewpoint; for example, Dr. Rick Strassman, in his book *DMT: The Spirit Molecule* (2001), explains that psychedelics can induce "firsthand knowledge of the sublime" and adds that this "may help develop a more broad-minded and universal approach to the spiritual." Again, Huxley's theory of spiritual awakening as the core of religion and the goal of our lives fills so much of our field of vision that we have trouble recognizing it, and Huston played a key role in making this so. He was, for five decades, speaking at conferences, publishing books, and championing the pan-religious value of perennialism.

CLEANSING THE DOORS OF PERCEPTION

I sometimes describe Huston as a popular defender of unpopular theories, given his support for mysticism and the perennial philosophy, but no theory he ever embraced was so unpopular as that which held psychedelic drugs can produce real mystical experiences, including an intimacy with the Divine Ground. Despite strong opposition, Huston defended this theory in print for more than forty years, beginning in 1965 in the *Journal of Philosophy,* with "Do Drugs Have Religious Import?" That article, which went on to become the most reprinted in the history of the journal, also had something to do with Huston's friend, Huxley.

In 1960 Huston invited Aldous to MIT as a visiting professor for the institute's centenary year, and during that visit Huston quizzed Huxley about his experiments with mescaline, first detailed in *The Doors of Perception.* Over dinner one night, Huxley told Huston that if he was really curious he should meet a young psychologist at Harvard's Center for Personality Research, Dr. Timothy Leary, who was then studying the psychological effects, and possible benefits, of psilocybin. When Huston contacted Leary, he learned that several of Leary's test subjects were reporting what sounded like mystical experiences, and Leary became eager to show Huston the reports—to see if Huston, as an expert on religion, could shed light on the experiences.

After reading the reports, Huston became intrigued and decided to try the psilocybin—which was not then illegal—out of professional curiosity. So on New Year's Day, 1961, he and his wife, Kendra, drove to Leary's house to take their first trip. The experience, though somewhat unpleasant, convinced Huston that psychedelics *could* trigger mystical experiences—experiences indistinguishable from those of the traditional mystics. To broaden his experience in support of this theory, he and Kendra undertook several more experiments with psychedelics, and on several of these occasions they were joined by Paul Lee, a friend who was then studying at Harvard Divinity School. Speaking of their first trip together, Lee once told me how positively Huston had reacted to the experience. "I couldn't wait to try it," Lee remarked, "but my first experience turned out to be a very odd session. Someone had built a fire and the fireplace had backed up, so the whole room filled with smoke, which was not agreeable at all, and someone got sick. Then someone else put 'Flight of Valkyrie' on the stereo, which was also disagreeable! But Huston didn't seem perturbed at all. He was lying down on the carpet right next to me, and about every two hours he would sit up, look at me, and go, "wooonderfull.' And then down he'd go again. Two hours later he'd sit back up and 'wooonderful.' He was really terrific that day, and his reaction was comforting to me. It helped steady me a bit."

Lee soon joined Leary's Harvard Psychedelic Project, along with Huston, Richard Alpert, Ralph Metzner, Walter Houston Clark, and a few others. As their work together progressed, and the first blush of enthusiasm for psychedelics faded, they looked for clinical ways to test whether or not psychedelics could produce religious experiences. One of the group, Dr. Walter Pahnke, a physician then completing a Ph.D. degree at Harvard Divinity, proposed a double-blind experiment in which one half of a group of graduate students and guides would be given psilocybin while the other half would be given niacin as a placebo, but neither half would know who had been given what. Huston and everyone else immediately agreed to the test, and since it eventually took place in the Marsh Chapel of Boston University on Good Friday, 1962, it came to known as the Good Friday Experiment.

Huston, working that day as a guide, found himself in the half who received the psychedelic, and a few days later, after filling out a detailed questionnaire, he learned, to no surprise of his own, that many of his experiences matched those reported by traditional mystics. Pahnke had put together a list of nine parameters of mystical experience gleaned from traditional accounts, and this was used as a yardstick to determine the relevance of the reports from the questionnaires. As it turned out, almost everyone who had taken the psilocybin that day had experienced something strongly in resonance with Pahnke's typology, providing the first empirical evidence for the theory that psychedelic experiences can actually *be* mystical experiences. Today, this position is far less controversial (the Good Friday Experiment having been clinically repeated with the same results at Johns Hopkins University in 2006), but in 1962 the only people convinced of Pahnke's conclusions were in the Harvard Psychedelic Project.

Bolstered by the positive outcome of Pahnke's experiment, Huston, Leary, and Alpert began working on ways to apply this new spiritual tool. Huston followed Huxley's lead that people who were mature enough to handle the experience could undertake a course in what Huston called "empirical mysticism," testing in their own experience whether or not mystical insight could be triggered by psychedelics and whether or not such insight had value for them. Leary on the other hand believed psychedelic drugs could—and should—be used to create a cultural and social revolution that would free the Western mind of all its hang-ups. Soon after the Marsh Chapel experiment, Leary and Alpert were dismissed from Harvard on various and sundry claims of misconduct and went on to become leaders of the counterculture. Huston remained friends with Leary and Alpert but peeled off from them professionally—worried that their wholesale endorsement of psychedelics would create a public outcry, which of course it did. Huston later publicly expressed his dismay with Leary's "turn on, tune in, drop out" ethos at a conference on psychedelics in San Francisco, in 1966. He criticized Leary, who was in the audience, not only for acting irresponsibly toward America's youth but also because he had come to doubt that psychedelics could create, in and of themselves, religious and moral lives. He agreed that they can produce "altered states," but he wasn't so sure they could produce "altered traits" of behavior—and Leary's own actions gave him room to doubt. Huston advised Leary to proceed more cautiously, but what actually happened is, as they say, history. Leary broke lose from academic research altogether, and the next year, for better and worse, helped spur San Francisco's infamous "Summer of Love."

Huston would rather have seen the doors of perception opened more slowly. But given the flood of interest that followed when Leary let the genie out of the bottle, and the equally intense backlash that followed that, Huston's writings on psychedelics became a thoughtful and measured reference point for scholars and seeker alike—and they still are today.

A RELENTLESS EXPLORER

Eventually, Huston summarized his experiments with psychedelics, both during and after his time with Leary, in *Cleansing the Doors of Perception* (2000), a book that references and builds from Huxley's earlier title. Some critics have seen this interest as a compromise of his professionalism, but those who know Huston best, both as a scholar and as a man, recognize it for what it is: just one expression of his deep curiosity about all spiritual matters. Huston has devoted himself in the past sixty years to a wide variety of explorations, both intellectual and experiential, of inner space. An avid meditator, he also undertook Sufi practices, yoga practices, and experiments in Native American sweat lodges. Like Huxley and Heard before him and his good friends Joseph Campbell, Stanislav Grof, and Ram Dass in his own time, Huston has been a key explorer and key interpreter of the inner landscape, looking for ways to improve the human condition by cultivating our latent potentialities of mind and spirit. If his experiments were bold, well, from his perspective they needed to be. He has never backed down from a serious search, and as a consequence he has been a regular at such retreat facilities as the Easlen Institute in California and the Omega Institute in upstate New York. In these places, Huston finds the cutting edge of experiential inquiry into the perennial philosophy, attempts to uncover the "highest common factor" at the core of each of us—intimating that we are not only connected to the Sacred but that we *are* sacred. "Over the years," Michael Murphy, one of the two founders of Esalen, once told me, "we've had only a handful of presenters who really glowed in the dark, and Huston is one of them."

Huston's courage as an explorer first came out during his travels around the globe to learn about the world's religions, and we see it again in his research with meditation and psychedelics, but we find it at its zenith in his lifelong support for the traditional faiths of the world. Huston has tirelessly defended religion in all its manifestations for fifty years, most recently in *Why Religion Matters* (2001) and subsequent volumes on Buddhism, Islam, and Christianity. He has fought for the religious freedom of the Tibetan people, the Chinese people, and also Native Americans. Regarding the latter, Huston once journeyed to Mazatlán, at the age of seventy-five, to undergo a four-day peyote rite in order to help defend their traditional ways. The Native American Church was, in the early nineties, prevented from using peyote as its religious sacrament, and Huston was asked to help plead their case before the U.S. Congress. To better understand the issue, and inspire his testimony, Huston sat up for four nights with the elders of the church and took the sacred peyote. In short, both the experience and Huston's testimony were a success. After passing unanimously in both houses of Congress, the Native American Religious Freedom Act was signed into law by Bill Clinton on October 6, 1994. "To call peyote—as they used it—a drug," Huston explained to Phil Cousineau, a filmmaker with whom he was collaborating on the case, "would be like calling the wine at Catholic Mass, 'boooooze.'"

RELIGION'S ROCK STAR

To summarize Huston's overall significance, there hasn't been a single supporter of the traditional religions in the last century who has had more influence than Huston Smith. He has argued that every tradition has value, and none should trump the others. Each should be followed religiously and not watered down into a New Age mush, although there are benefits to be gained from comparative study. He has argued that we are diminished if the impact of that comparative study is to lessen our commitment to our own tradition, but there is an advantage if we deepen our understanding of one another and learn respect for every tradition. He has also argued that comparative study is worthwhile if it helps us gain insight into the "highest common factor" of the perennial philosophy that underlies all religion—and in this regard his viewpoint again converges with Huxley's and Joseph Campbell's. This, in brief, is a summary of Huston's viewpoint, and it has drawn tremendous support to him over the years, which is why the *Christian Science Monitor* once called him "religion's rock star." Huston, as a scholar, teacher, seeker, social critic, philosopher, and bridge builder between cultures, has been an inspiration to people all over the world who love their religion—and to all those who believe we are more than the sum of our genetic code and that life contains a mystery that only the soul can fathom.

WORKS BY HUSTON SMITH

BOOKS

The Purposes of Higher Education. New York: Harper & Bros., 1955.

The Religions of Man. New York: Harper & Row, 1958.

The Search for America (editor). Englewood Cliffs, NJ: Prentice-Hall, 1959.

Condemned to Meaning. New York: Harper & Row, 1965.

Forgotten Truth: The Common Vision of the World's Religions. San Franciso: HarperCollins, 1976.

Beyond the Post-Modern Mind. New York: Crossroad Press, 1982.

Primordial Truth and Postmodern Theology. With David Ray Griffin. Albany: State University of New York Press, 1989.

The World's Religions. Revised and expanded edition of *The Religions of Man.* San Francisco: HarperSanFrancisco, 1991.

Cleansing the Doors of Perception: The Religious Significance of Entheogenic Plants and Chemicals. New York: J. P. Tarcher/Putnam, 2000.

Why Religion Matters: The Fate of the Human Spirit in an Age of Disbelief. San Francisco: HarperCollins, 2001.

Buddhism: A Concise Introduction. With Phil Novak. San Francisco: HarperSanFranciso, 2003.

The Way Things Are: Conversations with Huston Smith on the Spiritual Life. With Phil Cousineau. Berkeley: University of California Press, 2003.

The Soul of Christianity: Restoring the Great Tradition. San Francisco: HarperSanFranciso, 2005.

The Almost Chosen People. With Kendra Smith. Kalamazoo, MI: Fetzer Institute, 2006.

A Seat at the Table: In Conversation with Native Americans on Religious Freedom. With Phil Cousineau. Berkeley: University of California Press, 2006.

Tales of Wonder: Adventures Chasing the Divine. With Jeffery Paine. San Francisco: HarperOne, 2009.

ARTICLES (SELECTED)

"The Operational View of God: A Study in the Impact of Metaphysics on Religious Thought." *Journal of Religion* 31, no. 2 (1951).

"Accents of the World's Philosophies." *Philosophy East and West* 7, nos. 1–2 (1957).

"Values: Academic and Human." In *The Larger Learning,* edited by Marjorie Carpenter. Dubuque, IA: William C. Brown Co., 1960. Reprinted in *Christian Scholar* 43 (Winter 1960).

"The Accents of the World's Religions." *Australian Bulletin of Comparative Religions* 1 (1961). Reprinted in *Comparative Religion,* edited by John Bowman (Leiden: Brill, 1972).

"The Revolution in Western Thought." *Saturday Evening Post,* Adventures of the Mind Series, August 26, 1961. Reprinted in *Dialogue on Science,* edited by W. Cozart (Indianapolis: Bobbs-Merrill, 1967); and *Iqbal Review* 25, no. 1 (April 1984).

"Twenty Years of the Atom." *Nation* 195, no. 20 (December 15, 1962). Reprinted as "The New Age," in *Rockefeller Chapel Sermons,* edited by Donovan Smucher (Chicago: University of Chicago Press, 1967); and *University of Chicago Magazine* 51, no. 8 (May 1967).

"Between Syncretism and the Ghetto." *Theology Today* 20, no. 1 (April 1963).

"Empiricism Revisited." In *The Empirical Theology of Henry Nelson Wieman,* edited by Charles Brettal. New York: Macmillan, 1963.

"The Death and Rebirth of Metaphysics." In *Process and Divinity: The Hartshore Festschrift,* edited by William Reese and E. Freeman. La Salle, IL: Open Court, 1964.

"Do Drugs Have Religious Import?" *Journal of Philosophy* 61, no. 18 (October 1964). Reprinted in *LSD: The Consciousness Expanding Drug,* edited by David Solomon (New York: Putnam, 1964); *Reason and Responsibility,* edited by Joel Feinberg (Belmont, CA: Dickenson, 1965); *Introductory Philosophy,* edited by Frank A. Tillman (New York: Harper & Row, 1967); *Basic Philosophical Analysis,* edited by Charles L. Reid (Encino, CA: Dickenson, 1971); *Philosophy: A Modern Encounter,* edited by Robert Wolff (Englewood Cliffs, NJ: Prentice-Hall, 1971); *Religiose Erfahrung und die Droge,* edited by Hanscarl Leuner (Stuttgart: W. Kohlhammer, 1972); *Religion's Influence in Contemporary Society,* edited by Joseph Faulkner (Columbus, OH: Charles Merrill, 1972); *Philosophy of Religion,* edited by William L. Row and William J. Wainwright (New York: Harcourt Brace Jovanovich, 1973); *Ways of Being Religious,* edited by F. Streng, C. Lloyd, and J. Allen (Englewood, Cliffs, NJ: Prentice-Hall, 1973); *Philosophical Issues,* edited by J. Rachels and F. Tillman (New York: Harper & Row, 1972); [in part] *Psyche and Spirit,* edited by John J. Heaney (New York: Paulist Press, 1973); *The Problems of Philosophy,* edited by William Alston and Richard Brandt (Boston: Allyn and Bacon, 1974); *Philosophy Looks to the Future,* edited by W. L. Fogg and P. E. Richter (Boston: Holbrook Press, 1974); and William Bruening, *Self, Society, and the Search for Transcendence,* edited by William Bruening (Palo Alto, CA: National Press Books, 1974).

"The Humanities and Man's New Condition." *Liberal Education* 50, no. 2 (May 1964).

"The Irenic Potential of Religions." *Theology Today* 23, no. 3 (October 1966). Reprinted in *Religious Pluralism and World Community,* edited by Edward Jurji (Leiden: Brill, 1969).

"Valid Materialism: A Western Offering to Hocking's 'Civilization in the Singular.'" In

Philosophy, Religion, and the Coming World Civilization, edited by Leroy Rouner. The Hague: Martinus Nijhoff, 1966.

"Transcendence in Traditional China." *Religious Studies* 2 (1967). Reprinted in *Traditional China,* edited by James Liu and Wei-Ming Tu (Englewood Cliffs, NJ: Prentice-Hall, 1970).

"Unique Vocal Ability of Certain Tibetan Lamas." With K. Stevens. *American Anthropologist* 69, no. 2 (April 1967).

"On an Unusual Mode of Chanting by Certain Tibetan Lamas." With K. Stevens and R. Tomlinson. *Journal of the Accoustical Society of America* 41, no. 5 (May 1967).

"Human versus Artificial Intelligence." In *The Human Mind,* edited by John Roslansky Amsterdam: North Holland, 1967. Reprinted in *Renew* (Winter 1970).

"Psychedelic Theophanies and the Religious Life." *Christianity and Crisis* 27, no. 11 (June 26, 1967). Reprinted in *Journal of Psychedelic Drugs* 3, no. 1 (September 1970).

"Technology and Human Values." In *Human Values and Advancing Technology,* edited by Cameron Hall. New York: Friendship Press, 1967.

"Empirical Metaphysics." In *The Ecstatic Adventure,* edited by Ralph Metzner. NewYork: Macmillan, 1968.

"Secularization and the Scared." In *The Religion Situation,* edited by Donald Cutler. Boston: Beacon Press, 1968.

"Empiricism: Scientific and Religious." In *The Future of Empirical Theology,* edited by Bernard Meland. Chicago: University of Chicago Press, 1969.

"Like It Is: The University Today." *Key Reporter* 34, no. 2 (Winter 1968–69). Reprinted in *Wall Street Journal,* March 20, 1969.

"The Reach and the Grasp: Transcendence Today." In *Transcendence,* edited by H. Richardson and D. Cutler. Boston: Beacon Press, 1969. Reprinted in *The Philosophy of Religion,* edited by Norbert Schedler (New York: Macmillan, 1974).

"Tao Now: An Ecological Testament." In *Earth Might Be Fair,* edited by Ian Barbour. Englewood Cliffs, NJ: Prentice-Hall, 1972.

"The Well of Awareness: A Review Article." *Eastern Buddhist* 5, no. 1 (May 1972).

"Man's Western Way: An Essay on Reason and the Given." *Philosophy East and West* 22, no. 4 (October 1972).

"Wasson's SOMA: A Review Article." *Journal of the American Academy of Religion* 40, no. 4 (December 1972).

"The Jesus Prayer." *Christian Century* 90, no. 13 (March 28, 1973).

"The Relation between Religions." *Main Currents in Modern Thought* 30, no. 2 (November–December 1973). Reprinted in *Traditional Modes of Contemplation and Action,* edited by Yusuf Ibish and Peter Wilson (Tehran: Imperial Iranian Academy of Philosophy, 1977).

"The Point of Death." With Samuel Todes. In *The Patient, Death, and the Family,* edited by Stanley Troup and William Greene. New York: Scribner, 1974.

"Two Kinds of Teaching." In *Excellence in University Teaching,* edited by Thomas Buxton and Keith Prichard. Columbia: University of South Carolina Press, 1975. Reprinted in *Key Reporter* 38, no. 4 (Summer 1973); *Journal of Humanistic Psychology* 15, no. 4 (Fall 1975); *The Healthy Personality,* edited by H. Chiang and A. Maslow (New York:

D. Van Nostrand, 1977); and *Teaching Philosophy Today,* edited by T. W. Bynum and S. Reisberg (Bowling Green, OH: Bowling Green University, Philosophy Documentation Center, 1977).

"Frithjof Schuon's *The Transcendent Unity of Religions:* Pro." *Journal of the American Academy of Religion* 44, no. 4 (December 1976).

"The Meaning of Tradition: A Conversation with Huston Smith." *Parabola* 1, no. 1 (Winter 1976).

"Four Theological Negotiables." *Eastern Buddhist* 10, no. 2 (October 1977).

"Excluded Knowledge: A Critique of the Modern Western Mind Set." *Teachers College Record* 80, no. 3 (February 1979). Reprinted in *Education and Values,* edited by Douglas Sloan (New York: Teachers College Press, 1980).

"Features Review Article: Coomaraswamy, Selected Papers and Biography." *Philosophy East and West* 29, no. 3 (July 1979).

"The Sacred Unconscious." *Re-Vision* 2, no. 2 (Summer–Fall 1979). Reprinted in *Beyond Health and Normality,* edited by R. Walsh and D. H. Shapiro (New York: Van Nostrand Reinhold, 1983); *What Is Enlightenment?,* edited by John White (Los Angeles: J. Tarcher, 1985); and [expanded] *Journal of Humanistic Psychology* 25, no. 3 (Summer 1985).

"Western Philosophy as a Great Religion." In *Transcendence and the Sacred,* edited by Alan Olson and Leroy Rouner. Notre Dame, IN: University of Notre Dame Press, 1981.

"Beyond the Modern Western Mindset." *Teachers College Record* 32, no. 3 (Spring 1981).

"Science and Theology: The Unstable Detente." *Anglican Theological Review* 63, no. 4 (October 1981).

"What Wilfred Smith's Against, and For." *Religious Studies Review* 7, no. 4 (October 1981).

"Scientism in Sole Command." *Christianity and Crisis* 42, no. 11 (January 21, 1982).

"Evolution and Evolutionism." *Christian Century* 99, no. 23 (July 7–14, 1982). Reprinted in *National Forum* 63, no. 2 (Spring 1983).

"Spiritual Discipline in Zen and Comparative Perspective." *Eastern Buddhist* 16, no. 2 (Autumn 1983). Revised version in *Ultimate Reality and Spiritual Discipline,* edited by James Duerlinger (New York: Paragon House, 1984).

"Two Evolutions." In *On Nature,* edited by Leroy Rouner. Notre Dame, IN: University of Notre Dame Press, 1984.

"Truth and Transformation in Psychological and Spiritual Paths." With Daniel Goleman and Ram Das. *Journal of Transpersonal Psychology* 17, no. 2 (1985).

"Can Religion Endure the Death of Metaphysics?" *Religion and Intellectual Life* 3, no. 3 (Spring 1986).

"Spiritual Personality Types." *Hamline Review* 10 (Spring 1986).

"Another World to Live In, or How I Teach the Introductory Course." *Religious Studies and Theology* 7, no. 1 (January 1987).

"Is There a Perennial Philosophy?" *Journal of the American Academy of Religion* 55, no. 3 (Fall 1987).

"Can Modernity Accommodate Transcendence?" In *Modernity and Religion,* edited by William Nicholls. Waterloo, ON: Wilfrid Laurier University Press, 1988.

"This Ecumenical Moment: What Are We Seeking?" *Japanese Religions* 15, no. 1 (January 1988).

"The Crisis in Philosophy." *Behaviourism* 16, no. 1 (Spring 1988).

"The Conceptual Crisis in the Modern West." In *Synthesis of Science and Religion,* edited by D. T. Singh and Ravi Gomatam. San Francisco and Bombay: Bhaktivedanta Institute, 1988.

"Philosophy, Theology, and the Primordial Claim." *Cross Currents* 38, no. 3 (Fall 1988). Reprinted in *God, the Self, and Nothingness,* edited by Robert Carter (New York: Paragon House, 1990).

"Has Process Theology Dismantled Classical Theism?" 1988 Bellarmine Lecture, St. Louis University. *Theology Digest* 35, no. 4 (Winter 1988).

"Remembering Aldous Huxley." *Los Angeles Times Book Review,* November 20, 1988. Reprinted in *Journal of Humanistic Psychology* 29, no. 3 (Summer 1989).

"The View from Everywhere: Ontotheology and the Post-Neitzschean Deconstruction of Metaphysics." In *Religion, Ontotheology, and Deconstruction,* edited by Henry Ruf. New York: Paragon House, 1989.

Featured Book Review of *The Essential Writings of Frithjof Schuon. Philosophy East and West* 39, no. 4 (October 1989).

"The Central Curricular Issue of Our Age." In *Rethinking the Curriculum,* edited by Mary Clark and Sandra Wawrytko. New York: Greenwood Press, 1990.

"Chinese Religion in World Perspective." *Dialogue and Alliance* 4, no. 2 (Summer 1990).

"Encountering God." In *For the Love of God,* edited by Benjamin Shield and Richard Carlson. San Rafael, CA: New World Library, 1990.

"Postmodernism's Impact on the Study of Religion." *Journal of the American Academy of Religion* 58, no. 4 (Winter 1990). Reprinted as "Hierarchy Essential to Religion," *Contemporary Philosophy* 13, no. 8 (March–April 1991).

"Dignity in Difference: Organic Realism and the Search for Community." In *On Community,* edited by Leroy Rouner. Notre Dame, IN: Notre Dame University Press, 1991.

"Turning *The Religions of Man* into *The World's Religions:* Reflections on the New Edition." *Anima* (Summer 1991).

"Two Traditions—and Philosophy." In *Religion of the Heart: Essays in Honour of Frithjof Schuon,* edited by S. H. Nasr and W. Stoddart. Washington, DC: Foundation for Traditional Studies, 1991.

"Do Drugs Have Religious Import? A Thirty-Five-Year Retrospect." In *Psychoactive Sacraments,* edited by Thomas B. Roberts. San Francisco: Council on Spiritual Practices, 2001.

"Engaging Huston Smith's *Why Religion Matters;* Huston Smith Replies to Critiques by Ursula Goodenough, Ian Barbour, and Gregory Peterson." *Zygon* 36, no. 2 (June 2001).

"Nasr's Defense of the Perennial Philosophy." In *The Philosophy of Seyyed Hossein Nasr.* Library of Living Philosophers. Carbondale: Southern Illinois University Press, 2001.

"Intimations of Immortality: Three Case Studies." 1901 Ingersoll Lecture. *Harvard Divinity Bulletin* 30, no. 3 (2001–2).

"The Good Friday Experiment." In *Hallucinogens: A Reader,* edited by Charles Grob. New York: Tarcher/Putnam, 2002.

"A Life of Exploring Religious Frontiers." *Quest* (July–August 2002).

"The Long Way Home." In *Paths to the Heart: Sufism and the Christian East,* edited by James Cutsinger. Bloomington, IN: World Wisdom Books, 2002.

"Perspectives on East-West Dialogue, Wanderings: Brush and Pen." In *Philosophical Reflection,* by Peimin Ni and Stephen Rowe. Chicago, IL: Art Media Resources, 2002.

"Retreat: Withdrawal and Return." In *Monkscript.* Louisville, KY: Fons Vita, 2002.

"Science and the Great Chain of Being." In *Neoplatonism and Contemporary Thought,* edited by R. Blaine Harris. Albany: State University of New York Press, 2002.

"Scientism: The Bedrock of the Modern Worldview." In *Science and the Myth of Progress,* edited by M. Zarandi. Bloomington, IN: World Wisdom Books, 2002.

"Terrorism." *Journal of Transpersonal Psychology* 34, no. 1 (2002).

"Water from a Deeper Well: Huston Smith on Why Spirituality without Religion Is Not Enough." *Sun,* October 2002.

"Awe as Promise and Peril: The Entheogenic Evidence." In *Promise and Peril: The Paradox of Religion as Resource and Threat,* edited by Anna Lannstrom. Notre Dame, IN: Notre Dame University Press, 2003.

"Reclaim Your Sacred Self." *Yoga International,* May 2003.

"Scientism: The World's Littlest Religion." In *Creed and Culture,* edited by James M. Kushiner. Wilmington, DE: ISI Books, 2003..

"Do Drugs Have Religious Import: A 40-Year Retrospective." *Journal of Humanistic Psychology* 44, no. 2 (Spring 2004).

The Master-Disciple Relationship." 2003 Victor Daniel Memorial Lecture, Indiana University. *Sophia* 10, no. 1 (2004). Reprinted in *The Best Spiritual Writing of 2005,* edited by Philip Zaleski and Barry Lopez (New York: Houghton Mifflin, 2005).

"The News of Eternity." In *Healing Our Planet, Healing Our Selves,* edited by Dawson Church and Geralyn Gendreau. Santa Rosa, CA: Elite Books, 2004.

"Remembering Arthur." In *Arthur Young, Nested in Time: An Astrological Biography.* Cambria, CA: Anodos Foundation, 2004.

"The Search for Universal Values." In *Universal Values: An International Symposium.* Athens: Academy of Athens, 2004.

"Why Fundamentalism Matters." *Parabola* 20, no. 4 (Winter 2005).

"God Is Winning." *Parabola* 33 (Summer 2008).

FOREWORDS, INTRODUCTIONS, AND PREFACES

Foreword to *The Three Pillars of Zen,* by Philip Kapleau. Boston: Beacon Press, 1967.

Introduction to *A Buddhist Bible,* edited by Dwight Goddard. Boston: Beacon Press, 1970.

Introduction to *Zen Mind, Beginner's Mind,* by Shunryu Suzuki. New York: Weatherhill, 1970.

"The Relevance of the Great Religions for the Modern World." Introduction to *The World Religions Speak,* edited by Finley P. Dunne Jr. The Hague: W. Junk, 1970. Reprinted in *Insight* 2, no. 2 (Winter 1977–78).

"Let There Be Light." Introduction to *Great Religions of the World.* Washington, DC: National Geographic Society, 1971.

Preface to *Ideals and Realities of Islam*, by Seyyed Hossein Nasr. Boston: Beacon Press, 1972. Reprinted in *Iqbal Review* 25, no. 3 (October 1983).

Introduction to *The Transcendent Unity of Religions*, by Frithjof Schuon. New York: Harper Torchbook, 1975.

Foreword to *Speculum Spinozanum*, edited by Siegfried Hessing. London and Boston: Henley and Routledge & Kegan Paul, 1977.

Introduction to *Buddha: The Quest for Serenity*, by George Marshall. Boston: Beacon Press, 1978.

Foreword to *The Spiritual Heritage of India*, by Swami Prabhavananda. Hollywood, CA: Vedanta Press, 1979. Reprinted in *Vedanta for East and West* 171 (January–February 1980).

Preface to *Meister Eckhart*, translated by E. Colledge and B. McGinn. New York: Paulist Press, 1981.

Foreword to *On Having No Head*, by D. E. Harding. London and New York: Arkana and Methuen, 1986. German edition: *ZEN und die Wiederentdeckung des Offensichtlichen.* Basel: Sphinx Verlag, 1986.

Preface to *Vedanta: Voice of Freedom*, by Swami Vivekananda, edited by Swami Chetananda. New York: Philosophical Library, 1986.

Preface to *An Experience of Enlightenment*, by Flora Courtois. Wheaton, IL: Theosophical Quest Miniature, 1986.

Preface to *A Treasury of Traditional Wisdom*, by Whitall Perry. San Francisco: Harper & Row, 1986.

Foreword to *Death and Dying: The Tibetan Tradition*, by Glenn Mullin. Boston: Routledge & Kegan Paul, 1986.

"Does Spirit Matter? The Worldwide Impact of Religion on Contemporary Politics." Introduction to *Spirit Matters*, edited by Richard Rubenstein. New York: Paragon House, 1987.

Foreword to *Mysticism and Philosophy*, by W. T. Stace. Los Angeles: Jeremy P. Tarcher, 1987.

Foreword to *The Wheel of Life*, by John Blofeld. Boston: Shambala, 1988.

Introduction to *The Concise Encyclopedia of Islam*, by Cyril Glasse. New York: Harper & Row, 1989.

Foreword to *The Way of a Pilgrim and the Pilgrim Continues His Way*, by R. M. French. San Francisco: HarperSanFrancisco, 1991.

Preface to *Beacons of Knowledge: Essays in Honor of Seyyed Hossein Nasr*, edited by Mohammad H. Faghfoory. Lexington, KY: Fons Vita, 2003.

Foreword to *Journeys East: 20th-Century Encounters with Eastern Religious Traditions*, by Harry Oldmeadow. Bloomington, IN: Wisdom Books, 2004.

Foreword to *Pain, Sex, and Time*, by Gerald Heard. Rhinebeck, NY: Monkfish, 2004.

Introduction to *Return to the Center*, by Martin Lings. Lewisburg, KY: Fons Vitae, 2005.

Foreword to *Talking to God: Portrait of a World at Prayer*, edited by John Gattuso. Milford, NJ: Stone Creek , 2006.

Foreword to *Epiphanies: Where Science and Miracles Meet*, by Ann Jauregui. New York: Atria Books, 2007.

Foreword to *The Ultimate Journey: Consciousness and the Mystery of Death*, by Stanislav Grof. Santa Cruz, CA: MAPS, 2007.

CREDITS

Grateful acknowledgment is made to HarperCollins Publishers for permission to reprint the following selections.

Chapter 5: "Light," from *Why Religion Matters: The Fate of the Human Spirit in an Age of Disbelief,* by Huston Smith. San Francisco: HarperCollins, 2001.

Chapters 8 and 23: "My Three Other Religions" and "Reflections upon Turning Ninety," from *Tales of Wonder: Adventures Chasing the Divine,* by Huston Smith, with Jeffery Paine. San Francisco: HarperOne, 2009.

Chapters 19 and 20: "The Levels of Reality" and "The Levels of Selfhood," from *Forgotten Truth: The Common Vision of the World's Religions,* by Huston Smith. San Francisco: HarperCollins, 1976.

The other essays in this volume were first published in the following publications:

Chapter 1: "No Wasted Journey." *Dialog* 33, no. 4 (Fall 1994).

Chapter 2: "The Way Things Are." Originally published as "The Way Things Are: A Conversation with World Religions Scholar Huston Smith," interview by Timothy Beneke, *East Bay Express,* March 8, 1996.

Chapter 3: "Two Kinds of Teaching." *Journal of Humanistic Psychology* 15, no. 4 (Fall 1975).

Chapter 4: "The Sacred Dimension of Everyday Life." *Holistic Education Review* 6, no. 4 (Winter 1993).

Chapter 5: "Light." In *Why Religion Matters: The Fate of the Human Spirit in an Age of Disbelief,* by Huston Smith. San Francisco: HarperSanFranciso, 2001.

Chapter 6: "The Revolution in Western Thought." *Saturday Evening Post,* August 26, 1961.

Chapter 7: "Empirical Metaphysics." In *The Ecstatic Adventure,* edited by Ralph Metzner. New York: Macmillan, 1968.

Chapter 8: "My Three Other Religions." In *Tales of Wonder: Adventures Chasing the Divine*, by Huston Smith, with Jeffery Paine. San Francisco: HarperOne, 2009.

Chapter 9: "Explaining Fundamentalism." *Parabola* 30, no. 4 (Winter 2005).

Chapter 10: "What They Have That We Lack: On Native American Religion." In *Best Spiritual Writing of 1998*, edited by Philip Zaleski. San Franciso: HarperSan Francisco, 1998.

Chapter 11: "Three Ways of Relating to the World. Three Geographies. Three Religious Traditions." An earlier version of this essay, "Accents of the World's Religions," was delivered as the first Charles Strong Memorial Lecture, Australia, 1961.

Chapter 12: "Shinto: A Japanese Sense of the Sacred." *Athenaeum Society Review* (Spring 1985).

Chapter 13: "The Spiritual Heritage of India." *Vedanta for East and West* 171 (1980).

Chapter 14: "The Importance of the Buddha." In *Buddha, the Quest for Serenity*, by George M. Marshall. Boston: Beacon Press, 1978.

Chapter 15: "Tibetan Chanting." Originally published as "Unique Vocal Abilities of Certain Tibetan Lamas," *American Anthropologist* 69, no. 2 (April 1967).

Chapter 16: "The Relevance of the Great Religions for the Modern World." Originally delivered as the concluding address of the First Spiritual Summit Conference, Calcutta, October 1968. Published as the introduction to *The World Religions Speak*, edited by Finley P. Dunne Jr. The Hague: W. Junk, 1970.

Chapter 17: "Educating the Intellect: On Opening the Eye of the Heart." In *Can Virtue Be Taught?*, edited by Barbara Darling-Smith. Notre Dame, IN: University of Notre Dame Press, 1993.

Chapter 18: "Do Drugs Have Religious Import?" *Journal of Philosophy* 61, no. 18 (October 1964).

Chapter 19: "The Levels of Reality." In *Forgotten Truth: The Common Vision of the World's Religions*, by Huston Smith. San Francisco: HarperCollins, 1976.

Chapter 20: "The Levels of Selfhood." In *Forgotten Truth: The Common Vision of the World's Religions*, by Huston Smith. San Francisco: HarperCollins, 1976.

Chapter 21: "Western Philosophy as a Great Religion." In *Transcendence and the Sacred*, edited by Alan M. Olson and Leroy S. Rouner. Notre Dame, IN: University of Notre Dame Press, 1981.

Chapter 22: "Encountering God." In *For the Love of God*, edited by Richard Carlson and Benjamin Shield. New York: New World Library, 1992.

Chapter 23: "Reflections upon Turning Ninety." In *Tales of Wonder: Adventures Chasing the Divine*, by Huston Smith, with Jeffery Paine. San Francisco: HarperOne, 2009.

"Conclusion: The Sacred Unconscious": In *Beyond Health and Normality: The Exploration of Extreme Psychological Well-Being*, edited by Roger Walsh and Dean Shapiro. New York: Van Nostrand Reinhold, 1982.

TEXT:
10/12.5 Minion Pro

DISPLAY:
Minion Pro

COMPOSITOR:
BookMatters, Berkeley

PRINTER AND BINDER:
Maple-Vail Book Manufacturing Group